"Bill, this is an Eastern Western and I'm Geronimo."

— John Wayne, Actor
Snow Canyon, UT – 1954
Page 3

"Ernie Borgnine can be Ernie Borgnine all his life."

— Glenn Ford, Actor
Beverly Hills, California – 1970
Page 28

"We can shoot it on the back lot and cover up the palm trees."

— Television Executive – The Black Tower
Universal City – Hollywood, California – 1972
Page 15

"It might be worth a few bucks."

— William Conrad, Actor
Burbank, California – 1982
Page 25

"Keeping your innocence and enthusiasm in the face of terrible rejection."

— John Wayne, Actor
Newport Beach, California – 1977
Page 89

"Which way to the flight deck?"

— President Richard Nixon
U.S.S. Saratoga – 1969
Page 68

"I don't want them to."

— Anthony Hopkins, Actor
Hollywood, California – 1982
Page 122

"Paranoid man, really paranoid."

— Hal Ashby, Director/Editor
Hollywood Hills – 1972
Page 144

"We worked it out with wooden matches on my kitchen table."

— Navy Ace, Admiral "Jimmy" Thatch
Coronado, California – 1973
Page 77

"So, we couldn't get the church, but Pappy Ford had a better idea."

— John Wayne, Actor
Newport Beach, California – 1977
Page 119

"For this money,
he could hit me with a baseball bat."

— Danny Trejo, Actor/Inmate
Los Angeles, California – 1985
Page 153

"I just hope I ain't next."

— Pee Wee Reese, Baseball Player
Los Angeles, California – 1993
Page 250

"The recovering addict or alcoholic
must be on guard against a well-meaning
but ill-informed doctor from harming him/her
with his prescription pad."

— Joseph A. Pursch, M.D.
On numerous Occasions, at Numerous Locations
Page 159

"Did you spot it Bill — did you see it?"

— Borden Chase, Author/Screenwriter
Hollywood, California – 1948
Page 172

"Just like that, there was gold in my closet."

— Rod Serling, Writer
Brentwood, California – 1973
Page 122

"Scared of what?"

— Bob Hope, Comedian/Actor
Beirut, Lebanon – 1982
Page 20

"And the old bastard didn't die
for another 25 years."

— Jackie Cooper, Actor/Director/Producer
Beverly Hills, California – 1980
Page 230

"The Navy owes me nothing.
I feel I owe the Navy something."

— Ernest Borgnine, Actor
Hollywood Hills, California – 1997
Page 175

"*The rosary in his hand, the Bible in his lap — it just wasn't him.*"

— Maureen, USO Person
Pacific Palisades, California – 1970
Page 150

"*Mister Tucker, ah, um, is it true?*"

— Attractive Matron
Las Vegas, Nevada – 1981
Page 82

"*Mind it? I didn't mind it at all. I enjoyed it actually.*"

— Troy Donahue, Actor
Pacific Palisades, California – 1995
Page 42

"*Just stay here; he'll come up for you.*"

— Gallery Marshal – Bob Hope Classic
Bermuda Dunes, California – 2009
Page 237

"*I'll sign for you after the round.*"

— Tiger Woods, Golfer
Sherwood Country Club – Tiger Woods Challenge
Thousand Oaks, California – 2010
Page 244

"*They looked like vultures.*"

— Jason Robards, Actor
Culver City, California – 1980
Page 53

"*Charles, what is it? What's the matter?*"

— Robert Young, Actor
MGM Studios – 1944
Page 42

"*This is cruelty to an old woman.*"

— Phyllis Diller, Comedienne/Actor
Beverly Hills, California – 2006
Page 57

"*Is that your bike, kid?*"

— Humphrey Bogart, Actor
Warner Brothers Studios
Burbank, California – 1947
Page 139

"*You're somebody, ain't cha?*"

— Prisoner, Lincoln Heights Jail
Los Angeles, California – 1950s
Page 168

"I loved those movies —
I didn't have to dance."

— Donald O'Connor, Actor/Dancer
Sherman Oaks, California – 1980
Page 32

"And what do you do?"

— Paul Keyes, Producer
Burbank, California – 1971
Page 73

"You'll know when you know that you don't know."

— Mo Freedman, Football Player/Coach
Los Angeles, California – on numerous occasions
Page 265

He was just the same old asshole."

— Evelyn Keyes, Actress
Beverly Hills, California – 2001
Page 36

"They really hated... despised each other.
It was sad, really"

— Julie Harris, Actress
Hollywood, California – 1989
Page 47

Not getting a role I wanted,
a setback of any kind...
I just kept thinking something
better will be coming along?"

— Ernest Borgnine, Actor
Hollywood Hills, California – 2003
Page 38

"I loved being a child star."

— Margaret O'Brien, Actress
Hollywood, California – On numerous occasions
Page 42

"Bullshit!"

— Jackie Cooper, Actor/Director/Producer
Hollywood, California – 1984
Page 102

"Have a Texas roadmap, cousin."

— Chill Wills, Actor
Eugene, Oregon – 1962
Page 32

"Come on over to the set today;
I get to kill six guys."

— James Drury, Actor *The Virginian*
Studio City, California – 1970
Page 131

"Sorry, you will have to wait a moment.
I have to sign John's balls first."

— Carol Channing, Entertainer
Newport Beach, California – 2002
Page 57

"Admiral I don't suppose the Russians
would give us that second pass?"

— John F. Kennedy
President of the United States
USS Enterprise (CVN-65),
Atlantic Ocean – April 1962
Page 170

"Wayne Newton just went off."

— Shecky Greene, Comedian
Las Vegas, Nevada – 1980s
Page 232

"I fell in last night with evil companions."

— Gene Autry, Actor/Singer/Songwriter/Mogul
Oklahoma – 1940s
Page 84

"MGM was a fairyland of talent and beauty.
Work was a pleasure.
What a wonderful place and time."

— Mickey Rooney, Actor/Performer/Author
Sugar Babies – Backstage Pantages Theater
Hollywood, California – 1984
Page 102

"What are all these people coming to see me for? I ain't dyin'. Give me my pants, I'm going home."

— Ernest Borgnine, Actor
Cedars Sinai Hospital
Los Angeles, California – 2012
Page 38

The Man from Planet X?

— Sir John Mills, Actor
Studio City, California – 1999
Page 108

"Alcoholism is not a valium deficiency."

— Joseph A. Pursch, M.D.
On numerous Occasions,
at Numerous Locations – 1970s
Page 159

"You don't understand... it's over... it's over."

— James Dean, Actor
Burbank, California – 1954
Page 47

"The water began to rise — up to my knees — waist — shoulders — I wanted to die."

— Pearl Harbor Survivor
Honolulu, Hawaii – 1980
Page 98

"My tits and toes are killing me."

— William Shatner, Actor/Director/Producer, etc.
Manhattan Beach, California – 2005
Page 126

"Where is Jimmy Nasser?"

— Francis Ford Coppola, Director/Writer
Hollywood, California – 1980
Page 284

"Hello, my name is Carol Channing."

— Carol Channing, Entertainer
Newport Beach, California – 2002
Page 57

"There's tigers down there, snakes and shit."

— Navy Vietnam Ace, William "Willie" Driscoll
Miramar Naval Air Station – 1974
Page 77

"George, it is my good fortune to announce the dedication of the George Burns and Gracie Allen stage here at Hollywood General Studios."

— Johnny Grant, Mayor of Hollywood
Hollywood, California — 1979
Page 280

"One Option is that I will go and tell the ladies that they must move."

— Joseph A. Pursch, M.D.
Long Beach, California — 1978
Page 160

"I tried to keep half the ball on the black."

— Warren Spahn, Pitcher
Biltmore Hotel, Los Angeles, California — 1990s
Page 246

"Only if he was cleaning it with his teeth."

— Deputy Sheriff
Ketchum, Idaho — 1962
Page 218

"It's the 3-2-1 Syndrome."

— Joseph A. Pursch, M.D.
On numerous Occasions, at Numerous Locations
Page 159

"I think Tom has to step up."

— Charlton Heston, Actor/Author/Activist
Beverly Hills, California — 1991
Page 275

"If I had my way, I'd have made them all that way."

— John Frankenheimer, Director
Brentwood, California — 1998
Page 288

"It's him. It's HIM!"

— Barbara Eden, Actress/Singer/Author
Rancho Mirage, California — 1982
Page 291

"We had three options, depending on the condition he was in that day."

— Vance Skarstedt, Actor/Writer
Hollywood, California – 1974
Page 94

Nothing happens out there until I throw the baseball."

— Bob Welch, Pitcher
Los Angeles, California – 1980
Page 255

With respect, but check your six."

— Vietnam Navy Ace, Randy "Duke" Cunningham
Miramar Naval Air Station – 1974
Page 77

"The Navy made a man of me."

— Jackie Cooper, Actor/Director
Beverly Hills, California – 1980
Page 176

"They were real heroes."

— Charles Durning, Actor
Studio City, California – 2001
Page 175

"Guilty? Of course he's guilty — guilty as hell!"

— Thomas Henderson, Football Player/ Motivational Speaker
Austin, Texas – 1994
Page 260

"Forty... a million... who's counting?"

— Samuel Z. Arkoff
Hollywood, California – 1998
Page 62

"All the heroes are dead."

— Jimmy Stewart, Actor
Hollywood, California – 1946
Page 175

AND FOR EVERY QUOTE THERE IS A STORY

StarCatcher

A True Life Hollywood Fantasy

By John Frederick

MOVIES & TV	PUBLIC & MILITARY FIGURES	SPORTS

MOVIES & TV		PUBLIC & MILITARY FIGURES	SPORTS
John Wayne	Charlton Heston	John Kennedy	Tiger Woods
Jack Nicholson	George Burns	Richard Nixon	Arnold Palmer
Bob Hope	Barbara Eden	Harry Truman	Joe Namath
Humphrey Bogart	James Dean	Ronald Reagan	Muhammed Ali
Carol Channing	Julie Harris	Gerald Ford	Warren Spahn
Gene Autry	Roy Rogers	Dwight Eisenhower	Pee Wee Reese
Carol Burnett	and more...	Navy Aces	Hollywood Henderson
		and more...	and more...

Robert D. Reed Publishers   .   Bandon, OR

Robert D. Reed Publishers
P.O. Box 1992
Bandon, OR 97411
Phone: 541-347-9882; Fax: -9883
E-mail: 4bobreed@msn.com
Website: www.rdrpublishers.com

Editor: Cleone Reed
Designer: Amy Cole
Cover: Joe Cibere, Westlake Marketing Works

Soft Cover ISBN: 978-1-944297-84-8
EBook ISBN: 978-1-944297-85-5

Library of Congress Control Number: 2020947438

Designed, Formatted, and Printed in the United States of America

Dedication

To all the baseball players
who entered the Baseball Hall of Fame,
some of whom graced me with your acquaintance
and others who gave me immense joy
just watching you from the stands,
and to anyone who played the game.

To my fellow documentarians,
who speak to the important issues of the day,
and entertain as they inform.
Keep up the good work.

To all who serve in our military,
every single one of you
is owed an enormous debt of gratitude
for your service.
I stood with you for 36 years.

For me, it all began in the movies.
To all who entertained me
in this magical, mystical, luminescent world
of thrills and laughter,
I am in your debt.

To my wives and children
who put up with me
even though I was not always my best self.

And finally, to Irene Robertson,
who was kind enough to share her sunshine.

Acknowledgments

I have so much to be grateful for, so many people to thank.

First of all, my greatest warmth and respect for those I have written about, many of whom I was able to get to know and, however briefly, enjoy their company. To those teachers and life coaches: my parents; my younger sister and role model, Paula; Hank Juran; John Lewis; Vice Admiral B. J. Semmes; Captain Walter Sessums, USN; Herm Saunders, and many others, who believed in me when I did not believe in myself. To my raft of proof readers for giving it the good old college try. And especially to my life companion, Irene, without whose love and support *StarCatcher* would never have been completed.

Many thanks to my God-sent publisher Robert Reed and eagle-eyed editor Cleone Reed, without whom I was going nowhere with great speed. To my indefatigable typist Cathy Medeiros, who endured more typos, changes on changes, and corrections more than there should have been. Thank you to Joe Cibere, who took my thoughts and dreams and turned the front and back covers of this book into artistic reality. Great job. To Amy Cole, who has a wonderful talent for book design and has made my book a better one, for which I am very proud. And if I had not thanked them elsewhere, to my good friends Judy Woods-Knight and George Vercessi, fellow authors who encouraged me to publish.

Lastly to my anonymous friends for their love and support, and to the great character Allen Jenkins, whose mantra in his best Brooklyn accent was, "Your Highah Powah will never let you down." Amen, Allen.

Table of Contents

Introduction 1

   John Wayne 3

   Jack Nicholson 8

   Television Executive — The Black Tower 15

   Bob Hope 20

   William Conrad 25

   Glenn Ford 28

   Chill Willis and Donald O'Connor 32

   Evelyn Keyes 36

   Ernest Borgnine 38

   Troy Donahue, Margaret O'Brien, and Robert Young ... 42

   James Dean and Julie Harris 47

   Jason Robards 53

   Carol Channing and Phyllis Diller 57

   Samuel Z. Arkoff 62

   President Richard Nixon 68

   Paul Keyes 73

   Randy "Duke" Cunningham, William "Willie" Driscoll, and Admiral "Jimmy" Thatch 77

   Forrest Tucker 82

   Gene Autry 84

   John Wayne 89

   Vance Skarstedt 94

   Pearl Harbor Survivor 98

   Mickey Rooney and Jackie Cooper 102

   Sir John Mills 108

   Studio Kids 112

   John Wayne 119

   Anthony Hopkins and Rod Serling 122

   William Shatner 126

James Drury 131

Humphrey Bogart 139

Jonathan Winters 141

Hal Ashby 144

Maureen 150

Danny Trejo 153

The Incredible Dr. Pursch 159

Prisoner 168

President John F. Kennedy 170

Borden Chase 172

Jimmy Stewart, Charles Durning, Ernest Borgnine,
and Jackie Cooper 175

Short Takes and Incidental Contact 182

Nick Nolte and Liza Minnelli 183

Keystone Kop 187

Rock Hudson 189

Burt Lancaster and Charles Bronson 191

Dean Martin and Lena Horne 194

Robert Young's Luncheon Companion 196

Henry King 198

William Conrad 200

Sean Connery 202

Roy Rogers and Dale Evans 204

Jack Lemmon, Dick Van Dyke, and Carol Burnett 208

Audrey Totter, Dorothy McGuire, and Jane Wyatt 211

John Frederick 215

Hemingway, Rex Allen, and the Smothers Brothers 218

Disney Studios Gate Guard 222

Dana Andrews, Rod Cameron, Jan Clayton, and Gary Crosby 224

Fast Cutting 228

Tom Hanks 229

Jackie Cooper 230

Shecky Greene 232

Peng Meng-ji 234

Short Takes and Incidental Contact Sports 236

Gallery Marshal 237

Paul Azinger 239

Pádraig Harrington 240

Jim Furyk 242

Ian Poulter 243

Tiger Woods 244

Warren Spahn 246

Darrell Evans 248

Pee Wee Reese 250

Joe Namath 252

Bob Welch 255

Thomas Henderson 260

Mo Freedman 265

Muhammad Ali and Miguel Cabrera 1980s/2011 267

Dean Chance and Bo Belinsky 269

Five Good Ones to Quit On And More 272

Five Good Ones to Quit On and More 273

Charlton Heston 275

Johnny Grant and George Burns 280

Francis Ford Coppola 284

John Frankenheimer 288

Barbara Eden 291

Sneak Preview 294

Sneak Preview 295

The American Society for the Prevention of Progress

Santa Rosa, California – 1950s 297

About the Author 300

Introduction

Where do dreams come from? How can a fantasy, by some earthly magic, turn into reality? John Wayne and Winston Churchill are regularly featured in my dreams. They are both willing to sign baseballs. But, I can't find a ball that doesn't already have signatures on it. Dreams, like movies, don't always have happy endings. The fantasy was all about the movies. I was movie struck about the time I learned to walk. Mom and Dad, God bless them, took me to all the Disney classics of the time: *Snow White, Pinocchio, Bambi*, and *Dumbo*. It was wartime, and a darkness hung over, not just our country, but the entire world. We faced harsher strictures and restrictions then than we do now in the era of Covid-19. There were limits on how far we could travel, where we could go, and, in many cases, what we could say. Air raid wardens moved about at night to check if your house was properly blacked out. Gas was rationed, and certain foods and personal items, liquor, and cigarettes were scarce or disappeared, not for weeks or months, but for years. Then, as now, we had an enemy to fight. The difference then seemed to be, even to a child, that we were all united against a common foe. There was no political posturing or partisanship. We all did our bit. As a child, I collected scrap metal, giant balls of tinfoil, even fats from pots and kettles on the stove. Still and always, there were movies. The Great Escape. By 1944, I was allowed to see more mature fare, like *The Princess and the Pirate* with Bob Hope, and *Up In Arms* with Danny Kaye. I am kidding here, because to William Goldman, one of the best writers to ever write about Hollywood, *Bambi* was a far more serious movie than the two I have just named. And here is where the fantasy comes in. Almost before I knew it (actually 30 years or so) I found myself in Hollywood. I met Bob Hope many times, once in the presence of President Ford and Betty. He was also in a TV Special that my company produced. Dana Andrews, the male lead in *Up In Arms*, appeared in two films of mine. I also found myself on the practice tee, exchanging pleasantries with songstress and television host Dinah Shore, another *Up In Arms* star. And this was just the beginning. John Wayne, Charlton Heston, Rod Steiger, Julie Harris, Carol Burnett, Dick Van Dyke, and many other famous names in entertainment, sports, politics, the military and just in life, were in my future. And in yours. Just turn the page and you'll see.

So, now you know of my hopes and dreams. The good news — though this book is autobiographical, it is really not about me. It is more precisely about quotes, as you may have noticed. Quotes may live down the centuries, and still have meaning. "These are the times that try men's souls." Would work nicely, or chillingly, right now. Most all of us have heard, or read, something that stuck with us for the rest of our lives. The quotes in this book offer a buffet of story choices, and a buffet of any kind is hard to find these days. With *StarCatcher*, you can begin at the beginning and plow on through, as you would with any book, or you can pick out a person and/or a quote that catches your fancy, and chances are you will know something you did not know before, about this motion picture or television star, sports figure, even a President or two. Most every quote and the following story have been overheard or elicited by me. A very few are second or third hand, but come from what political reporters would deem, "reliable sources." I will tell you when they are not originals. As I reach back in my memory bag for a quote, I recall where and when and sometimes why I heard them, and a smile or chuckle may come unbidden. Some of these tales are funny or frivolous; they can also be insightful and profound. I hope you enjoy them, as I have greatly enjoyed the life that enabled me to offer them to you.

John Wayne

*"Bill, this is an Eastern Western,
and I'm Geronimo."*

**— John Wayne, Actor
Snow Canyon, UT — 1954**

The Duke was speaking — in this case to William Conrad, who was to play his brother in the RKO/Howard Hughes epic, *The Conqueror*. Conrad arrived at the St. George location two days ahead of the beginning of shooting, probably for not having read the script, which may have led to the question that elicited the Wayne quote above.

We will get back to Conrad's aversion to reading scripts later, but let us concentrate on the tragic/comic nature of the picture and the story behind it.

The Conqueror is acknowledged by both critics and viewers to be one of the very worst pictures of all time. It also may have been the unluckiest. We begin, and for many it will end, with cancer. Of the 220 cast and crew who worked on the film, 91 developed cancer, with at least 46 fatalities attributed to the disease. The primary reasons for this would seem to have been the filming locations in the St. George, Utah area, almost all of which were in close proximity to the Nevada atomic bomb test sites. There were no tests slated for this period, a tiny micro dot of good news to an area that was already thoroughly saturated by fallout. Starting with the principals in *The Conqueror*, the grim tally is as follows: John Wayne died of cancer; Susan Hayward died of cancer in her fifties; Dick Powell (director) died of cancer in his fifties; Pedro Armendáriz killed himself when he found out his cancer was terminal; Agnes Moorhead died of cancer in her sixties; Lee Van Cleef died of cancer in his sixties; John Hoyt died of cancer. Of course, there may have been other causes. Wayne, Hayward, Moorhead, and Hoyt were heavy smokers, and Van Cleef had a heart problem as well, but the obituaries above defy coincidence. While not fatal, the spectacular, legendary miscasting in the picture is worthy of a serious postmortem. John Wayne played Genghis Khan. One has to read this sentence two or three times to grasp the enormity of it all. The mind and body boggle and comparisons are elusive, if not impossible. Perhaps Pee Wee Herman as Adolph Hitler would come close. Then we have a famous Mexican movie star Pedro Armendáriz as a rival Tartar chieftain — bad but not up to the Wayne/Khan standard. Susan Hayward's only qualification for her role as a Tatar princess would seem to be the fact that she was born in Brooklyn. Aggie Moorhead was believable as a witch on television, but her essaying an Asiatic bitch was — let us be polite to the departed — cursed from the start. Then there was Thomas Gomez, a Hispanic/American actor, whose role as Wang was just… Wong. Forgive me, but you get the picture of the picture. Poor Dick Powell's directorial effort was one that most certainly would have been downplayed in his autobiography, which he never got to write. William Conrad was spared from cancer, but he suffered right along with everybody else aboard this cinematic Titanic.

The film did not officially sink until its opening in 1956, two years after shooting had begun, though the picture did not actually sink-sink. It lost money of course. The budget had ballooned to six million dollars, an enormous amount at the time. The amazing thing was that it brought in a respectable 4.5-million dollars in the U.S., which may have proved that a provocative title promising action, blood, and gore can at least open a film. It did prove, definitively, that diehard John Wayne fans will accept their hero in any role this side of Shakespeare.

The awfulness of *The Conqueror* brings to mind the old saying, "Victory has a thousand fathers, but defeat is an orphan." A more apt quotation comes from William Goldman's work, *Adventures in the Screen Trade*. Therein is found this bit of wisdom, "The secret of Hollywood is that nobody knows." Nobody knows what makes a movie star, nobody knows what makes a hit, nobody knows what genre will work at any given time, and nobody knows whether a script is any good or not, especially actors. If blame is to be levied, the Duke comes in for a full share. After all, he had read the script and wanted to do the film anyway. He had also worked with Howard Hughes (who was Wayne's good friend) in an earlier disaster, *Jet Pilot*. That picture featured Wayne as an USAF fighter pilot, a possibility, and the lovely Janet Leigh as a Russian aviatrix and part-time spy, far less likely.

Jet Pilot was meant to showcase the state of aviation at the time shooting began (1950), but it was not released until RKO had disappeared as a movie studio in 1957, which meant that the planes were obsolete and the aviation sequences — the only distraction from a worn, hackneyed plot — were outdated and boring. Hughes diddled, dawdled, and fiddled with the film for years, shooting endless footage of clouds that never seemed to look dramatic enough to the enigmatic billionaire. His pursuit of suspected Communist subversives at the studio was also cause for delay and distraction.

Now, back, reluctantly, to *The Conqueror*.

Actually one should not be reluctant to examine a colossal failure. Who really learns from a great success? *Gone with the Wind* could never be duplicated, but another *Conqueror* might be avoided.

As a modestly successful baseball pitcher in high school and college, I can attest that I never learned a thing when I won easily, but a great deal when my stuff had vanished and hitters were licking their chops and spraying line drives all over the ballpark. Let's turn back to a relatively innocent bystander, the aforementioned William Conrad. When Conrad arrived at the location and met with the Duke, the latter had already donned his costume, the better to "'get the feel" of the great barbarian. Bill did say that was a warning, and from that point on he regarded himself not as an actor but as a reluctant witness.

Further proof came with the first setup. The scene was set at the base of a mountain, or a rock formation that could double for a mountain. Khan/Wayne was to rally his kinsman to mighty deeds as yet unspecified. Dick Powell and the assistant directors artfully scattered the few hundred extras, Navajo Indians from a nearby reservation, the better to fill the frame. This proved to be somewhat difficult. Movie making is a time-consuming, boring business and many of the would-be Asian tribesmen relieved their boredom by consuming the 20th century equivalent of fermented Yak milk. Eventually this would prove a plus, as some in the group would have to respond with vocal enthusiasm to the Great Khan's pep talk. Their war whoops and battle cries would be most impressive, the most notable part of the sequence according to Bill Conrad who was there. At the first call for "action," Wayne stood for a long time surveying his troops and glowering a fearsome Khan glower. At length, he spoke in ringing tones that Charlton Heston as Moses would have appreciated. "SEE HERE ALL YOU MONGOLS!!!" he roared. It was at that moment, Conrad said, "I knew we were dead."

Lessons learned?

See *Ishtar*, *Heaven's Gate*, *Waterworld*, etc. Those who do not learn from history are doomed to repeat it. Tricky business making movies. At one point in history and in secret, the studios tasked the Rand Corporation to build a machine that could look at a script, evaluate it and determine how much money it would make. I was interviewed for a job on that project. I would have loved to have been able to prove that the impossible... is impossible. *The Conqueror* proved nothing then, save that bad movies will always be with us. There is even a ghastly postscript to the story of *The Conqueror*.

After the company returned to Hollywood to shoot the interiors, a careful scrutiny of the dailies and a comparison to the California dirt that covered the floors of several sound stages, it was determined that the Golden State dirt did not match St. George soil in color, texture, and perhaps in radioactivity. The offending dirt was discarded as if it were — well, dirt. Truckloads of the real stuff were brought in from Utah. This proved a satisfactory solution, and further opportunity to radiate the entire company.

In the end, no one knows what happened to that suspicious topsoil, though it is unlikely they would have taken the trouble to return it to its source.

Who knows? If you live in Southern California, your backyard could be a part of movie history...

Jack Nicholson

*"It's a stiff, the worst. Forget the percentage;
I want the money."*

**— Jack Nicholson, Actor
Salem, Oregon – 1975**

For most of the quotes and stories, like Bill Conrad's, I was there, and it was a privilege. I loved being the fly on the wall... I take that back; the analogy is disgusting. Think of me as a hummingbird at the window — who reads lips. A few were told to me by trusted, close personal friends who were Jane/Johnny on the spot. One such example follows:

The above observation, though credited to Jack Nicholson, was told to me by Dr. Dean Brooks who was present at the scene that provoked it. Dr. Brooks is still famous in Oregon for his work with the mentally ill. For 27 years, he was Superintendent of the Oregon State Hospital, the primary state facility for treating mental patients. I know this because I went to school in Salem, home of the hospital, and was born in Salem General, just a 5 iron from OSH. My parents knew and admired Dr. Brooks, as did I. In 1976, when trying to get my writing career started, I went to Oregon in search of subject matter and immediately thought of Dr. Brooks. The reason? Just a few months before, Dr. Brooks had permitted the filming of *One Flew Over the Cuckoo's Nest*, one of the most successful pictures of that year, or any year. I was seeking another "Cuckoo." With my family connections, I got an invitation to meet with Dr. Brooks at the hospital. I got a tour of the grounds, during which Dean showed me the building and the room where he in the role of Psychiatrist Dr. Spivey had conducted the famous intake interview with Randle P. McMurphy/a.k.a. Jack Nicholson. The director of the picture, Miloš Forman, allowed both the actor and the doctor considerable latitude while filming and practically the whole sequence was ad-libbed. Nicholson took advantage of the novice in one scene by an old actor's trick, "catching flies," reaching out and grabbing invisible insects. Dr. Brooks' reaction to this was a classic, but he quickly resumed his screen persona questioning of this odd new patient.

Dr. Brooks always had a bit of the actor in him, which helped his cause with the state legislature where he was a popular figure who got his needs filled with a regularity that many a government supplicant would envy. Although he is recognized for his many contributions to the mentally infirmed, I think it is ironic that his Wikipedia bio lists him as an actor first and a medical practitioner second.

Dr. Brooks also had a way with corporate Oregon. Timber giants like Weyerhaeuser supported a Brooks program that had appeared in *Life Magazine* in a photo article titled, "Roughing It Back to Sanity." Brooks had long believed that the system was failing the patients who were not getting well, while staff members were developing problems of their own. His answer was to pair off a patient with a staff member, doctors and nurses included, and send them off to Eastern Oregon for a survival experience that included whitewater rafting, rock climbing, and wilderness survival. It was a marked success. The picture of a rock-climbing doctor depending on the patient who was holding the doctor's climbing rope excited me.

I wrote a fifteen-page treatment. Dean Brooks, never adverse to favorable publicity, gave me his complete support. Before I had returned to Hollywood, my business partner Herm Saunders (*Adam-12, F Troop*) had snagged a meeting at CBS. One did not snag a meeting in those days; one "took" them. Actually, it was a big deal. It was 1976 and the three networks were the only game in town, with CBS on top of the heap. Perhaps a fitting analogy. Our company was weeks old, totally unknown and little heralded.

Though Herm had a reputation, I had none. Nevertheless and to my amazement, the meeting was a total success, and this project was green-lighted on the spot. Since I believed (later confirmed) they had not read my submission, this development remained a mystery until one of the suits said that my comment, "You can't tell the doctors from the patients," had won the day. I got the go ahead to write a script. I had never written a treatment before, let alone a script, and my first reaction was to seek help. My business partner Herm, though he was a producer, was also a member of the Writer's Guild. Like many writers/producers (hyphenates in the biz), creativity comes from an outside source. In Herm's case, it was from young Steve Cannell, whom Herm had tapped to be story editor for *Adam-12* at the age of 19.

In the background we can hear the Friday voice of Jack Webb, threatening, "He better be good pally." He was better than good. The young man became Stephen J. Cannell, and he wrote and produced quality television shows like *The Rockford Files*, *Baretta*, *Baa Baa Black Sheep* and many, many others. Stephen J. tired from all the hassle of shooting shows in Vancouver and the myriad headaches involved in running a production company, no matter how successful. He gave up that life and settled for writing successful crime novels until he died, too young, of cancer.

FLASHBACK to me still waiting for my business partner to help me, which he didn't and probably couldn't. It was my idea and it was not his kind of thing. Herm was very supportive of my efforts, however, and after several days of facing a blank page in panic, trending toward terror, the reluctant Underwood slowly but surely began to make some progress. Herm would read the new pages, pat me on the back and say, "You got it kid." A 32-year-old novice likes to hear those things. I finished the damn thing in a month and a half, and we Rocket Messengered it to CBS.

A week of nail biting silence followed, and then... and then... GOOD NEWS! Another meeting at CBS, this time to sign a go-ahead deal. This was BIG!

My script was called *A Walk in the Forest*. I had seen and been impressed by a post-WWII movie about a platoon that participated in the invasion of Italy. It was called *A Walk in the Sun*, and, if you love films, you should take a look. My submission was followed by several tense weeks of silence, finally broken by promises and words of enthusiastic praise. According to the execs it was to be a highlight of the season, a four-hour special event. Back to CBS for a celebratory meeting, the best kind.

There was only one problem as it turned out — ME. Though my work was praised as having "met all of the parameters" (whatever that meant), it would now be necessary, due to my lack of reputation, to bring in one of their "A" writers for a "polish." Translation is necessary here; "We don't trust our instincts, so we are going to turn it over to someone who has been there before." I wanted to tell CBS to screw off, but an entry to the Writer's Guild was hard to come by and harder to get, so I folded. They were way ahead of me anyway; my collaborator had already been chosen. He was what every network exec and producer looked for in a writer. He was fast. Let us call him Bill Forrest.

The polish became a full rewrite. They were right though; he was fast. I had expected him to want to talk over script with me at some point, but it would only have slowed him down. With a speed that I envied, three copies of the new script were messengered to our office at General Service Studios. I quickly noted with relief that they had kept the title. *A Walk in the Forest* was safe for now. They were the only positives I could find in the "polish" that had become a complete rewrite.

My little touchy-feely story of uplift and growth was now populated by *Cuckoo*-like characters and a hero/patient/protagonist whose dreams were punctuated by the sounds of gnashing of teeth emanating from a giant, steel mouse. This disturbed our hero, almost as much as it disturbed me. The writer Mr. Forrest had told me he disliked his mother, and so there was a mother-villain in the new *Walk*. It seemed that everything was all her fault. I must say here that I really liked the writer, who had promised not to "compromise" my work. I even liked him after reading the script.

When we first met I had initially asked the writer about his most recent credits. His latest for CBS was called *Death Car on the Freeway*, which he assured me was "not his title." I was amused but not comforted.

Now I was distraught, leaning toward rage. To make matters worse, from my now limited vantage point, it had already gone to the big boss, or bb (small letters intended), as he will briefly be known.

It turned out that bb was a hunter/sportsman who was appalled at the thought of "crazy people" in his woods. The project died, and, unlike many others who were killed and revived like the Frankenstein monster, this death was permanent. I realize here that I had gone far afield, but I wanted to confirm that the sad position of the writers in Hollywood is basically true. It is also true that 90% of the green-lighted scripts are never made. One considers that there must be some worthwhile stories in that 90% that would better serve the viewing audience than some of the crap we are getting today, especially — most especially — on network television. My deepest apologies to you and to the late Dr. Brooks, whom I have left warming up in the heavenly bullpen.

To rescue us all, I will again utilize a writer's device called a FLASHBACK. While calling on Dr. Brooks to research *Walk*, I had many questions for him about the making of *Cuckoo's Nest*. Over many visits I got the whole story.

The producers of the film, Saul Zaentz and Michael Douglas, had been turned down by every mental health facility in California and elsewhere. The approached institutions had cited privacy problems, legal problems, and problems they had not yet thought of — and anyway, the answer was NO!

Someone, possibly a *Life Magazine* subscriber, had told them about Dean Brooks, and they were getting desperate. Money was being spent, the not-that-big budget was being impacted, time was ticking away, and the prospects for a movie on the mentally ill, even considering the past successes of the writer's book and play, were marginal at best.

The production team was more than happy to go to Dr. Brooks' hospital in Oregon. Dean insisted on a number of conditions, namely that the patients be shown as human beings with problems and not just as freaks of nature. Also he insisted that the production crew, including the actors, producers, and the director spend at least two weeks on the wards interacting with the patients.

The cast and crew were not only well received by patients and staff, but firm friendships were begun that outlasted the filming of the picture. All was going along nicely.

There was still the problem that there were no major stars in the film. Most of the roles were filled by stage actors who were not all that familiar to the general public. Nurse Ratched was to be played by Louise Fletcher who was also an unknown factor but who would go on to win a Best Supporting Actress Oscar. The biggest star by far was Jack Nicholson but he, as yet, was not a superstar. The film would make him one. The producers had made him a nice offer for a nova of medium stature. He was offered ten percent of the gross or 750 thousand dollars straight up. The final decision was postponed until filming started, but in the meantime he could have half of the dough. The gross offer was exceptional but not quite as good as it looked. If the film bombed, Jack would get very little. If it was a smash, the producers could afford it. Then too, the contract could be written in such a way that there would be a laundry list of expenses written against the project, making it a net gross deal — a typical Hollywood contract.

A month or so into filming, Nicholson approached Dean Brooks to ask for the use of his office, as his agent was flying up from L.A. Brooks agreed, but for legal reasons, he would have to be present. And so he was. Jack spoke of all the problems the film was having. He had lost faith in its success — and HE WANTED THE REST OF THE MONEY!

It should be noted here that performers are not always the best judges of their material.

A few years before, Elliot Gould, a star at the time, had done at least one interview in which he described his latest picture in terms of human excrement. The picture was *MASH*. Spencer Tracy, finally free of the paternal arms of MGM, opted for a 20th Century Fox effort entitled *The Mountain*, in which

Robert Wagner, a hundred or so years younger than the veteran Tracy, played his brother. The picture was lousy anyway.

And Jack's decision? It cost him the better part of 20 million bucks. Thirty some years later in one of the Batman films, he played the Joker, asking and getting ten percent of the gross (no deductions), thus making his money back plus interest.

A final note or two on this wonderful film *Cuckoo's Nest.* Dr. Brooks did not lay aside his medical duties during the making of the picture. He diagnosed a major player, William Redfield (who had appeared in the NY stage version) as having leukemia. Sadly, the noted actor would die within the year. On a brighter note, the water cooler that Chief Bromden, played by newcomer Will Sampson, threw through a barred window to gain his freedom was rescued and now resides as a permanent resident of Dr. Brooks' old office — a forever memory of *Cuckoo's Nest* at Oregon State Hospital.

Television Executive – The Black Tower

"We can shoot it on the back lot and cover up the palm trees."

— Television Executive – The Black Tower
Universal City – Hollywood, California – 1972

T he Black Tower is a naturally dark and forbidding thirty-story edifice that stands inside the entrance to Universal Studios. Terrible events have come to pass there.

At the time and on the day I entered the Black Tower it was ruled by a king, Lew Wasserman. There had been rulers in Hollywood before — Mayer, Cohn, Zanuck, Warner, Disney, and a few others — but even Walt Disney was not a king. They were only princes. Some, like Louis B. Mayer, were more princely than others, as Orwell would have put it, but they all paled before King Lew. Some high officials of his court had not only paled, they had fainted, vomited, wept, and peed in their pants when faced with the famous Wasserman ire. To put a better face on this departed legend, I must add that Wasserman had the respect, if not the love, of every element of Hollywood society, the only person who could bring all fractious elements together. He was an astute businessman and philanthropist, honored by popes and presidents. He was

15

many other things too, but I won't go into them because this story isn't about Lew Wasserman.

This is a tale that involves me and some of Wasserman's choice vassals. One of them had gained me entrance to the castle. He was Taft Schreiber, a big dog, a vice president in charge of other vice presidents of something or other, and the official house Republican. They didn't miss a beat at Universal.

I was going to add that King Lew, though a liberal Democrat, had given aid and comfort to Ronald Reagan as an actor and through his transition to bigger things. That Lew could pick 'em, could he not? I won't go there though because this is not about Lew Wasserman.

Back to Taft Schreiber, a powerful man in his own right, a fixture at the studio. He was involved in a coup, along with MCA founder Jules Stein. The coup failed and, though Taft Schreiber kept his job and title, most of his power was severely curtailed. He had most probably also been a vomiteer, though not voluntarily. I had obtained a job interview with Schreiber, thanks to my Navy connections where my last assignment on active duty had been as a motion picture and television officer at the Navy's Office of Information in Los Angeles. In that capacity I had aided Universal in the making of a motion picture.

The movie was *Silent Running*, a story of a space freighter in the future. I took a call from one of their producers who had come up with a clever but stupid idea. What he/they wanted was to borrow an active duty aircraft carrier whose cavernous hanger bays would provide a perfect backdrop to their futuristic tale, while saving the cost of myriad sound stages. The notion that the Navy would take a carrier off operations to make a movie was an immediate deal breaker, and I said so as diplomatically as one can when speaking to someone with an idiotic idea. I said I would get back to him, a lie we both understood. He was very disappointed, and I went back to my coffee.

A few days later I drove down the 405 to the Long Beach Naval Station on assignment. As I was crossing over the Vincent Thomas Bridge, I noticed a forlorn-looking vessel moored on an out-of-the-way pier. The hull numbers had been removed and there were other significant signs of decay and abandonment. The Valley Forge, one of 24 Essex class carriers built during and just after WWII, was no longer a ship of the line. A little checking on my part found that its next destination was the scrap heap at the naval shipyard Mare Island, near San Francisco.

We have stayed far afield from the Black Tower, so I will cut to the chase, as my fellow writers like to say. I did call that producer back and a deal was brokered to rent the ship to Universal for the six months it would be sitting in Long Beach awaiting its fate. An agreement was struck between the studio and the Navy for a weekly rental of ten grand or so. Chump change for the government, but it was found money, the best kind. For Universal, it was a real windfall. A special effects film with no stars (Bruce Dern was the biggest) would save on locations, and its budget could stay in the B-feature class.

I received nothing for initiating the deal. It was my job, after all. I did extract the promise of future employment from the producer when I left the Navy. I hoped for nothing special — just a soft, cushy job that would set me on the road to Hollywood success and fortune. Oddly, when I called after my separation to redeem that promise, the producer never seemed to be in his office and had also lost my phone number. Shame on you, Michael Gruskoff!

I soon discovered that similar evanescent promises had also evanesced, leaving me out on the street hat in hand.

Thus I sat before Taft Schreiber, pleading my case for employment. I mentioned to him my *Silent Running* contribution, and he seemed favorably impressed. "But what is it that you do?" he asked. At one time he would have had me there, but by now I was ready for him. "I'm a writer," I lied straight-faced.

"We can always use those," he said.

And so it was that two weeks later I was on my way to the very top of the Tower to meet with a bigwig or two in charge of television programming. I did not go unarmed or unassisted. In the previous fourteen days, I had developed a concept for a TV series called *Trouble Man*. It was the story of an ombudsman, once a famous athlete at a state university, and a former rodeo star, now a successful rancher. This puffed up hero resume fitted James Drury, who had been the star of Universal's mega hit, *The Virginian.* Jim also happened to be a schoolmate of mine. I had pitched the idea to him over the phone and he said he was interested. Close enough.

What hooked James Drury was the idea of an official driving all over the state setting up shop in malls and parking lots and inviting citizens to air their grievances. There would be tales of graft and corruption, stupidity and unfairness, and perhaps something sinister — in short, the story of a typical sprawling government entity. I was also accompanied in my quest by Jackie Cooper, a veteran of the movie wars, a former child star who had faced rejection (and temporary eviction) from MGM, which frowned on acne in its adolescent luminaries, and theft from a stepfather who made off with most of his childhood earnings.

Jackie credited the Navy for "making a man" of him during WWII; and returning to civilian life, he had clawed his way back up the ladder to a firm position as a working actor and a successful producer/director. Captain Jack (he had retained his loyalty to the Navy) received a commission and was a Captain USNR. More to the point for me, he had also taken a bite out of *Trouble Man,* and since he knew the mysteries of the entertainment lingo, he would do all of the heavy lifting in the interview while I filled in the blanks, if any.

Captain Cooper exceeded my wildest expectations. Not only did he hold the interest of the chief vassal and two accompanying serfs, he filled in most of the blanks and plugged the holes in my 13 story ideas, which were a few sentences, bare bones at best. Cooper also invented out of thin air a kind of Sancho Panza companion for my hero. Cooper described this character as "Kildare and Gillespie upside down and backwards." This referred to a popular movie and television series with a wise old doctor (Lionel Barrymore/Raymond Massey) and a young, handsome, in-need-of-help-sometimes doctor (Lew Ayres/Richard Chamberlain). In short and in translation, the young hero was the smart one and the older man was more like a sidekick in old Western movies — lovable, loyal, slow, yet capable of pithy sayings à la Charlie Chan. We all solemnly agreed he should not be a boob but should have "pathos." I noticed that none of the traits of character or twists of plots were unfamiliar. There is absolutely nothing new in the creation of these things. Besides, the vassal and serfs seemed much more at ease with the already known. Anything different and revolutionary might have frightened them away. We are talking 70s television here.

I was called on once in a while for a word or two and an occasional nod of assent. It could not have possibly gone any better, I thought. The pitch meeting ended. "I love it!" said the head vassal. The serfs loved it too! As we were leaving, the boss walked us by a window and looked out at the lot.

"Where did you say this thing was set?" he asked.

"The Pacific Northwest," I answered.

"That's all right," he mused, "We can shoot it on the back lot and cover up the palm trees."

Forty some years later, I still think that was one of the funniest things ever said to me.

On the way down in the elevator, I remarked to Jack, "Did you hear what he said about the palm trees?" Jack had been around a long time. He had heard enough.

"No," he said.

I asked Captain Jack how he thought it had gone.

"Great," he said smiling.

I always thought that ready smile was forced. There was a lot of rejection behind that boyish grin. Of course I did not think that at the time. I remember driving home in a high so great it was scary. "There's no business like show business," I sang over and over and over. In what other business can a total nonentity walk into an office and tell people he had never met what they should be doing next in their particular endeavor?

Amazing.

Unbelievable.

In three days we received an answer from Universal. They had passed. Tough love. Welcome to Hollywood.

Bob Hope

"Scared of what?"

— Bob Hope, Comedian/Actor
Beirut, Lebanon – 1982

They changed the name of Bob Hope Airport the other day. Hollywood Burbank is the new moniker which makes sense geographically speaking — in sentimental terms, not so much. I don't suppose that many people under 20 have any idea who Bob Hope was. That is a shame, because he was really something.

Speaking as a vet, I know of no one outside the services who has done more for the military than Hope. I saw his Christmas show in 1962 in Taipei, Taiwan. A lot of the old gang was along — Jerry Colonna, Les Brown and his band, but I was there to see Hope. Away from America for over a year, Hope brought a touch of home to me. I was always a big Hope fan, on radio and in the movies mostly. I have several books and posters signed by him to me and my family.

A friend of mine, Harry Flynn, one of Hope's many publicists, told me that, no matter how busy Hope was, and he was always busy, he always tried to spend an hour or so a day answering fan mail, requests for photos and such.

Hope and his good friend Arnold Palmer were among the most prolific celebrity signers of all time.

As an autograph collector/addict, I have several Hope books signed to others. One is of particular interest. "To Shirley, I miss you." An innocent explanation would be that it was signed to his Big Broadcast of 1938 costar Shirley Ross; however, Shirley Ross was dead when the book was signed.

I have to wonder how the "Me Too" movement might have reacted to the stars of the Golden Age. Hope, Errol Flynn, Gary Cooper, and David Niven were only a few of the possible suspects. Even Leslie Howard, of all people, was said to have been a womanizer of the first rank. With the downfall of a noxious slug like Harvey Weinstein, a host of contemporary stars have come under fire, and even possible prosecution. That is all well and good, but an accusation is not a conviction. The abuse defense is a virtual must in the cases of women accused of murdering their husbands or boyfriends, which is okay if it can be proved but lame if it can't.

I have tried to emphasize the values and virtues of the 20th century man and woman, but there were vices and defects there, and I should know because I had plenty of both. Which reminds me, as long as I am on this extended detour, to proclaim that we had a better class of criminals in my day. It is impossible to think of bank robber Willie Sutton and other lawbreakers of my era who would stoop to pleading not guilty when caught with their hands in the till — or around someone's throat. Even gang members mostly targeted one another and made efforts to keep innocent civilians out of the line of fire.

There is simply too much firepower available today, and an automatic weapons ban is a no-brainer to me. There should also be a ban on lawyers who advertise in the media that they can get their clients off, no matter the circumstances.

Oh yes, Bob Hope. I came to Hollywood in 1969 with the Navy. It was inevitable, on military occasions or matters, our paths would cross. I was luckier than that. We met briefly several times. He was friendly but not particularly forthcoming. He was never funny — never tried to be. He wanted to talk about Vietnam. I didn't, but I listened.

After I left active duty, my company produced two outtakes or bloopers shows on NBC. Hope was in one of them and had opened his vast vault of material to let us use a few good ones. In my pursuit of autographs, I am ashamed to report that I got Hope to sign a baseball as he and his wife were talking to President and Mrs. Ford at a post golf tournament dinner in Rancho Mirage. Shameless, and worse, I sold it too cheaply.

Two other occasions come to mind. The first was in Vegas at a celebrity benefit. It was at the old Sands, and I was sitting in a booth at the entrance and exit of the main showroom. Hope was first on the bill, with customary entrance theme and exit theme. "Thanks for the Memory." Another big star followed, but I wasn't paying attention to him or her. I observed that Hope had exited the stage and was walking around the showroom so that he would pass directly past me. As he moved closer I turned away from the stage toward which everyone else was looking and mimed "applause, applause." Hope saw me out of the corner of his eye and, as he passed, he reached for my arm and squeezed it — twice. It was the second squeeze that did it for me. No wonder he's such a big deal, I thought — that was personal PR at its best.

Harry Flynn, the aforementioned publicist, gave me another instance that was never reported anywhere. Hope always went as close as he could to where the action was.

In 1983 it was in Lebanon, which provided another good reason for not getting in the middle of what goes on in the Middle East. In October of '83 the Marine barracks in Beirut were attacked with a deadly truck bomb. 241 American military personnel were killed, including 220 Marines, the largest one-day Marine casualty total since Iwo Jima. Hope immediately began to pester Harry Flynn, who was also Commander Harry Flynn, USNR, to work something out so that he and his troupe could get over there. Harry had a hand in arranging some of the USO tours and other military events, where Hope was in constant demand.

What Hope wanted Hope got, and in December, Hope and Harry Flynn and a group of willing entertainers left Van Nuys Airport for the Middle East.

Because of the dangers involved, it was decided by the Pentagon top brass that Hope and his party could not go into Beirut proper, but the shows could be performed on the ships at sea nearby. The Marines ashore would be helicoptered out to various ships, and the shows would be staged there. The USS Guam LPH-9, an Iwo Jima class amphibious assault ship with a large flight deck, was the host for both the Hope troupe and the first of the shows. Hope had no complaint with this set up, but he still wanted to go into Beirut and perform for the Marines at the Beirut airport. The answer was no, many times. "Too dangerous." "Impossible."

After performing for Vice Admiral Edward Martin, the admiral asked Harry Flynn if it was possible to pay for one of the special Hope troupe jackets that had been made especially for this trip. Harry took off his own jacket and gave it to the admiral.

A week later, what was impossible was now reality.

No one was to know, and measures would be taken to assure a total news blackout. Within minutes, every Marine in Beirut knew that Bob Hope was coming their way. Four of the roughest, toughest Navy SEALs would be accompanying the Hope party flying in, with a second helicopter flying cover and support. The dangers of this evolution can only be imagined.

On the flight in, one of the SEALs talking to Harry Flynn asked if he thought Bob Hope was scared. Hope heard him. "Scared of what?" he asked. The SEAL thought Hope had been praying, but as was the

A signed poster to me by Bob Hope and Jane Russell

entertainer's habit, he was just dozing. Upon landing, they went to the base hospital where there were troops still recovering from their wounds from the barracks bombing two months earlier. There was a meet and greet at the airport, and Hope went around to many of the Marines in the area. None of the visits were filmed, but there were some still photos taken.

The story did not come out till the Hope expedition was back in the USA.

The final Bob Hope kicker to this, for me, was that Hope took the time and trouble to find that Harry Flynn had been on no one's payroll. Hope Enterprises thought the Navy was taking care of Flynn, but this was not the case. Back in Toluca Lake, Hope invited Harry to drop by for a chat. Flynn lived just a few blocks away and thought that Hope might want to relive some of the experiences on the trip. He did, but he also wrote Harry Flynn a personal check for ten thousand dollars. He could write it off, of course, but he went out of his way to reward a valued member of his team.

Please don't talk badly about Bob Hope to me. I am liable to wallop you.

William Conrad

"It might be worth a few bucks."

— William Conrad, Actor
Burbank, California — 1982

The name may not be all that familiar now, but William Conrad was a presence, bluff, hearty with the girth and appetites of Henry VIII (and some of the menace, which he used to good effect playing heavies in numerous film noirs). To be fair, he had a lot of Falstaff in him too. Bill was a familiar, constant voice on the radio for decades. He appeared in over 7,500 radio shows. He played all the roles on an episode of *Suspense*, was the voice of Matt Dillon on *Gunsmoke* and was the announcer (on TV) of the *Rocky and Bullwinkle Show*.

Bill described the madhouse atmosphere of the latter show as equally as funny as the program itself. Producer Jay Ward was constantly urging him to read "faster and faster," which inevitably would arouse the noted Conrad temper. Bill laughed at the memory of "The weird and terrible events that took place on Veronica Lake." Bill also pitched everything from automobiles to pet food.

In the 50s, the parts on films decreased, but Bill was still Matt Dillon. He had high hopes for landing the same role when it came to television. So he lost weight and got himself into what for him was great shape.

But when John Wayne was asked for his opinion on the part, he recommended Jim Arness, who had appeared in several recent Wayne films.

Rejection is always a part of the business, but Bill Conrad was terribly disappointed. There was always dinner though, and back went the pounds, this time to stay.

Bill was both multi-talented and resilient. In 1960, he went to Warner Brothers at the behest of the studio head, Jack Warner. While there Bill fulfilled many roles — actor, director, producer, narrator, and all-around creative force. Warner was so pleased with Bill's efforts that as a bonus he was given an iconic prop — one of the two Black Birds from the film noir classic *The Maltese Falcon* which starred Humphrey Bogart and perhaps the best cast ever assembled for a studio film. It included Peter Lorre, Sydney Greenstreet (in his film debut at 62), Mary Astor, Gladys George, Ward Bond, Barton MacLane, Jerome Cowan, Elisha Cook, Jr., and other talented players.

There were actually two Falcons because one had to be defaced as part of the plot, and the other had to be available for possible retakes.

Bill was telling me this story at a lunch at the Smoke House in Burbank after narrating a Navy documentary that I had written. I had begun my collection of movie autographs and memorabilia then, but this was way out of my league.

Bill Conrad was grateful to Jack Warner but hardly impressed.

I asked Bill where the Black Bird was. "Somewhere in the closet at home — it could be worth a few bucks."

A few bucks indeed.

After Bill's death some years later, his widow, Tippy, put it up for auction for thirty-five thousand dollars. It sold for just slightly under $400K. Then it was quickly resold to a mystery buyer for over a million.

At around this time, Falcons began popping up like dandelions in May. Lead Falcons, plaster Falcons, all manner of Black Birds. Steve Wynn is alleged to have purchased a 45-pound lead falcon for 4.2 million. Whatever happens with the birds, one thing is certain: William Conrad owned one of the originals. It was presented to him, scratches and all, from the head of the studio where the movie was made. And you can't beat that for provenance.

I have often wondered what would have happened if I had made an offer. But then, neither Bill nor I would have any idea what people would be willing to pay for an iconic bit of Hollywood history that is right up there with Dorothy's red shoes.

William Conrad would later star in such popular shows as *Cannon* and *Jake and the Fat Man*, which we will visit later. My memory of his narrating my film was amazement at just how good he was and how fast it all went. I don't remember there being more than two takes on any line, and one of those, Bill called himself.

When he had finished, he nodded to me and observed, "This was high-grade shit." I cherish the compliment, and he was nice enough to inscribe that sentiment on my copy of the script.

Bill is too fine a talent to limit to a single quote. We will visit him again.

Glenn Ford

"Ernie Borgnine can be Ernie Borgnine all his life."

— Glenn Ford, Actor
Beverly Hills, California — 1970

With the beginning of motion pictures, a very strange event began to occur. Women in their mid-forties or younger began to disappear. It started with Mary Pickford, "America's Sweetheart." When her "little girl" persona began to unravel as time marched on, she retired. A superlative business woman as well as an actress, she seriously considered burning the negatives on all her pictures, which she owned. "Little Mary" retired to Pickfair and the loving care of her husband, Buddy Rogers, there to peacefully drink herself to death away from the prying eyes of fans and columnists.

As a founder of United Artists Mary Pickford retained much of her power but you never saw her again on film. At the same time on the stage, great actresses were allowed to age without prejudice. Helen Hayes, Ethel Barrymore, Katharine Cornell, Lynn Fontanne, Julie Harris, and many others had long and successful careers on the boards.

Not so in the movies.

There were exceptions of course — Hepburn, Bette Davis, and Joan Crawford come to mind, possibly Irene Dunne and Myrna Loy. This was in the heyday of so-called "women's pictures." But opportunities for romance, older woman and younger man, were not there. Davis and Crawford were pushed into shock or horror pictures that showed the ravages of old age which were, frankly, beneath them.

Fans loved them as old hags though.

Meanwhile the Sandra Dees and Meg Ryans vanished before their forties. Men were treated much more gently. Clark Gable, Gary Cooper, Cary Grant, James Stewart, and William Holden appeared in films with leading ladies who could have been their daughters or even their granddaughters. Meanwhile, their costars of yesteryear were either dead, discarded, or had become princesses — Susan Hayward, Rita Hayworth, Lana Turner, Gene Tierney, Linda Darnell, Roz Russell, and Grace Kelly come to mind.

It was about the time of *Love in the Afternoon*, featuring the very mature Gary Cooper and the young and vulnerable Audrey Hepburn, that some began to question the believability of such December and May unions. Cary Grant began to get the message late in his career. *Walk, Don't Run*, his final film, being the best example. Duke Wayne got the word even sooner. In his last decade or so in feature films, Wayne opted for Rooster Cogburn-type roles or "buddy" pictures with the likes of Kirk Douglas and Robert Mitchum and others. When romance was involved, ever so slightly, it was with someone like Coleen Dewhurst, which made more sense. Of course in real life Wayne was paired with a much younger woman, his longtime secretary, Pat Stacy, and he may have felt some guilt about that. That is, however, a whole other story, which brings us back in my roundabout, circuitous fashion, to Glenn Ford.

People may not remember this today, but Glenn Ford was a STAR, a Fifties Superstar, Number One at the box office in 1955. The stars of that era still have a hold on today's public — Bogart and Wayne for sure, Gable for *Gone with the Wind*; Grant, Tracy, Stewart, and Kirk Douglas strong maybes. Not so Glenn Ford. Perhaps it was because none of his films, while popular at the time, are regarded as classics — *Casablanca*, *Gone with the Wind*, *The Searchers*, etc. *Gilda* had a cult following, but that is about it.

Glenn Ford got caught up in the May/December thing mostly of his own choosing.

I was at the Navy Office of Information from 1969 to 1971, and producers would generally send us scripts with a Ford character, perhaps hoping to go around his agent, CMA, or ICM, or whatever it was. We would send them along to the agency, and usually the agent who handled Ford would call before actually reading the script and say something like, "Does it have some romance in it? Glenn likes that kind of thing."

On set on a Navy film. Captain Glenn Ford (USNR) was the star.

Glenn was pushing sixty at the time and the good scripts and the offers were not as frequent as they had been just a few years before. His persona had always been of Mr. Everyman, youthful, handsome, sometimes shy and hesitant, but fearless when aroused, moved, or crossed. Jimmy Stewart had had that "aw shucks" kind of character, but in the last half of his career he turned to harder, darker heroes, some even obsessed, cynical, or neurotic. In short, Stewart matured. Ford was more comfortable with his standard character with a love interest. That was no longer cinematic reality.

The May/December thing had caught up with Glenn Ford. Westerns were going out of style too, and Westerns had been Ford's biggest successes in recent years. Since 1939 there was hardly a day when there was not a script to be read or a role to perform. Time lay heavier on Ford's hands. He began to show a greater interest in the Navy.

Glenn Ford had been a Naval Reservist since 1958 and now was a Captain, USNR. This development took me to Ford's home occasionally. Glenn lived in a Spanish-style place on Oxford, just behind the Beverly Hills Hotel. It was nice, north of the Boulevard (Sunset) in a rich neighborhood, but hardly a movie star mansion.

Frank Capra had just written his autobiography in which he described Ford as "difficult" and amplified this theme on several pages that dealt with the film *A Pocketful of Miracles*, on which they had worked together but not necessarily in harness. Though Glenn took his movie star status seriously, he was always extremely nice to me. Of course, I liked him in consequence. I was a movie nut anyway, impressed by his career. I enjoyed many of his films.

Between pictures Ford had let his hair turn gray. He belatedly was turning to television and character parts. We discussed several Navy matters, our conversation interrupted by a loud sound that seemed to come from above. "Rita," he said, referring to his costar, current neighbor and former lover. "She throws her empty champagne bottles on my roof." He grinned that boyish, Glenn Ford grin. "You get used to it." I don't think I could have — I mean having Rita Hayworth as a neighbor, much less throwing her empties on my roof. Rita, as it turns out, had an alcohol problem and the beginning of Alzheimer's. Glenn understood and said he was trying to help her.

It was about this time, out of the blue, Ford said what he said, "Ernie Borgnine can play Ernie Borgnine parts, roles of all kinds, for as long as he lives." And he did too. Ernie Borgnine continued to work in films and television till his death at ninety-five. People loved Ernie, and Ernie loved them back.

Sometimes it pays to be ordinary and a little ugly. Sometimes you can feel sorry for a movie star...

Chill Willis and Donald O'Connor

"Have a Texas roadmap, cousin"

— Chill Wills, Actor
Eugene, Oregon – 1962

"I loved those movies — I didn't have to dance."
— Donald O'Connor, Actor/Dancer
Sherman Oaks, California – 1980

C hill Wills and Donald O'Connor may have seemed an odd combination, but they had one thing in common — a mule, and a talking mule at that. O'Connor was the star of a series of *Francis* films produced by Universal-International in the early fifties. These light but popular pictures detailed the misadventures of Francis, an Army mule with Chill Wills' voice, and a hapless but winning buddy/foil, Peter Sterling, played by O'Connor.

Donald had been paired with Peggy Ryan at Universal in half a dozen musical comedies. They were a junior varsity version of Rooney and Garland over at MGM. The Universal efforts did highlight O'Connor's singing and dancing talents, which were considerable. Playing second fiddle to a long-eared beast must have seemed a bit of comedown, even though every one of those films made money.

The public loved the pairing.

Early in the series, O'Connor went to MGM for *Singin' in the Rain*, one of the best movies ever made about Hollywood. That was 1952, a year in which *Singin' in the Rain* was not even nominated for Best Picture. *Rain* was a smash, and O'Connor's "Make 'Em Laugh" dance routine was perhaps the best thing in the film. I thought it must have been difficult for Donald O'Connor to go back to being second fiddle ("Fit as a Fiddle,") another great *Singin' in the Rain* number, to a mule.

In 1980 Donald O'Connor was one of many stars who appeared in a telethon for the National Council on Alcoholism, which I was co-producing. We shot an interview with him at his comfortable home in Sherman Oaks, and I asked him about his feelings about being sidekick to a donkey. He "loved those pictures," he said. "I about killed myself in *Singin' in the Rain*. I never worked so hard in my life. I was smoking four or five packs of cigarettes a day. Going back to *Francis* was like a vacation."

Chill Wills was something else again, in more ways than one. I met him at a telethon as well. I was a Navy volunteer/phone answerer for a *March of Dimes* telethon in Eugene, Oregon, in 1963. Actually, I was ordered to the event. I learned early in my service never to volunteer for anything, a position I have rigidly adhered to ever since.

Chill had willingly volunteered his services for free. Chill is little known these days, except for fans of Turner Classic Movies and AMC, but he was a consistent presence in film from the forties through the sixties. He had begun his career as a singer with the Avalon Four, a group he founded. You can hear him singing bass over the charming Laurel and Hardy dance sequence in *Way Out West*. After 1940, Chill concentrated on acting. He usually played a professional Texan, a role he continued off stage as well. When we were introduced, he reached in his pocket and handed me what he termed "A Texas road map." It was a color postcard of Chill, a Texas flag, sagebrush, and an armadillo or two.

Chill was quite the self-promoter, no doubt. Like all Texans he loved servicemen, and conversation was easy. He was dressed like a frontier mortician — dark suit, string tie, and great looking cowboy boots. The telethon was held at the local Elks Club, and it took but a few steps for Chill to walk off stage to the bar. This is where we met. He had a bottle of Jack Daniels Black Label set aside for him, and he consulted it at regular intervals throughout the day.

The booze had little effect, save to make Chill more effusive, loquacious, and down-homey than ever. He spoke to the audience as if he were a friend or neighbor, perhaps a redneck cousin, eccentric but lovable. "Ah would love to make you folks honorary Texans. I met your Governor (later Senator Mark Hatfield). I looked him in the eye — he's good."

It worked. The phones were ringing, the people were giving, and the telethon was breaking records.

Late in the day, back in the bar, I noticed that the first bottle of Jack Daniels had been replaced by a twin brother. Chill was now to the point of confiding in me. He was going to Hawaii after this to play Fleet Admiral Chester Nimitz in a John Wayne movie. Nimitz was a fellow Texan, but a totally different personality. Nimitz was dignified and somewhat reserved. It would be quite a stretch, but watching Chill, I thought that anyone who could knock back a quart of booze and carry on as if nothing was amiss could do almost anything.

Chill was on the air for another three or four hours before returning to his hotel for a few hours of sleep. Promptly the next morning, there he was again. If bright-eyed and bushy-tailed were not an accurate description, he was on time, hitting his marks, and ready to go. For breakfast he made a six-pack of beer disappear with a speed that David Copperfield would have envied. The man was indestructible. He wasn't, of course. It got him in the end, to the point that his publicist had to put out a release that Chill Wills was off the sauce and had been for many a moon, or quite a few months anyway.

There are few secrets in Hollywood. Chill Willis was up there on the list of great characters I have encountered. I was his willing, private audience. He spoke to me of many things, probably including cabbages and kings. But he never, in two whole days, said a word about Francis the mule. Francis must have stolen scenes from Chill's voice.

Working a Telethon
with Michele Lee

Michele Lee is known for her role as Karen Cooper Fairgate MacKenzie on the 1980s prime-time soap opera "Knots Landing" (1979–93), for which she was nominated for a 1982 Emmy Award and won the Soap Opera Digest Award for Best Actress in 1988, 1991, and 1992. She was the only performer to appear in all 344 episodes of the series.

Evelyn Keyes

"He was just the same old asshole."

— Evelyn Keyes, Actress
Beverly Hills, California — 2001

Evelyn Keyes was best known for her role in *Gone with the Wind*, where she played Scarlett O'Hara's younger sister. That was far from the whole story. She was an accomplished and versatile performer who appeared in fifty films in all genres: comedy, drama, Westerns, even a musical or two. We met at one of the Round Table Book Club luncheons that I have mentioned elsewhere. She and two other women of film noir — Coleen Gray and Ann Savage — and author Eddie Muller were on hand at the Beverly Wilshire Hotel to sign the book *Dark City Dames: The Women of Film Noir*. I purchased three books; I should have gotten a couple of dozen. Ms. Keyes and I exchanged a few pleasantries, one thing led to another, and I asked her to lunch. She countered with an offer of coffee at her apartment condo on Beverly Drive, which I naturally accepted.

Ms. Keyes was still a very attractive woman, but romance was never on the agenda. I was interested in her career in film, plus she had led a very interesting personal life. She was married four times, and also had a long affair with showman Mike Todd. Two of her other husbands were directors of some temperament: Charles Vidor and John Huston. Number one had committed suicide early on. He was never discussed. Her last husband, the longest running by far, was musician-turned-author Artie Shaw. I never met Shaw, but we had talked

36

on the phone about his books. It seemed odd to many that he had given up a world-class career as bandleader and musician to become a less than successful writer. Mostly Ms. Keyes talked about Shaw, who also had a marital history of some note. He was married eight times, Lana Turner and Ava Gardner among the flock. The Shaw/Keyes relationship lasted longer than all their other hitchings put together.

Artie Shaw and Evelyn Keyes built a house in Spain and moved there to an isolated location — the better to provide inspiration for Shaw's writing career, which was drooping. Ms. Keyes had temporarily given up her own career to further Shaw's. They were happy there for a while. Ms. Keyes had never done the housewife thing, but she actually enjoyed it. Isolated inspiration did not translate to a book, however, and a frustrated Artie Shaw began to fall back into one of his character defects, pointing out the defects of another, namely his wife. She was a strong woman. The battle was joined.

They left Spain.

She resumed her career. It was over, though not finalized for several more years. Still there had been many happy times.

As Ms. Keyes sat around sipping coffee, she told me that a wave of nostalgia had passed over her recently. Artie Shaw had settled in Newbury Park, California, just thirty miles up the 101. She thought about it and decided to give him a call. Shaw seemed happy to hear from her and the two of them chatted pleasantly for a time, until the musician-turned-author began to go into detail as to why it was Ms. Keyes fault that they had gotten a divorce. The conversation became more and more strained until finally, she hung up on him. There would be no further calls she said, passing judgment on her attempt at recapturing the best of the past.

My business partner Herman Saunders had been a big-band musician. I had heard that most of the leaders of the great bands were autocratic disciplinarians. Perhaps unwilling to take the word of an ex-wife, I asked Herm if Artie Shaw was a nice guy.

"Not really," he said.

Ernest Borgnine

"Not getting a role I wanted,
a setback of any kind...

I just kept thinking something
better will be coming along?"

— **Ernest Borgnine, Actor**
Hollywood Hills, California — 2003

"What are all these people
coming to see me for? I ain't dyin'.
Give me my pants, I'm going home."

— **Ernest Borgnine, Actor**
Cedars Sinai Hospital
Los Angeles, California — 2012

This was the type of heady optimism that made Ernie Borgnine a true Hollywood success story. Even on the day before his death at age 95 in Cedars Sinai Hospital, Ernie was still sounding optimistic. He did not let WWII and ten years in the Navy stop him, nor did a number of misses in everyday jobs deter him from what must have seemed impossible to friends and family.

Ernie wanted to become an actor.

A break here and there and a meaty role as a sadistic sergeant in *From Here to Eternity* set him on the path to cinematic fame, and briefly, villainy. That did not last and *McHale's Navy* transformed him into the Ernest Borgnine we knew and loved.

Because of our Navy connection, I was invited to Ernie's house several times over the years. On two occasions, I was photographed holding his Academy Award from *Marty*. The photographs were taken by friends, but I neglected to ask for prints, and my only chance at posing with the iconic statue has been lost forever.

Ernie was not only the most approachable of actors — he would often approach you first.

Between assignments, Ernie and a friend would travel about the country in a motor home, stopping here and there to chat with folks who happened along. Ernie loved life and the people in it, most of whom felt the same way about him. He also loved the ladies and married quite a few of them.

One of Ernie's wives was the fiery Mexican actress Katy Jurado. During one of their disagreements, Katy grabbed a photo of her husband, tore it up, and peed on it on their living room carpet.

Another of his brides was entertainer Ethel Merman. The marriage turned out to be as much of a mismatch on the inside as it did to everyone else in the outside world. But Ernie had a sense of humor about it. The marriage lasted fewer than forty days. Their honeymoon to the Far East turned out to be a McHale love fest, with no one recognizing Merman at all. This did not sit well with La Merman, a woman of strong ego, and it all blew up before they got back to California.

In her autobiography, Merman had a chapter headed "My Marriage to Ernest Borgnine." The page that followed it was blank. I heard the story from Ernie himself. He thought it was very funny.

Ernie had a large collection of Lincoln memorabilia in his den that was valuable both historically and monetarily. Another prized item was a photo of his friend Lee Marvin. They were in several films together. I believe this picture was from *Cat Ballou*, for which Marvin had been honored with an Oscar for Best Actor. The photo was inscribed to his old buddy Ernie, but Lee signed it "Randolph Scott." Another picture on his wall was of a Navy ship and the shipmates with whom Ernie had served.

Ernie continued to speak and appear on behalf of the Navy, in person and on camera throughout his career. He was made an honorary Chief Petty Officer in 2004 and, as he had requested, his funeral in 2012 was complete with a flag for the family and military honors. Many Navy men and women participated or attended.

Ernie lived to be 95, and his career lasted as long as he did.

Ernie's autobiography, ghosted by his longtime publicist Harry Flynn, came out in 2008. Though over 90, Ernie had traveled the country, appearing on talk shows and at book signings in cities from coast to coast. I went to many book signings. The book

With Ernie Borgnine. Besides being a great actor, Ernie always remembered how lucky he was, and where he had come from. Everyone loved Ernie.

seller's people would always caution, "No inscriptions or pictures, please." Ernie would then say, "Forget that stuff!" and he would pose for pictures and sign any inscription that his book-buying fans wanted.

The first time I met Borgnine to drive him to a Navy event he was in front of his house, lowering the Stars and Stripes at sundown.

That was vintage Ernie.

Troy Donahue, Margaret O'Brien, and Robert Young

> *"Mind it? I didn't mind it at all.*
> *I enjoyed it actually."*
>
> **— Troy Donahue, Actor**
> **Pacific Palisades, California – 1995**

> *"I loved being a child star."*
> **— Margaret O'Brien, Actress**
> **Hollywood, California – On numerous occasions**

> *"Charles, what is it? What's the matter?"*
> **— Robert Young, Actor**
> **MGM Studios – 1944**

The Norma Desmond syndrome is alive and well in Hollywood and elsewhere. Call it Sunset Boulevard revisited. Many an actor or actress has succumbed to this dreadful condition. What is worse, almost none of them have Norma's mansion or money. They are individuals whose star,

150 Years of Hollywood History: Robert Young appeared in his first film in 1931. Turhan Bey was a star in the 1940s ("The Mummy"), and Margaret O'Brien, perhaps the best child actress ever, whose career began in 1941's "Journey for Margaret" (with Robert Young).

an uncertain description at best, has dimmed or whose moment has passed and who refuse to accept the new reality. They are sad and pathetic and we don't want to talk about them. So, we won't. Instead let's meet someone who played the cards as they were dealt, with a little bit of help from an anonymous fellowship.

Troy Donahue was a huge star in the 1950s and 60s in such films as *A Summer Place*, *Parrish,* and *Rome Adventure*. We first met in the late 1980s at Turnoff in Desert Hot Springs, California, a long-term recovery home for young alcoholics and addicts who had been totally given up on by the system and their parents. The ones who made it stayed a full year. It was really Alcoholics Anonymous meetings around the clock.

Troy had kind of adopted the place, and though the teens and sub-teens who were going through the process had no idea who Troy Donahue was — that was fine with the actor. He found recovery in 1982, and after that it was his number-one priority. He found work, not always of the quality he might have liked, but he was grateful to get it. Holland America Cruise Lines paid him to give talks on acting and the movies. Some would have found it demeaning. Troy didn't. "Love those little old ladies," he said. He had loved young ladies too — four marriages that lasted a total of nine years. This was in the years of trouble. Suzanne Pleshette was one of them, and they later renewed their friendship.

With Troy Donahue, one of the good guys

Troy was often confused with another actor in his agent Henry Wilson's stable of gay hunks — Tab Hunter being the Troy Donahue double.

Rock Hudson was another Wilson hunk.

I met Hunter, though I did not know him. He was another actor who endured a diminished cinematic persona and survived nicely. Troy was good-natured about having people think he was gay. "At least they're thinking of me," he said. He had a wry, honest sense of humor about himself. One of his favorite song lyrics was that from *A Chorus Line*: "If Troy Donahue can be a movie star, then I can be a movie star." He was self-deprecating, but serious.

In the last years of his life, Troy found love with the gifted Mezzo Soprano Zheng Cao, who liked everything about Troy. They were together for almost as long as all his marriages combined. They lived a quiet and contented life, with lots of adventurous travel involved. There was good work as well. His final acting appearances were in the nationwide road company of *Bye Bye Birdie* as the father (the Paul Lynde part), and the cast looked upon him as a beloved father figure. They loved him a lot, and he enjoyed himself immensely. A heart attack took him out in 2002.

"Too much ice cream," Troy would have said.

Troy touched and helped save a lot of lives. Sandra Dee, his costar in *A Summer Place*, did not conquer her addiction demons. She and Troy had actually appeared together in reunion screenings of *A Summer Place* — it turned out there was as audience for those sixties melodramas. The TCM audience is also alive and well. Troy tried to help Sandra, I am sure of it. He was that kind of special person.

Margaret O'Brien, thankfully, is still with us. She was the finest child actress of her day, perhaps the best child actress ever. Lionel Barrymore called her the greatest American actress. The old scene stealer should know — she outperformed him in a film or two. It may be apocryphal, but according to several survivors of the Golden Age at MGM, one of Margaret's directors asked her if she could cry in a particular scene. She replied, "Which eye, and how far down do you want the tears to go?"

She was that good.

Every mature actor or actress who worked with Margaret knew they had to be at their best to hold their own in competition with her for the audience's attention.

Charles Laughton was not an MGM contract player, but in 1944, he came to the studio to star with Margaret and Robert Young in the escapist fantasy, *The Canterville Ghost*. World War II was still raging and any diversion from the realities of that deadly conflict was welcome. At MGM, the only battle raging was the competition between Laughton and a talented, charming child. Charles, another scene swiper, had spent a morning trying to do just that in scenes with the lovable moppet. It had not gone well for the Englishman that day. Robert Young came upon him later that morning, head down on a table, moaning softly. Concerned, Young thought Laughton to be seriously ill and asked for a situation report.

Charles raised his head and sadly murmured, "I simply must kill that child."

Laughton was an Academy Award winner, though many in the profession thought that he had a tendency to ham it up. After his death, Katherine Hepburn had asked Spencer Tracy, her longtime companion, what disease had the veteran thespian succumbed to.

Tracy answered with one word. "Acting," he said.

James Dean and Julie Harris

"You don't understand... it's over... it's over."

— James Dean, Actor
Burbank, California – 1954

"They really hated... despised each other.
It was sad, really"
— Julie Harris, Actress
Hollywood, California – 1989

James Dean died in 1955. I was a junior in high school at the time, so I never got to meet him. Someone once said that the art of newspaper writing was a matter of explaining the headline, "Charles Bogle Dead," to people that who didn't know Charles Bogle was alive. Not so with the youth of America.

We pre-baby boomers all knew James Dean though more than a few of us refused to believe he was dead. Like most of my peers I was a member of the Dean cult. Girls were in love with him and boys wanted to be just like him — a real rebel.

John Frederick

The 1950s were peaceful, tranquil and, face it, boring to most of us. To be sure, there was a lot simmering on the underside of this sliced, white-bread life. We were looking for something different, but we were not sure of what it was.

The decade had begun with number one hits like "Shrimp Boats is a Comin'" and "How Much is that Doggie in the Window?" Things turned around completely when "Rock Around the Clock" and Elvis, Chuck Berry, Johnny Cash, and James Dean showed up.

I went to a concert in 1956 that took place in my high-school gym. It featured Chuck Berry and Fats Domino. I think it was seven or eight bucks to get a ticket. As I was looking for my seat, I passed Berry in a heated discussion under the grandstand with the promoter. He wanted to be paid — paid more, in fact, than he had agreed to be paid — or he wouldn't go on. The producer had no choice, and I am sure Chuck did not either, having been cheated by countless promoters back down the road.

Chuck Berry was a rebel. He also played the guitar, which I didn't — and was black, and I wasn't, so I didn't identify with him that much.

James Dean was a rebel who could have been in my class at school. I might have bumped into him or passed him on the street. He was like me but wilder and stranger. We saw all of his movies, wanted to look like him, dress like him, slouch, and bitch to his parents and other authority figures as he did. He was cool before the word was.

Conditioned as I was by the slam-bang pace of B Westerns, I found it difficult to sit through long, slogging epics like *East of Eden* and *Giant*. I actually like *East of Eden*, primarily because I had found John Steinbeck. *Giant* I thought was a bore, though I would never admit it even to close friends. I wouldn't see it twice though. The only Dean film I went to twice was *Rebel Without a Cause*. Warner Brothers re-released *Rebel* after his death and, though I can't prove it, I believe it made almost as much as it did on its first run. Dean was hotter than ever. Entire magazines told his story, while the tabloids reported that he was not dead but had defected to Russia or was lying on a tropic beach someplace and living under an assumed name.

This went on for at least a year, well into 1956.

When *Rebel* reappeared I seized the opportunity to ask a girl to go with me. Her name was Kerri, and she was not like other girls I had pursued IF they had shown interest in me first. My self-esteem and ego were very fragile at this time.

Kerri was exotic; she used mascara and eye liner, had dark black hair and big Flo red lips. She looked like Queen Nefertiti without the headdress.

What Kerri was really about I had no idea — it had been small talk only.

As we stood in a long line at the Capitol Theater, I attempted to open her up a little and ventured a story about "the late James Dean." She batted her long lashes at me and responded, "Were there two of them?"

Once in gear Kerri wouldn't shut up. She had embarked on a self-improvement program whereby she learned a new word every day. I asked her what the word for the day was. "Trifari," she said, "like what you go to Africa for."

I could not wait to get Kerri home to her mother, who was also exotic, had false teeth, and was screwing a friend of mine. The last I heard of Kerri, she had been married ten times, was worth millions, and was dead, all of which has little to do with James Dean; but when one is not totally familiar with a subject, one has to tap dance a little.

Anyhow, the few people I met who knew or worked with James Dean described him as a surly, self-indulgent, non-communicative, sloppy drunk, difficult, weirdo — with a death wish — rather like his screen persona.

Not Julie Harris. She loved James Dean and was his good friend till he died. I don't remember if they had ever met back East, but it was in 1954 in Hollywood that their real relationship began. Julie was Dean's costar and on-screen love interest in *East of Eden*, Steinbeck's Cain and Abel tale. They discussed the script when Dean abruptly dropped everything to take her for a ride in his sports car. They sped along the Valley on Laurel Canyon, up into the Hollywood Hills, onto Mulholland Drive with Dean driving like the maniac daredevil he tried to be. Julie was terrified but, great actress that she was, gave no sign that it was anything other than a leisurely drive into the country. "We're going to have fun," Dean said. "We're going to have a great time."

The filming began. Dean fell into hate with his costar father, Raymond Massey, who returned the emotion in kind. Massey had no use for the method acting, erratic and unprofessional behavior of his "son." It came across that way on film too. They truly looked as if they hated each other.

When Dean's emotions got the better of him, he always had one shoulder to lean on. Julie counseled him, consoled him, and encouraged him on the set and in his or her dressing room. It was not a sexual relationship. Julie just wanted to help. It must be said here that I thought Julie Harris was not only the nicest person I met in Hollywood, she was probably the nicest person I ever met.

Julie Harris was a tiny thing but I looked up to her from the moment I saw her. We worked on several projects together and she was the ultimate professional. After a reading in a sound studio, I asked if she was satisfied with the take. "That isn't important, John," she said. "Are *you* satisfied?"

When *Eden* wrapped, Julie went to Dean's dressing room to congratulate him one last time on his performance and express the wish that someday they would work together again.

Chin on his chest, Dean was weeping, crying uncontrollably, and saying again and again, "It's over... it's over!" Julie Harris tried for an hour to comfort him with words of love and the possibilities before them both.

Nothing helped.

When she left, James Dean was still bawling. "You don't understand... it's over!"

Julie Harris stayed in touch with her friend, tried to help him when and if she could. Perhaps Bogart put it best when he heard of Dean's death. "It's probably just as well," he said. "He could never live up to his press clippings."

Dean didn't have to.

The good news out of this tragic tale is, every other year or so, I got to work with Julie Harris again. She was back on stage, her real métier, doing *Driving Miss Daisy* at the Henry Fonda in Hollywood. She was still active in films and on television, but the theater was her life. She was born in Grosse Point, Michigan, not a hot bed of poverty. But bad things can happen in Grosse Point, too. Her father was a financial success and an alcoholic. While her mother watched, Julie packed Dad's suitcase for another visit to the sanitarium. When she had finished, her mother ventured the thought that, "You did that rather well." Julie claimed it was the only nice thing her mother had ever said to her.

Is it any wonder that Julie Harris longed for the applause a live audience can give?

I had the privilege of working with Julie Harris
on several projects. She was a warm and gracious lady.
We corresponded and stayed friends until her death.

I called her at her hotel and asked if I could meet her backstage, saying that I was a friend of Barbara P., who was actually my therapist — very Hollywood. BP was a black belt Al Anon from the Marine Corps/SEAL Team group of Alcoholics Anonymous known as the Pacific Group and she had given me Julie's number. Julie waved away Barbara's name. "But John, you're a friend of mine."

Julie always had the right words. After the performance, wife Gayle and I went backstage to see Julie, who introduced us to her costar, Brock Peters, and we all had coffee. I remember the final scene of *Daisy* so well.

Julie is in a home and has just been given a piece of cake from her driver, the Peters character. She uttered a sound of delight, so soft and sweet, but in some freak of nature it could have been heard across the street and was heard in the back of the Fonda, where my wife and I had been lucky to get tickets.

Julie was so good in the part. I asked her if she was going to do the movie version. "No, Jessica Tandy's going to do it," she said. "She'll be wonderful." She meant it — there was not the slightest bit of envy, bitterness or rancor on her face.

That was Julie Harris, a Great, Great lady.

Jason Robards

"They looked like vultures."

— Jason Robards, Actor
Culver City, California – 1980

Jason Robards wasn't just an actor — he was a helluva good actor. Like many of his generation (born 1922), WWII got in the way. He joined the Navy in 1940 and was aboard the USS *Northampton* at sea off Hawaii when the Japanese struck. In a night action off Guadalcanal, the *Northampton* was sunk by Japanese torpedoes. Like his surviving shipmates, Jason had to swim for it till they were rescued.

Later in the war aboard another cruiser USS *Nashville*, Jason's ship was struck by a kamikaze attack. More than 200 sailors were killed, and the ship was forced to return to Mare Island Naval Shipyard near San Francisco. Jason had risen to the rank of Radioman First Class by the time the war ended but always said that "World War II scared me to death." Little wonder his acting career started slowly. His father, also Jason Robards, had been an actor whose early successes turned to failure and alcoholism. The war and decline of his father's career were such traumatic events to the son that he sought refuge in analysis — and alcohol. This combination is not recommended.

At 35, Jason finally made it big, in Eugene O'Neill's *The Iceman Cometh*. The playwright's works would define Robards' career. His father had passed and Jason took the "Jr." off his name. His career continued an upward path

Talking to Jason Robards about his participation on a telethon for
the National Council on Alcoholism and Drug Dependency (NCADD).
President Reagan, Betty Ford, and Bob Hope also took part.

in plays and film. There were also four marriages and six children, one of the wives being actress Lauren Bacall. They had a son, Sam. Throughout this period, alcohol was a corrosive thread. He was unable to enjoy his successes, and his failures as a husband and parent gnawed at him.

When I met Jason Robards in 1980, he had been sober for many years and seemed to be a truly happy man. With the help of his supportive wife, Lois, and his personal physician, Dr. Nick Pace, a family and friends support system was created that worked for Jason as long as he lived. He had also claimed two Academy Awards, an Emmy and a Tony along the way, and was surely ranked as one of America's greatest actors. We were making a promotional film for the National Council on Alcoholism, and recovering alcoholics in sports and enter-tainment were lending a hand. Jason Robards would be in good company. Non-alcoholics were in the film too, speaking of their experiences with the disease or the hope of recovery — President Reagan, Bob Hope, Barbara Eden, Rod

Steiger, and Melissa Gilbert among them. The latter two, as the years passed, would join their brothers and sisters in recovery, ironic but fitting somehow.

Jason Robards, luckily enough, was in Hollywood for a film, and a simple shoot was arranged in a Century City condo where Jason would talk about what it was like, what happened, and what it was like now. Our hosts were relatives of the film's co-producer, Stephen Fisch, and three generations of family women were on hand to see a star. Robards came to the shoot unaccompanied, a rarity among Hollywood's top echelon, and we discussed the nature of his participation. There would be no script, just Jason Robards telling his own story. He introduced himself to the host family, to their obvious pleasure, and acknowledged every member of the crew. He then introduced himself on camera, and we were off. Robards started at the beginning when alcohol "took the pressure off," which soon morphed into incidents and accidents, including a car crash on a California mountain road that was serious enough for extensive plastic surgery. This happening was eerily similar to one that happened to Montgomery Clift, an almost too handsome young star of the fifties, whose features were severely altered, even with plastic surgery. Jason's looks, fortunately, were not his livelihood, and his career as a character star was only briefly interrupted.

The real turning point came, fittingly, while Jason was appearing in another O'Neill play. Between the matinee and evening shows on that day, Jason broke his self-imposed rule and had a number of drinks between performances. In the middle of the evening performance, Jason "went up," his mind went blank, and he began to panic. He glanced about helplessly and noticed that offstage, the producers of the play were staring at him, eyes like daggers. His fears multiplied, and he could not summon the words. It seemed to Jason like an eternity before his memory and composure returned. By the time the curtain had fallen, he made up his mind, something had to be done. I believe he remained sober from that very day. It was quite a story, very powerful.

Before Jason left the set, he shook hands with every member of the crew and, of course, our hostesses. He could not have been more thoughtful or more professional. I was very curious to ask the ladies what they thought about what they had seen and heard. They were our very first audience, after all, as members of the crew, including me, and were only looking and listening for technical problems and not content. The grandmother spoke first. "Did he really believe what he said?" God, what an odd question, I thought. They did not relate. This was not good.

"Well," I offered, "what if he had been talking about medication, pills and such?" There were quick nods of recognition. "How about food?" I continued. Jackpot! They got it, sort of. Jason Robards went on to support the sober life in print and television public service ads. He continued working and being happy in his life to the very end.

Carol Channing and Phyllis Diller

"Hello, my name is Carol Channing."

— **Carol Channing, Entertainer**
Newport Beach, California — 2002

"Sorry, you will have to wait a moment. I have to sign John's balls first."

— **Carol Channing, Entertainer**
Newport Beach, California — 2002

"This is cruelty to an old woman."
— **Phyllis Diller, Comedienne/Actor**
Beverly Hills, California — 2006

---

always preferred movies to the theater. When I watch a play I cannot help thinking, I am in a theater and I'm watching a play. Movies took me away from where I was. I guess I just wanted to be somebody else, somewhere else.

Carol Channing was a great and gifted talent who never really made it in the movies. She did win a Golden Globe for *Thoroughly Modern Millie*, a film that reminded me too much of a play. On stage, well that was something else again. Audiences could not get enough of her in *Gentlemen Prefer Blondes* and *Hello Dolly!* Doofus that I am, I never saw her in either one, but I did get to meet her, and that in itself was unforgettable. Ms. Channing had just written her autobiography, *Just Lucky I Guess,* and was preparing for a nationwide book tour. The Los Angeles based Literary Club, Round Table West, had snagged her for a talk and book signing at one of their monthly meetings. At its peak in the last quarter of the 20th century, Round Table held three monthly meetings — at the Beverly Wilshire in LA, La Quinta Hotel in the desert, and the Newport Country Club in Orange County. This enabled RTW to reach affluent women, their friends and companions in almost all of Southern California.

Their audience was well served. Bob Hope, Jimmy Stewart, Walter Cronkite, Neil Armstrong, Ray Bradbury, Dean Koontz, Benny Goodman, Betty Ford, Alan Shepard, Gloria Swanson, and 2000 other authors and luminaries made appearances at the varied RTW locales.

As often as we could, my wife Gayle and I attended these events, becoming close friends with one of the founders, Margaret Burk. Often Margaret would favor us by making sure we were seated next to the talent.

So it was that we found ourselves in Newport Beach at the Country Club seated beside Carol Channing and astronaut and aquanaut Scott Carpenter — pretty heady stuff. Carol greeted us by getting up and extending her hand across the table, not forgetting to mention her name. To which I wanted to reply, "No shit!" I didn't, of course. I was told by others that Cary Grant would say, "Hello, my name is Cary Grant." I would have wanted to say, "No shit," twice. As much as I wanted to hear from Scott Carpenter — the Mercury 7 crew members were heroes of mine — Carol did most of the talking. And she was funny, hilarious actually. I don't remember the funnies, but it was mostly about her days at Bennington and early experiences of breaking into the theater. Scott Carpenter seemed as interested and entertained as I was. Later, he would talk about his book, *For Spacious Skies*, so I got to hear about his life too.

Carol's breathy little girl voice, with a rasp, as she told her tales, was somehow mesmerizing. It was as if Marilyn Monroe had finished graduate school. The luncheon menu was a cut above rubber chicken, but Carol would have none of it. When not speaking, she snacked on a mixture of plants and nuts that she had brought along in a paper bag. Awful looking stuff. There must be something to it, though, as she lived to be two weeks shy of 98.

After the authors' presentations, it was time for book signing. I had purchased several of my tablemates' books but, greedy bastard that I am, I wanted more. In my tote bag I had half a dozen major league baseballs. I connect baseball and signed baseballs with all the good things in life. Taking advantage of my proximity, I asked Carol and Scott Carpenter to sign the balls "on the sweet spot." A line had been formed and others were waiting to have their books signed. It was at this point that Carol, in a voice heard around the spacious dining room, said that she would soon be signing for everyone, but she had to sign my balls first. Nobody was offended. Only Carol Channing could get away with saying something like that and making it sound completely innocent.

A further payoff for me came later. Carol had been hitting the talk shows. I never watch the morning shows but, touched by her magic and seeing that she would be on, I watched *Good Morning America*. Six weeks went by and I heard that Carol Channing would be the special guest at a special screening of *Thoroughly Modern Millie* at the Egyptian Theatre. Gayle and I went, parking out back, and as we were walking around to the box office, a limo pulled up and Carol Channing emerged, looking as if she had been on an extended vacation. She spotted me as I walked by and said, "John, what are you doing here?" After what should have been an exhausting schedule all around the country, she remembered ME. I have heard it said that politicians like Jim Farley and Gerald Ford could remember the names of thousands of people. Carol Channing would have made one helluva politician.

Phyllis Diller, maybe not magic, was unique, a survivor, and one tough cookie. She too made an appearance at a Round Table West event, this time at the Beverly Wilshire. Diller's book, *Like a Lampshade in a Whorehouse: My life in Comedy*, was just starting to appear in bookstores. I was not invited to sit with her because, though the luncheon was well along, she had not arrived. She was said to be on the way, but a worried Margaret Burk sent me down to the porte cochère to check things out. Phyllis had just arrived, and she was mad as hell about it.

Thanks to a dozen or more successful surgeries, Phyllis was well-preserved but moved about like Tim Conway's little old man. She was accompanied by her secretary/caregiver, an officious sort of the type that gravitate to the faded famous. The woman had a small sack full of pills, which Miss Diller seemed to need every few yards or so. "I told them I didn't want to do this," she said to me. I pleaded not guilty. The journey from the car to the hotel, roughly 30 feet, must have taken five minutes.

I had the horrible feeling that she was going to die on me and that I would be held responsible. The elevator seemed an impossible dream, but we made it. Phyllis was moaning all the way.

Another interminable totter to the ballroom. Once there, Phyllis's whole persona changed. She seemed to have gotten a massive injection of speed. Phyllis practically bounced up to the microphone. She had, almost instantly, turned into herself. She did ten minutes of some of the funniest stuff I had ever heard and had enough left over to pose for pictures.

Wife Gayle was going in the next week for plastic surgery, and Diller penned a note to the doctor threatening physical harm if he

Gayle with Phyllis Diller, who does not look pleased.

bungled the job. Gayle was so grateful she gave Phyllis a big hug. Mental note: Do not try to touch Phyllis Diller. She hates it. This advice, sadly, comes too late.

Before I was asked to escort Miss D back to her car, discretion being the better part of valor, I hid in the washroom — shades of my John Wayne experience, which is revealed somewhere in this book.

Samuel Z. Arkoff

"Forty... a million... who's counting?"

— Samuel Z. Arkoff
Hollywood, California – 1998

There are so many talented and creative people in Hollywood who you never see; you only see their work. I'd like to take a look at three of them, beginning with a man whose name I do not know.

It was in 1970 or so when I was on my job as a Navy technical advisor on a television show called *The F.B.I.* that starred Efrem Zimbalist, Jr. Zimbalist was nowhere to be seen in this sequence that was shot at the Naval Construction Battalion Center at Port Hueneme, California. This particular location was a staging area for tanks, trucks, and other war material on the way to Vietnam. Bad things were going to be happening that the FBI would have to look into. One was about a young actor named Don Grady who had been one of *My Three Sons*, a popular family show a few years before. Grady demonstrated to me the dangers of too much preparation for a role.

Before the cameras rolled, Grady had been practicing his part by leaping up and doing pull-ups on a tank gun barrel, a bit of ad-libbing he had thought up himself. When the time came to shoot the scene, however, he had run out of leaps and had merely to stand under the barrel, which was the public's loss. Another scene featured a large explosion and revealed a talent of an unusual nature — the special effects coordinator. A man appeared to be running into the blast and was blown in the air. Shooting with a long lens ten feet away from the explosion, the special effects guy had made a five-gallon can of gas and five inches of cork atop it look like the end of the world. He also had invented a machine that could project fire or smoke from either side of the frame.

This was a man I had to know, and between takes he told me his story.

He had been a butcher at Safeway in this little town in Northern California until a movie company showed up to shoot a motion picture called *Annie Oakley*. It was 1935. Barbara Stanwyck, perhaps the most popular actress in Hollywood with both fellow cast members and crew, was the star. The word went out in the town that what was needed was a great shot with a long gun, shotgun preferred. The butcher was their man. He was to hide in a barrel, and Stanwyck was to ride her horse around an arena. Our anonymous friend was to explode a series of glass balls as Barbara, or rather her stuntwoman, made a circle around the ring. The butcher executed his job perfectly and was told to report the next day to the production shack for payment.

Promptly the next morning, he got in line and received an envelope, which he took home before opening. Sitting around the kitchen table with his wife, he sliced it open and found a check for sixty dollars. He knew what he had to do. Sixty dollars was his weekly salary at Safeway. There had obviously been a mistake. He returned to the production office the next day and tried to give the check back. All he wanted was what he was owed — no more. The bookkeeper thumbed through a well-worn volume and must have found the section which referred to shooting glass balls from a barrel. "Sixty bucks is all it is," the book-keeper intoned, "nothing more."

Our man thought not of Poe's *Raven*, but, "How long has this shit been going on?"

He took a few days off from Safeway, made friends with the special effects man who owed him a favor for his great shooting. Eventually the butcher became one of the best explosion and fire illusionists in Hollywood. He always kept his little ranch in Northern California and returned to it after each picture or

TV show. He was going to retire after the 1970 season. What a pleasure it was to meet Mr. Nameless. In Hollywood there is a niche for just about everything.

My business partner and I had just been booted out of our offices at General Service Studios. The new Francis Coppola Zoetrope Productions owners had swept clean the old tenants, save for George Burns, who had been in residence there since God ordained it. No longer would I be able to walk to lunch past the Ozzie and Harriett cottage and to see the Incredible Hulk green his tan. Our fledgling company now had to make do with conventional offices on Vine Street opposite Capitol Records.

One could see, if so inclined, the Hollywood sign out the window of my business partner's office. We were documentary filmmakers, specializing in matters of social concern, and in a very short time had established a positive reputation in our field. In this first month or so in our new digs, a creative angel showed up. His name was Bill Scott and he was the voice of such iconic characters as Bullwinkle Moose, George of the Jungle, Dudley Do Right, and Tom Slick, race driver extraordinaire. Bill was more than that. He was an animator who, along with Jay Ward, had created one of the best adult shows on the air. Oh, I know it was a kid's show too, but so much of *Rocky and Bullwinkle* was funnier to people like me than any sitcom.

Bill had come to us, not to be funny, but to be serious. There was alcoholism and addiction in Bill's family, and he wanted to make a cartoon about it. I thought it was a fabulous idea. *Days of Wine and Roses* and *The Lost Weekend* would work for some, but I always felt that laughter and hope were better messages to reach those who needed help. Bill agreed completely, and we agreed to work together. The first steps included calling him at his home in Tujunga and even this held pleasant surprises. His answering machine was not a mechanical nonentity, but a mix of all the voices I loved so much. Later, I was also able to obtain Jonathan Winters number, and that was a riot as well. If I had a down day, all I had to do was call those two numbers and my tiny, transient mood of gloom would be lifted. If someone answered, I hung up.

Bill and I had meetings and made plans. As things moved along he invited me to a show that his little theater company was putting on at a church near his home. The morning of the show, still uncertain as to where Tujunga was, I called his house to get directions. He had already considered that other play-goers would need the same information, and both Bullwinkle and Dudley were made available to get us to the church on time. The play was standard little theater fare, nice but not particularly memorable. I was looking forward to intro-ducing my wife Gayle and two friends to the talented Mr. Scott after the perfor-mance. Immediately after the curtain fell, one of the players stepped out and said, "Tonight's performance was dedicated to the memory of Bill Scott, who died this morning." I was so stunned, the first thing I thought of was, "It can't be... I spoke with Bullwinkle just this morning."

Sam Arkoff, Samuel Z. Arkoff, actually. If this name had appeared in the NY Times crossword, it would have taken a movie fan of encyclopedic knowledge to come up with an answer. Yet Sam Arkoff produced over 350 films, almost all of them forgettable and of questionable quality, about which he could not have cared less. They made money, yes they did. Sam created the first studio without the usual sound stages, production offices, and other frills that cost too much. American International Pictures it was called, where titles became films and trends were hijacked and sometimes created. Initial production budgets at AIP were in the 60-grand range, and thanks to titles by cofounder James Nicholson and the creative genius on a budget of the legendary Roger Corman, such films as *Drag Strip Girl*, *The Beast from 12,000 Fathoms*, *The Terror*, *Beach Blanket Bingo* and *The Trip* offered a stream of mediocrity unparalleled in Hollywood history. Most of the pictures were for the fifties and sixties drive-in trade, some-thing to look at between romantic interludes.

AIP offered Westerns, Sci-Fi, Horror, Psychedelic, Beach, Hot Rod, dubbed Italian, and anything else that could conceivably make a buck. Nothing made Sam happier than turning nothing into something at the ticket counter.

I met Sam through a friend of my wife. Pearl Tucker was a gourmet cook and sometime counselor to Sam and his wife, Hilda, during their final years.

Gayle and I were invited during this time to screenings of new films before their release, something that had long been offered to heads of studios.

Sam had to fight for his screenings, as his major studio competitors were jealous of the new, upstart company. Theater owners and their young audiences would win the day for Sam. Unlike many old timers, Sam loved many of the new films. *Oh Brother Where Art Thou* was a particular favorite. Sometimes during pre- or post-discussions, Sam would have Pearl run down to Art's Deli on Ventura Boulevard to pick up a forbidden pastrami sandwich and hide it from Hilda.

Your seatmates at these screenings were interesting folk. I sat beside the man that had written the song "George of the Jungle," for example, and you just don't meet people like them every day.

I loved how Sam loved his work and how he still loved to talk about it after all was filmed and done. In his struggling early days, he had gone down a mine shaft to convince a miner, who was also the owner of the only theater in this small West Virginia town, to screen his films. According to Sam, in their first year Jim Nicholson had come up with the title *The Beast with a Million Eyes* and a similar kind of double feature for the drive-in trade.

The director, Roger Corman, had already done his work and moved on. When Sam screened the dailies, he had immediately noticed something was amiss. He called Roger, who was in Palm Springs shooting a picture for another company while dodging police and other officials who felt he should have obtained permits for such activities. "Roger, where the hell is *The Beast*?" Sam complained. Corman explained that he had spent the thirty grand that Sam had given him for the picture and *The Beast* was now Sam's problem. Sam grumbled but took it rather well, as he knew he would need Roger again. With a puff on his cigar and a grin, Sam explained that he had purchased a large metal object that looked somewhat like a large coffee pot, punched forty or so holes in it, lighted it from within like a jack-o'-lantern, put it in a dim cave about the size of a dog kennel, and it became The Beast. It looked like a Teletubby. Nobody complained.

Writers for AIP usually worked for only slightly more than scale. I had a friend who worked there and he was pushing a friend of his who was a television success but who wanted to break into features. "Sam, this guy is a real talent, and we can get him for scale," my friend said. Sam thought it over for a moment. "Can we get him for less?" That Sam, he was sure a careful man with a dollar... or less...

President Richard Nixon

"Which way to the flight deck?"

— President Richard Nixon
U.S.S. *Saratoga* – 1969

Nixon, Richard Nixon. Let's come back to him later. No one this side of the Nixon Library wants to rush in to meet Richard Nixon. Let me talk instead about presidents I have known. Okay, I actually only knew one, Gerald Ford. Our recovery films were utilized in Betty Ford's intervention process. As a result I was invited to both the groundbreaking and the dedication of the Betty Ford Center. I felt guilty — I had voted for Jimmy Carter. Somewhat later I heard from a Republican representative from California who had attended a conference at the White House on Western water rights. Carter knew all about them. Shirley Pettis said that is when she knew Carter would never be a success as president. He knew too much about everything. The lesson is clear. Never vote for a micromanager who knows everything and still has to decide who is to play on the White House tennis courts.

As for President Ford, I played in many golf tournaments that he and Betty sponsored. I always played behind him — to be ahead of him or to be a spectator watching him was said to be dangerous. Of course he teed off first, so that was never an issue. He was, and I do not hesitate to use the words, a lovely man. I was always humbled and proud when he always called me by name. Later, I found out that he knew the names and faces of 5,013 other people. That humbled me further.

There were four other presidents whom I saw in the flesh. George H. W. Bush was at the Betty Ford dedication and we exchanged a word or two. He was great as well. Then there was Harry Truman. The year was 1948. I was nine. In those days it was possible for nine-year-olds to walk alone without fear of being molested or mugged, though there was a tough twelve-year-old girl down the street who had it in for me. I avoided her house and walked two miles to the train station to see the president of the United States, Harry S. Truman. He was coming through Salem on a campaign swing that everyone called the whistle-stop tour. Oregon was a Republican state then but he came anyway. Truman spoke from a platform at the end of the caboose. He had a very red face and wore a white suit. He made sure to talk so everyone could hear him. He was rather small — I thought presidents would be bigger. Thirteen years later I was standing a mid-watch in a Navy comm center in Taipei, Taiwan, and I had time to write him a letter about his coming to my small town and what it meant to a little boy. I put my military address on the letter, and my boss, Lieutenant Beegle, hand-delivered Truman's response to me. He was very impressed. "You know him?" Beegle asked. "You mean Uncle Harry?" I answered. I always got along with Mister Beegle after that. I really like Harry Truman.

I liked Ike too. The year was 1957, and I was at Officer Candidate's school at the Naval Base, Newport, Rhode Island. I was there for the summer, and President Eisenhower spent part of that summer there also. Ike looked pink-cheeked and chipper, waving and grinning that famous grin as he was driven by, his wisps of hair fluttering in the wind. He looked old, a real grandfather type. Ike was great but also lucky, Napoleon's favorite trait in his generals. And the country was lucky right along with him. He got us out of one war and kept us out of others. The Cold War stayed cold, and we could live with that. Yes, I liked Ike, and Richard Nixon was his vice president. No one really knew if Ike liked that.

Ronald Reagan was my last presidential experience. My Navy unit was responsible for filming his arrivals and departures at the Naval Air Station, Point Mugu, as he returned to his California ranch or was here on campaign or fund-raising visits. Pretty routine stuff. I did see Nancy and him at the Reagan library. He was talking to a group of children about the evils of smoking. The president said that he had never smoked and that was a reason for his good health. He cited his brother, a smoker, as a negative example. Neil, the other brother, lived to be 88, so all that nicotine, all those nasty resins and tars did not slow him down that much. Whatever you thought about Reagan's policies or politics, if you had seen him with a bunch of kids, you would have liked him... and I did.

Then there was Nixon. I was neither a Nixon hater nor a Nixon lover. I had voted for Hubert Humphrey because I like jolly politicians who look as if they are enjoying their jobs. Nixon was not of this ilk, but I still preferred him to George McGovern whose supporters reminded me of me in my pantywaist rev-olutionary period in the mid-fifties.

While attending Willamette University I had participated in a walkout/boy-cott of compulsory chapel, a staple of that stern and noble Methodist institu-tion. I also railed against Air Force ROTC. Both these sins had terrified some older alumni who reported us to the FBI. We were hardly Weathermen, but one of the great flaws of the fifties was a tendency to look for Commies under every rock, or in our case, in every tavern. I was more a drink and dropout rebel than any kind of revolutionary.

By 1969 my view had shifted rightward and with the great mass of American voters, unable to foresee Watergate. I cast a ballot for Richard Milhous Nixon. It was, as they say, a landslide, 49 states to 1. Nixon was so pleased and buoyed up by this mighty triumph that he ushered in an era of peace and goodwill in politics and with all the people, or he would have if he were a normal politician and person. Instead he took this opportunity to rage against his foes, vowed vengeance, though I forget for what, and with his trusty aides began to compile an enemies list. Bad losers are bad enough, but bad winners are simply too much to bear, and we didn't. This was in the untarnished future. At the time, I was the public affairs officer for the United States Second Fleet. The Fleet wore a couple of other hats, one as Commander Joint Task Force 122, in case Castro or other of our Southern neighbors got frisky, and another as Commander NATO Striking Fleet Atlantic. I loved this one as it meant a yearly exercise in the North Sea with our British, Norwegian, Dutch, Danish, and German allies. The Russians also showed up. They were even a part of our Ops Plan and a good time was had by all.

In May of 1969, I was aboard U.S.S. *Saratoga*, a Forrestal-class aircraft carrier awaiting the visit on Armed Forces Day of President Richard Nixon. He would have high-powered company, including Chief of Naval Operations, Thomas Moorer and Commander-in-Chief Atlantic, Admiral, Ephraim Holmes. I think that the NATO foreign ministers were also invited. Quite a bunch. My job as a Public Affairs Officer was to brief and host the press. Even though Vietnam was fast becoming Nixon's war, there was little controversy expected. The event was to take place miles off the Virginia coast. It would consist of a firepower demo from ships and planes of the Atlantic fleet, to be followed by a presidential speech. There was to be no press conference. Carrier aviation is the greatest show on earth, and I was looking forward to that. The President/VIPs and the press were to be in separate viewing areas, which as usual pleased the former and irritated the latter. Most senior officers in the military regarded the press as the enemy. Part of my duty, as I saw it, was to explain to them that was not the case. I put it this way to one admiral, "This press isn't just against us, Admiral; they're against everybody. It's their job — the Constitution says so."

Two days before the big day, a group of Secret Service agents showed up. I gave them a walk-around, explaining where the president would be at all times in the schedule. While on the flight deck, one of the agents noticed several small ships in the area. He asked about them, and I explained that they were Russian trawlers who were spying on us, which was a normal part of their job. The nearest trawler was perhaps a couple miles or so away, bobbing about in the heavy swell. "Could a marksman on one of those vessels assassinate the president?" one of them asked me. I thought he was joking, before remembering that the Secret Service is not noted for its humor in regard to the safety of the Chief Executive. My "What a helluva shot that would be," line died a stillborn death, and I just said that seemed to be nearly impossible. I should not have said nearly, since they were only nearly satisfied.

Two days later, the president and his party arrived with the usual flourishes, "Hail to the Chief" and the national anthem. With the press well in hand, I decided to follow the presidential party around the flight deck looking over planes and personnel, and on up to the bridge to observe the first of the launches. The firepower demo was a hit, and when it ended I found myself next to the president of the United States. He was wearing his usual conservative blue suit and tie. Though his complexion was as healthy looking as any president I had seen, something seemed different. He did not seem real, as if someone had borrowed him from Madame Tussauds or Disney Hall of Presidents Animatronics. I could not shake the feeling that I was looking at a Stepford President. His voice broke the spell. "Which way to the flight deck, Lieutenant?" he inquired. "Down that ladder Mr. President," I answered — my contribution to presidential history ending this story. But not quite.

We have come to a time when countless numbers of our countrymen on both sides of the political divide are actually wishing for the demise of our current leader or his immediate predecessor. What has happened to us that perhaps millions of our citizens have become so toxically inoculated? I do not know for certain. I just wish we could go back to the fifties when presidents may have been joked about, even disliked, but were not on some kind of hit list.

Paul Keyes

"And what do you do?"

— Paul Keyes, Producer
Burbank, California – 1971

I don't know how anyone gets a job in Hollywood — I mean the job of their fantasies, the one they came for. Would-be movie stars come here and get jobs as waiters and waitresses. They give it the old college try for a while. The lucky ones give up in disgust and go back to Dubuque. The cattle call for actors in particular is one of the most humiliating experiences that anyone could wish for. I have a friend, Conlan Carter, who came west from Missouri and struck gold almost immediately. He was a bucolic, Southern cowboy type, a kind of young Walter Brennan with teeth. He and Strother Martin and Arthur Hunnicutt were the same type and immediately went to so many auditions together that they became good friends. They played poker and gin rummy while waiting for their call.

In his first few weeks in Hollywood, Conlan landed a part on an ABC series called *The Law and Mr. Jones,* which starred James Whitmore. He later was Doc on the long-running *Combat,* his name in the early credits. He made $750 a week and garnered an Emmy nomination. He worked as actors do, with a lot of pauses in between. During one of the breaks he learned to fly, became a commercial/corporate pilot, bought an orange grove in Florida, sold it and became a millionaire — a true Hollywood success story.

Personally, I knocked on many doors and was never granted entrance. I did get a peek over the transom once in a while. I finally co-started my own production/distribution business. We made and distributed documentary and educational films. Most were in areas of social concern such as addiction, child abuse, domestic violence, mental retardation, and the like. We made a nice living and I had job satisfaction, still in Hollywood, but mostly out of the main entertainment stream. I say mostly because, may God have mercy on my soul, my company produced the first "Outtakes" show on television.

This is when I discovered what nepotism means. Nepotism exists in Hollywood. The town couldn't run without it. Whom you know means how many relatives you have who are making it in "the biz." I am in the Writer's Guild, which is impossible to join unless you have sold something that is on the air or has hit the screen. You cannot do this if you don't have an agent. You can't get an agent of any quality unless you have sold something to somebody as per two sentences ago. Get the picture? Same with unions. You can't unless you did — OR if you have a relative who is a grip, a gaffer, an art director, or any one of a dozen other crafts. Immediate family is best but a distant cousin will do if powerful enough. I had none of these things going for me, until I finally met someone who knew some-one. She was a lady who had a powerful position in PR in Beverly Hills. You had to be organized about this, which I never was. In the Pentagon we used to say that we had to "have all our ducks in a row." Now I had a duck. Her name was Roz.

Roz was tight with a man named Paul Keyes, whom I had never heard of. Keyes, it turned out, was a writer who had written for the old Jack Paar *Tonight Show*. He now was on the top of the heap, having written and produced the immensely successful *Laugh In*. *Laugh In* starred Dan Rowan and Dick Martin and was produced by both Keyes and George Schlatter. The show had been on the air for several years and was a great success, which usually means it had reached the "inmates taking over the asylum stage." Nothing major, just three camps — R&M, Schlatter, and Paul Keyes. Keyes was my best bet and he was a lonely Republican. I would have better luck with him I thought, being in the military.

This was the height of the anti-Vietnam War protest season. While wearing my Navy uniform I had been both spat upon and called a "baby killer." *Laugh In* was the comic voice of protest. Still, I needed the job, I needed the money, and I had a wife and three kids to think about. And this job was a sure thing. It was "wired" in the vernacular of the time, which meant all I had to do was show up and the job was mine. I was to be the assistant to the producer, or the assistant to the assistant to the producer, I forget which. *Laugh In* had corporate offices in "beautiful downtown Burbank," and I went there one beautiful summer morning in 1971.

The office looked just like any other, with a deviation here and there. There was a man dressed as a tree, an oak as I recall, and I could hear the voices of writers trying to amuse one another. Comedy writers are different. Comedy is different. This was a time when youth was being served but not in comedy. There the ancients reigned. Writers from the 1930s were still being sought after because they knew secrets of laughter that youth could only dream about. I employed two of these old masters, Seaman Jacobs and Fred Fox, who had worked with the likes of Fred Allen, Jack Benny, Bob Hope, and others. They never laughed; they never as much as smiled. They delivered stories and one-liners to each other in voices that would have been better suited to announcing a death in the family. Eventually, one of them would say, somberly, "That's funny," and that bit would go in the show.

But, back to Paul Keyes who is still in his office waiting patiently to hire me. I had to wait of course. Everybody has to wait. I sat beside a young lady for whom the word gorgeous was coined. She was a knockout, blonde and beautiful. I wondered if perhaps she was to be the new Goldie Hawn, who had left the show. She had my vote and I wanted to hear all about her. She was more than willing, and with her first few sentences I could see she was as intelligent as she was attractive. She had just come from New York, where she had appeared on Broadway. She talked and I listened. It was a fair trade. She knew about the theater, far more than I. She spoke of Shaw and Ibsen, of Chekov and Moliere. She was just about to explain the plot of *The Cherry Orchard* to me when she was called to the inner sanctum. I picked up a copy of *Variety*, the show business *New York Times* which, along with the *Hollywood Reporter*, reports all the fake news in show business that's fit to print — and some that isn't. In a minute or so I heard her voice, lifted in song. She was singing "On the Good Ship Lollipop" in her best Shirley Temple imitation. I didn't know whether to laugh, and crying seemed pointless, so I did neither. When she came out a few minutes later, I congratulated her on her solo. She was smiling, a good sign. Ah Miss Ibsen, although we never kissed or even touched, I will never forget you.

Paul Keyes, looking very much the successful producer, stood in the doorway and invited me in. He sat behind his desk. I was not asked to sit, so I didn't. I mentioned my name. We stared at each other long enough that it became crystal clear to me that "the wire" had snapped at some point. Paul Keyes did not have the slightest idea who I was and what I was there for. "And what do you do?" he finally asked.

I plunged ahead, "First let me tell you what I don't do. I don't do Shirley Temple imitations." The silence was not golden and, of course, I didn't get the job. Never try to be funny to people who make a living that way. That, as they say, "is show biz." If I had to do it over again, I would say the same damn thing, only I would say it in my head.

Randy "Duke" Cunningham, William "Willie" Driscoll, and Admiral "Jimmy" Thatch

"With respect, but check your six."

— Vietnam Navy Ace, Randy "Duke" Cunningham
Miramar Naval Air Station – 1974

"There's tigers down there, snakes and shit."

— Navy Vietnam Ace, William "Willie" Driscoll
Miramar Naval Air Station – 1974

---

*"We worked it out with wooden
matches on my kitchen table."*

— Navy Ace, Admiral "Jimmy" Thatch
Coronado, California – 1973

Aces were a rare commodity in Vietnam. Only two pilots achieved this status, Air Force Captain Steve Ritchie and Navy Lieutenant Randy Cunningham. There were others in the cockpit who also qualified as aces. Willie Driscoll, a Navy Radar Intercept Officer, was one of them. Being an ace then was a two-person job. In 1974, the two of them would appear in a film I wrote and produced for the Naval Aviation Museum titled, *Wings of Eagles, Wings of Gold*. The picture was a history of Naval Aviation designed to raise money for the museum to be built in Pensacola, Florida, the home of Naval Air. As a history major in college, this was right up my alley. Besides being able to research the history of Naval Air, we filmed the aces and other pilots from WWII, which gave me a great chance to hear their stories. Admiral "Jimmy" Thatch, who was famed for the Thatch Weave, a two-plane defensive maneuver that saved many a Navy pilot, was over-matched when flying against the Japanese Zero, a quicker climbing and turning airplane than our early-in-the-war Grumman Wildcats and Brewster Buffaloes. Working with squadronmates and matches on his kitchen table, the Thatch Weave came together, saving countless American lives. Thatch had a big role in the film. Captain David McCampbell, the Navy's leading ace, and Admiral Thomas Moorer, who flew the slow but long-legged Catalina Flying Boat, a "super snooper" observation aircraft, were two other WWII vets who appeared in the film — a labor of love for me.

Cunningham and Driscoll were of more recent vintage, besides being the odd couple of flight. Cunningham, though born in L.A., spent a large portion of his childhood in Missouri. He spoke Southern to me and, fittingly, his idol was John Wayne, hence his nickname. Willie Driscoll was Boston born and bred, a city boy to the core. They made a great team. They had a three-kill day, a rarity in any war, but especially in Vietnam. Their final kill was rumored to be North Vietnam's leading ace, an alternative fact as it turned out. Whoever he was, he turned out to be the third victim and made them both aces. It proved to be even tougher than it sounds. The enemy was hit, but to make sure he crashed they followed him nearly down to the deck. Preoccupied to the max, their F-4 Phantom was struck by a SAM, a surface-to-air missile. The plane became uncontrollable, and a sinister, orange glow loomed in their rear-view mirrors. The sensible thing might have been to "punch out," eject before the plane blew up. Instead, in an amazing feat of airmanship, with control surfaces out or failing, Cunningham managed to keep altitude and some speed by barrel rolling the aircraft in the direction of the Gulf of Tonkin where he would have a chance of recovery. The fate of airman ejecting over North Vietnam was well known to them, but it must have been an act of sheer will to stay with the ship. They made the Gulf and parachuted, not into safety, but a firefight between the good and bad guys to see who got to them first. Good guys won, and they safely returned to their carrier to be hailed as heroes, who they were.

I was Commanding Officer of the Naval Reserve Combat Camera Group. Naval Air Station (NAS), Pt Mugu, CA, 1980's.

A few years later while doing a two-week Naval Reserve stint, I took them both around to LA TV stations while they told their stories. There had not been many positives coming out of Vietnam, and the tale of these two Navy Cross heroes was a welcome break in the stream of bad news. They were nice guys; they both had a little ham in them, and we all enjoyed the experience. I did ask Willie Driscoll why his first reaction had not been to hit the button and eject.

He had instead encouraged his pilot to keep going and stay with the Phantom. Willie looked at me with all seriousness and offered his first thought when his plane had been struck by the SAM. "Are you kidding? Do you know how many guys were killed by tigers in this war? There's snakes and all kinds of shit down there." Through a fear of snakes and tigers are war heroes made. I tried to insist he tell that version of their escape on the air, but he stuck to the old script. Was he kidding? Ask him.

During the making of *Wings of Gold*, we met again at Miramar Naval Air Station. We did some interviews by the Phantom, and Duke took the bird up for a touch-and-go or two and a fly-by. He made it look easy, which I knew it wasn't. Duke also had some observations on naval aviation. He said, "Ten percent of Navy pilots are outstanding, 10% are poor and may kill themselves and/or others, and the other 80% have good days and bad days." To anyone who has witnessed carrier operations at sea, this is virtual heresy. To me, these aviators have skills that almost seem unworldly. Remarks like this may have aroused some animosity or jealousy among his peers, as the Duke retired as a Commander, a modest rank for someone of his exploits. It was also alleged that he lobbied for a Medal of Honor nomination for his deeds. This is considered bad form and would be severely frowned upon.

So, what then becomes of heroes after heroism? I have not seen Bill Driscoll since the 70s, but it would seem that he has done quite well. He invested and worked in San Diego real estate and has had marked success in motivational speaking to numerous corporations and other organizations. He has also made appearances in military reunions and aviation-themed shows and events. He stayed in the Reserves and retired as a Commander after 20 years. Check out his website: https://www.willydriscoll.com.

Duke Cunningham's story is more complex. He attained great heights but then fell about as far as anybody. An eight-term Congressman, based on his war record and some gerrymandering, the former hero suffered what can only be called a major judgment bypass. Cunningham had a tendency all his life to "tell it like it is" or "shoot off his mouth," whichever you prefer. This led to much controversy, especially once in the halls of Congress. He lived, while in D.C., a lifestyle that was subsidized by individuals in the defense industry. This is known as conflict of interest. He lived on a yacht on the Potomac that was not his and hosted a number of ladies there who were not his wives. He was convicted of bribery and all manners of fraud and got eight plus years in the slammer. I wrote him there, a "hang-in-there-and-remember-you-are-a-hero" letter. I received no answer. I was merely returning a favor.

In 1974 Cunningham signed a picture of himself and Driscoll standing next to an F-4 Phantom. In his inscription he cautioned me to "check my six," which in Aviationese refers to the position directly behind you to see if anyone is sneaking up on you. Duke, you would have better served yourself to look forward to the future and make some better choices. Sic transit, buddy and you are still a hero — flawed, but a hero.

Forrest Tucker

"Mister Tucker, ah, um, is it true?"

**— Attractive Matron
Las Vegas, Nevada — 1981**

F orrest Tucker was one of a bunch of big, rugged actors who lost years or had a delayed entry into the business because of World War II. There were many others who later made their mark — Jim Arness and his brother Peter Graves, Clint Walker, and several more. Forrest Tucker had a long and successful career, which could have been longer had he taken a little better care of himself. Tuck was convivial shall we say. He could put away the booze, but it did not seem to hurt his work. Well, sometimes it did. He starred in a TV show my business partner Herm Saunders had produced called *F Troop*. *F Troop* is now considered a cult classic by its fans, even though it ran for only two years. They worked on several stages at Warner Brothers. Herm said that on one occasion Tuck (everybody called him that) had left one sound stage cold sober and by the time he had crashed his golf cart on the one he was going to, he would not have been able to pass a sobriety test. Quite a character.

Besides his rollicking ways, Tuck was also gifted in other areas. Along with Milton Berle, he was said to have the largest, ah, member of anyone in Hollywood. Another actor, John Ireland, was said to be a semifinalist. There may have been others. It is somewhat odd that only Hollywood, out of all the businesses in the world, has common knowledge or keeps score on these kinds of things. There is some of the same kind of record keeping in the sports world, but it usually stays in the locker room. The Hollywood thing, for good or ill, gets around.

I was paired with Forrest Tucker at the Shecky Greene tournament I have already written about in Vegas. Tuck was on the wagon that week and had been for quite a while. Unfortunately, there are those who make it difficult for someone trying to stay on the straight and narrow. Tuck was valiantly dry that week — I can attest to that.

One really great thing about Forrest Tucker the actor was how approachable he was. People liked him and he liked them back.

He was also a very good golfer, as many of his fellow members at Lakeside could attest to. We had a large and friendly gallery that day and Tuck, in his booming way, was making it fun for all of them. There was a particular lady, not old, not young, but quite attractive, who kept moving up in the gallery so that she was practically beside us. We were held up on a par 3, and she finally summoned up the nerve and made her move. She was embarrassed and spoke so softly that only Tuck and I heard her. He regarded her kindly. "Honey, The Chief is so big, that I have to unroll him like a fire hose," he said. Having gotten what she came for, the woman dropped back into the crowd. We didn't see her for the rest of the round.

As an aside in the dick derby, Marilyn Monroe was to have said concerning Milton Berle's asset, "So Milton Berle has the biggest prick in Hollywood. So, who cares?" Concerning Tucker, there was a story around Lakeside that, on a bet, Tuck sank a three-foot putt with his weapon, but I can't prove it.

Gene Autry

"I fell in last night with evil companions."

— Gene Autry, Actor/Singer/Songwriter/Mogul
Oklahoma — 1940s

From the 1920s and on into the 1960s, the Western was a boys' refuge from the realities of schoolwork, geometry, teachers, and mowing the lawn, which in Oregon seemed to grow back overnight.

My dad's hero was Ken Maynard, who in real life was an egotistical alcoholic. This was well before the "warts and all" school of journalism, and a good thing too. "Say it ain't so, Joe," spoken by a young lad to Shoeless Joe Jackson, the Black Sox slugger, true or not, is one of the saddest lines ever written.

We wanted our Western heroes to be clean-living, straight shooters, and Wild Bill Elliott surely filled the ball for me.

Bill Elliott was tall, wore his six guns ass-backwards, and was a great horseman. He played Red Ryder, a character based on a popular comic strip of the time. Republic Pictures cranked out eight of these a year. The titles were picked well before a scene was shot. Occasionally, this would be awkward, as in the case of a Ryder Elliot called *California Gold Rush*. The film had absolutely nothing to do with the gold rush, which necessitated an opening scene explaining the paucity of men in the town. They had all, you guessed it, run off to the gold rush. It was a simpler, less questioning time. Anyway, Red Ryder's "family" included a mother/grandmother figure called the Duchess, the obligatory

Gabby Hayes-type sidekick, and a young Indian boy, Little Beaver, played by Robert Blake.

This was well before Blake went for scene-chewing, overacting, and report-edly having his wife killed. His performance as Little Beaver was restrained. There was always a girl, usually Peggy Stewart or Anne Jeffries, but they seemed more sister than love interest.

These B oaters were probably the best edited, fastest-paced movies ever made. They each ran around 58 minutes and consisted almost entirely of fist fights, gun fights, posse chases, cattle stampedes (size of stampede based on budget or availability of stock footage), and very little else.

When I go to a film today and am asked my opinion of the picture my response is, "It was okay/it sucked/I liked it, but it was too long."

If your butt gets to aching at your local Cineplex when the film seems to be dragging, you are not alone.

I do tend to wander. Let us go back to or rather forward to the wonder that was Gene Autry. The Cowboy made 93 films and hundreds of television and radio broadcasts. I didn't like any of them. For one thing, he sang. If Gene is guilty of one thing in his life that was wicked, it was the singing Western. They were so popular for too many years that John Wayne, who was making B Westerns in filmdom's studio depths, was called on to play a character called "Singin' Sandy." The Duke did not win a gold record for his efforts, and if you asked him about it, you risked verbal or even physical abuse.

John Wayne looked like a hero. To me, Gene Autry didn't. He seemed short. He seemed, um, portly. He really was none of those things; it just seemed that way to me. Alan Ladd was actually much shorter, but he played tall, primarily because he stood on a box or had his leading lady standing in a ditch.

Leaving our anonymous woman in a hole, we turn to the good parts of Gene Autry.

He was the first and until now the only person to have five stars on the Hollywood walk of fame — radio, television, movies, music, and the performing arts. The Cowboy was a man of his word, a straight shooter if there ever was one.

His Cowboy Code, a list of do's and don'ts for youngsters, is Horatio Alger as an Eagle Scout. Gene lived it himself. He preferred a handshake to a contract.

While in negotiations for selling Melody Ranch, his studio Western location far away from Hollywood, he reportedly closed the deal himself. One of his employees involved reported to Gene that he had obtained a far better deal from another potential buyer. "That's fine, but I've already given my word," said the Cowboy, and that was that.

He also refused to sell until his horse, Champion, died well into his thirties. Nothing was going on at Melody Ranch by that time, but Champion was stabled there.

He had one wife. He was loyal to friends and fans. Touring England, he offered a job as the boss of his music department to the head of his British fan clubs. The man was still drawing a paycheck long after Gene had gone to the Big Corral in the Sky.

Gene took care of his people.

He owned a baseball team, the LA/Anaheim Angels. The fans and his players loved him.

He owned Golden West Broadcasting, a chain of radio and TV stations. His employees loved him.

In WWII, though over age, he qualified as a transport pilot and flew a modified B-24 Liberator over the Hump from China to India, taking precious supplies to our WWII ally.

Gene Autry was a patriot who loved this country. He was also friend and ally to Native Americans, helping to preserve their legacy and culture in the Gene Autry Museum of the West.

In 1982 I heard Iron Eyes Cody honor Gene's contributions to his people at a Pacific Pioneer Broadcasters tribute at the Sportsman's Lodge, which Gene owned and where Gene had spent many an afternoon and evening at the bar.

And now we come to a slight bump, or lurch, in the road. Gene Autry did like to consume strong waters. He was not a Jekyll and Hyde drinker; he just became more Gene than was usual or required.

His wife and true helpmate, Ina Mae, was a staunch Christian Scientist, which meant no drinking or smoking. Smoking was not a great issue, but Ina Mae sought to limit her husband's drinking opportunities. She asked Johnny Grant, an employee at the Golden West flagship station KMPC in Los Angeles and later the unofficial "Mayor of Hollywood" to assist by riding shotgun on the Cowboy and help him withstand temptation. Unfortunately, Johnny possessed at that time a thirst that may have exceeded that of the person he had been assigned to cure or curb. Strike one.

Pat Buttram, an Autry sidekick and a very funny man whose "country ways" in performance, belied a needle-sharp wit that is still quoted in Hollywood to this day. "Gene Autry used to ride off into the sunset — now he owns it," was one of his better lines about his boss. Pat Buttram was no help either and all this put quite a strain on Ina Mae. Strike two.

The stress on the mate of the alcoholic and alcohol abuser is many times greater than on the imbiber himself. He or she already has the medicine they need or want. As a Scientist, Ina Mae did not believe in doctors, and Gene found himself both saddened and shocked when Ina Mae dropped dead of a sudden heart attack. Strike three and out for Ina Mae.

Gene immediately and for some considerable time stopped drinking to honor Ina Mae's memory. Because of my inability to put events in the proper time frame, we are forced to use another FLASHBACK, to get back to the quote that launched this roaming tale.

It was around 1948 and Gene was touring with the Gene Autry Rodeo, another successful business venture that was bringing this traditional Western event to big cities from New York to Los Angeles, as well as to small towns all around the country. After a show in one of the smaller venues in Oklahoma, Gene, his partners and business associates, plus a few locals, set about painting the town several shades of crimson. Things had gotten so convivial and noisy, that a series of complaints were made and the local law was summoned, but Gene's group was just having good, clean, drunken fun. No one was hurt or arrested. The boys promised to tone it down and did. Gene signed autographs for all the deputies at the station. The next morning, full of remorse and Alka-Seltzer, Gene showed up at the local radio station and got on the air to explain what had happened to the local citizenry and, while he was at it, to shift some blame. His fellow revelers who were listening were surprised to hear that they were "evil companions," and the whole affair was quickly forgiven and forgotten by the local townsfolk. The thought that Gene Autry could be any kind of evil companion was never considered and he left town as unsullied as ever.

Though the Cowboy and his wife are no longer with us, we're going to let Ina Mae have the final word. Gene, a perfect gentleman, would have insisted on it. Ina Mae was anti-alcohol but she was no prude. She liked a good joke as much as the next person. The foibles of her husband could be both entertaining and amusing. Ina Mae told this one to a friend of mine who worked publicity at Golden West. Ina Mae had spent the day shopping while at her home in the Hollywood Hills, a beautiful Sherwood Green shag carpet was being laid wall to wall in the living room, dining room, and den. It was to be a surprise to Gene, who was finishing up a picture in the High Desert.

By the time Ina Mae arrived, Gene had already come home. The picture was "in the can," the wrap party had been a smashing success and Gene was fried to the eyeballs. Still dressed in colorful movie/Western garb, spurs jangling, the Cowboy had gotten his hands on a powerful mower and was taking it to the new rug. Spotting Ina Mae, over the noise, he yelled, "Damn thing is growing... it... it's everywhere, everywhere!" This is last shot we will see of the Cowboy — riding into the sunset, mowing his carpet. The End.

John Wayne

"Keeping your innocence and enthusiasm in the face of terrible rejection."

— John Wayne, Actor
Newport Beach, California — 1977

L ike most of my generation of boys and now old men, I was a John Wayne fan, though I never, ever thought there was a possibility I would meet him in person, and in my wildest dreams never imagined I would work with him on a movie. Beginning as a kid, I never missed a Wayne film. He rivaled Abbott and Costello in my affections.

When in the Navy and stationed in Taiwan in 1962, I ventured out of my Americanized comfort zone to a Chinese cinema where *The Man Who Shot Liberty Valance* was playing. I soon discovered that Wayne was a worldwide draw. Every seat was taken save one in the middle of the first row, which was three feet from the screen. Talk about larger than life. Try looking straight up at a 60-foot high image of the Duke for two hours. No don't; it will make you sick as it did me.

Fifteen years later, I was at his home on Bayshore in Newport Beach as part of a Navy delegation seeking his participation in a film to be made for the Seabees, the "We build, we fight" construction organization that has been a vital part of the Navy since 1942.

On location for *Home for the Seabees,*
CBC, Port Hueneme, CA. September 1977

In 1944, Wayne had starred in *The Fighting Seabees*. It was a natural fit. Wayne had a love for the military, though he had never been a member in anything but films. As part of the presentation, a film of mine, *Flight from Yesterday*, was shown. I was not close enough to see Duke's reaction, but in the half dark I could hear it. Everyone could. It was a profanity-filled appreciation of the film and the story it told.

My back-row status in the project took a leap forward. When the lights went on, the senior Navy rep from Washington asked Wayne directly if he would appear in the picture. "The Navy needs you," the admiral pleaded. I had already noticed that there was a bust of John Ford in a dining room alcove that showed the director in the uniform of a Navy admiral. That was a good sign, and his earthly rave about my movie did not hurt either. "Oh, I'll do it for ya," he said in that Wayne drawl, with a pause in the middle of a sentence. "I'll do it for ya, whether it's a good one or a bad one — but I'd like it to be like that movie we just saw." I was then introduced to the Duke as the writer/producer of the picture. He gave me a long, approving gaze. "He can do it — give him the power — watch him, mind you, but he can do it."

In later visits to Bayshore, I would come to know that POWER was one of John Wayne's very favorite words. Towards the end, both of us had come to the sad conclusion that this was going to be a "bad one." The script had been already written by civil service hacks and featured John Wayne in a PX surrounded by shoppers, in front of a bowling alley, and the like. My attempts to make drastic changes were resisted by the bureaucracy, though we were able to change the location to the Seabee Museum and work in some Seabee history.

Trying to make a chocolate-covered turd out of an ordinary turd is neither fulfilling nor rewarding. Wayne's thoughts roamed back to the 1944 film. "The trouble was that — the newspaper dame (Susan Hayward) was beatin' me to every island." He continued, "There was this scene, see, where Bill Frawley was dyin'... you remember Bill. He was in *I Love Lucy*..."

"Well, it was shot MOS," (a German émigré expression "Mit Out Sound," that is still abbreviated that way in script direction). "I lean over him; it's a long shot and his head's not in the frame, and he says to me... 'Duke, take me to a cool saloon.' I go to the director and say to him, 'Did you hear that? ... two buddies, one of em's dyin' and he says... take me to a cool saloon... it should be in the picture.'" Duke scowled an authentic Wayne scowl. "He wouldn't listen to me... the dumb son of a bitch... I didn't have the POWER then." He thumped a balled fist into a calloused palm. It was like the report of a .45. "We could have had a great picture!" He was still mad some forty years later. I screened the film again that night, and as much as I love John Wayne, nothing short of an exorcism could have saved it. Hopefully, it was good for civilian morale in wartime.

Over several trips to Newport Beach, when working on the script became too painful, John Wayne would talk of other times. I listened and took mental notes. That is, until the visit when, accompanied by Commander Harry Flynn, our floundering film's director, Wayne jabbed at both of us with an accusing finger and stated that we should both keep a journal. He had never kept one and now that he was considering an offer from a friend of his, author Wayne Warga, to write an authorized Wayne biography, John Wayne was frustrated by not being able to recall each and every event that had happened to him in his life and, more importantly, in his fifty-year motion-picture career. How impossible that would be, I thought, and began a daily diary.

The Duke was far more complex, funny, and intelligent than the John Wayne of the movies. With men he could be competitive and gruff, but when I saw him with women and children, he was he was unfailingly polite and courteous. He had great pride in his work, but like many of his generation — Cooper, Gable, Robert Young, and others — it was self-viewed as not a "manly" way to make a living.

Wayne's admiration for the men he portrayed in films kept him in heroic roles. He once chided Kirk Douglas for playing complex and troubled characters. Better to be a hero, he thought, and his fans remember him that way, and that way alone. There were stumbles along the way. After initial stardom in Raoul Walsh's *The Big Trail* in 1931, the Duke fell to B-Westerns and serials and adventure films that were even worse.

Speaking of the early oaters, he claimed that one of them had cost only ten grand and that the miniscule budget allowed for only one horse. He had to kayo the lead heavy and take his horse to give his role some mobility, or else he would have had to walk or run from scene to scene.

I don't know whether he invented the terms but he explained to me that there were two kinds of heavies: "brain heavies," who never fought, and "dog heavies," who did all the fighting and other nefarious misdeeds. Think of *Goldfinger* as a "brain heavy," demonstrating that the role spans all genres.

The Duke explained that "dog heavies" got the name from the abbreviated running times of the B-Western. In an opening scene, a villain would be seen crossing a dusty Western street, and when coming across a stray or anyone's dog, would pause long enough to give the poor beast a swift kick, hence the "dog heavy."

When I asked the Duke if he ever looked at his old films, he dismissed the early efforts with a mild profanity. He had, the previous evening, taken a look at *Wake of the Red Witch*, a Republic sea story from 1946 or so. As he watched, he thought to himself, "Look at that good-looking guy." His habit, like other royals, was to often refer to himself in the third person. Pausing from *Witch* to take a leak, he looked in the bathroom mirror and said, "Who is that old son of a bitch?" He had witnessed all the changes, from young romantic lead to Rooster Cogburn. One can only imagine what that must have felt like. "Surprise, it's me!"

The lost years were not entirely wasted. The Duke perfected the walk and the slow talk with a pause. He and fellow actor Yakima Canutt, a bad actor but a great stuntman, perfected the blocking moves that made fights on film totally realistic. In silent days and a little after, the combatants pounded each other on the shoulders, which looked as ridiculous as it sounds. He began to ride, fight, and act like John Wayne. He was ready when the time came, and Yak went with him. Check out his stunts in *Stagecoach*.

What surprised me about John Wayne was his sensitivity. He had a grin like a little boy and he could show sadness as well. When asked what had been the most difficult, the hardest thing to face in that long fifty-year journey, he thought for only a moment and did not hesitate. "Keeping your innocence and enthusiasm in the face of terrible rejection," he said. As he spoke the words, his face scrunched up in a look of pain that was hard to watch.

All those years in the Gower Gulch wilderness where, though the work was steady, the good roles, major roles, and studios had passed him by. John Ford and *Stagecoach* saved him in 1939 and he never looked back. No, that's not true. He did look back, and when he did with me forty plus years later, it still hurt. We will get back to the Duke in better times in other places in the book, but of all of his quotes, this one is my favorite.

Vance Skarstedt

"We had three options, depending on the condition he was in that day."

— **Vance Skarstedt, Actor/Writer**
Hollywood, California — 1974

Vance Skarstedt was a Hollywood journeyman — a tough way to make a living then and probably now. He made 20 appearances as an actor in low-budget, half-hour episodic television shows and a half dozen as writer of the same. He did write five screenplays that became features, including *The Slime People*, one of the worst sci-fi horror films of the Fifties. They scraped the bottom of the beast barrel with this one, including the unappetizing and un-frightening title. A couple of them were pretty good. *Man and Gun* featured recognized names, Macdonald Carey and Audrey Totter. The last of them, *Once Before I Die*, was filmed on location in the Philippines in 1968. It starred John Derek, a pretty but unremarkable actor, and Ursula Andress, one of his many beautiful wives. Linda Evans and Bo Derek were other famous ones. The latter set the record for Derek marriage longevity at 22 years, or until John died.

Anyway, what passed for glory days had passed for Vance Skarstedt when I met him in 1972. He was working, as I was, at Filmline, a small concern that would produce or edit for anyone who had a few bucks. For a beginner like me, it was a good place to learn. There was some talent there. Jack Reifert, who is still working, became one of the developers of the slam/bang MTV style, which has reduced the attention span of one third of America by half. Jack was actually a fabulous editor, and we teamed up together for many years.

Documentaries were made on 16 mm back then, and when tape came in, it all changed. The mixes in old-time sound houses with their multiple reels of film, music, sound effects, and the like were replaced by video engineers in small editing bays who often had no idea of what the material they were working on was about. They were button pushers, I thought. Wipes, fades, multiple images, fast and faster cuts were the norm. As Jack watched his art being manipulated, he turned to me and whispered, "They're killing my moments."

Jack was right, but he adjusted. Vance never did. He didn't live that long.

Vance was said to have been a B-24 pilot. He could have been; he looked the part — blond and handsome, a pipe smoker.

These days, alcohol was catching up to Vance, but when you asked him, "How are things?" his inevitable answer was, "Tip top." His eyes did not believe his words.

Though Vance's gifts were not of the major variety, he was a good man to have around. The wily owner of Filmline, Charles Bordwell, a close man with a buck, threw nickels around as if they were manhole covers. He kept Vance in booze, let him sleep in the back, and gave him small amounts of money on irregular occasions. Vance's wives and children, if any, were history and never discussed. All Vance liked to talk about was the movies. It is an odd reality that people who know better believe in the Hollywood dream, even as it kills them.

Vance had worked with some beauties, though. Robert Mitchum was one. Vance had a one-line gig in a movie called *The Last Time I Saw Archie*, a service comedy of sorts produced by Jack Webb, a man not noted for his sense of humor. The movie was partly filmed at March AFB near Riverside. The shot that opened the picture involved Mitchum, Vance, and a young girl dressed in WWII uniforms standing near a flight line with rows of planes stretching off into the distance.

A Chapman crane — a camera device on a long boom — mounted on a wheeled vehicle of huge proportions, was coming down the line, photographing the aircraft. As it reached the humans, it would stop and focus on them and their few lines. It took the better part of forever to set up, and to mess up would cost a whole day's shooting. Vance remembered Mitchum standing beside him, silent, strong and somnolent, eyes closed, bored as usual. As the camera beast bore down on them, red lights flashing, Vance frantically rehearsed his single line. As the two minor players stood there, nerves jangling, Mitchum opened up his eyes and spoke for the first time, offering a pornographic suggestion to the young actress. Vance forgot every word. The girl froze. "Showtime people," Mitchum whispered, and they all jumped back into character in time to make the shot happen the way it was supposed to. Mitch, who was seldom serious about himself or the film he was working in, suggested that they all go to the officer's club for a drink, which they did. Vance's name did not appear in the credits.

Vance's biggest continuing role was on television in the *Highway Patrol* series, which starred Broderick Crawford. Vance was Sergeant Larabee, the sidekick to Crawford's Chief Dan Matthews in the show. Larabee was the name of a street at the bottom of the Sunset Strip for those of you who would like to know where cinematic names come from. Broderick Crawford was a hulk of an actor who resembled a prize fighter with a long, losing record. He had played Lenny in *Of Mice and Men* on the stage and had even won a Best Actor Oscar in *All the Kings Men*, a political drama that mirrored the life of Senator Huey Long of Louisiana.

By the time of *Highway Patrol*, the cinematic heights were in Crawford's rear view mirror. He was lured to TV by an offer of ten percent of the gross on this Ziv production. There actually was a Ziv, who ran a cheapjack operation with program budgets of twenty-five grand a show. They made two a week, and the location where one show ended would be the start of the next one. Hoping that no one would notice, they mixed up the numbers of the episodes. Somewhat surprisingly, the show became a big hit and ran from 1945 to 1949, and in syndication ever after, or for quite a few years anyway.

Broderick Crawford drank. I can confirm this because I saw him in an alcohol treatment facility at St John's Hospital in Santa Monica some 20 years later.

A fellow actor and boozer, Aldo Ray, was also a patient. In a Q&A session at St. John's one evening, both actors came up with answers to every question, to which Dr. Joe Takamine, head of the rehab unit remarked, "If you guys know so damn much, why in hell have you been here half a dozen times?"

Alcohol is cunning, baffling, and powerful. So is good acting, by the way, and we should get back to it.

On *Highway Patrol*, according to Vance Skarstedt, Crawford could put away two bottles of brandy, give or take, on every shoot. From this reality came plans A, B, and C. Plan A, Brod could walk and talk. Plan B, he could talk sitting in his car ("10-4," a standard show line that became public property), but his mobility could not be predicted. Plan C, the emergency plan, was used only when he could not walk or speak. Brod could, however, sit in the car, while others divided up his lines, to which he would nod or emit sounds of approval or disapproval. There was also the problem of driving, since he had lost his license after accumulating an impressive number of 502s, the California code for "driving while under the influence."

The California Highway Patrol advisor on the show addressed Broderick Crawford as "Mr. 502." In the show Brod had to drive, but only on private roads, closely watched by CHP officers in their cars, and at the ready. Vance rode along with Crawford on these private road forays, holding on for dear life as Brod took a few pulls from a handy flask with one hand and steered with the other. It made for exciting television. Brod, by the way, hated to be called that, and I can only use it because he is in heaven's version of the Lambs Club, an actors' haunt in New York he loved to frequent. Once when a young director kept calling him that, after being warned, Crawford left the location and went to Paris, France. This was 1955 and getting to Paris and back took some time. The director was forced to look for employment elsewhere.

Vance Skarstedt died a few years ago, forgotten and alone. I miss him and all of the stories of the Hollywood he knew.

Pearl Harbor Survivor

"The water began to rise — up to my knees — waist — shoulders — I wanted to die."

**— Pearl Harbor Survivor
Honolulu, Hawaii – 1980**

For young men of my generation, the draft was always there — like a big, black hole dead ahead. The war we had then was a cold one, Korea was an inactive stalemate, Vietnam was a French problem, but the draft stayed put. Re-released war films were black, white, and scary. Even John Wayne died in one. In 1950 I saw a new war film, *Battleground*. It was made by MGM and featured a roster of their contract players: Van Johnson, Ricardo Montalbán, George Murphy, Marshall Thompson, James Whitmore, and a host of others, plus a sexy French girl named Denise Darcel. It was directed by William Wellman, who knew about war. He had been in one as a member of the Lafayette Escadrille in WWI. It did not have the realistic and bloody depictions of war that one sees today, but it was enough to scare the hell out of me. The GIs were cold and wet, frostbitten, shelled, shot at, and longing for home.

Years later I met General Tommy Franks, the General in charge of Iraq 2, and he asked if I had served and was it in the Army. "I'm Navy, sir," I said. When he asked why, I told him it was because of a movie. I didn't mention that as my 17th birthday loomed, I had decided that if I was going to die, somehow I was going to sleep in a bed or bunk with clean sheets. My family had not served since the Civil War, and my father was not anxious to break the string. He had one of the highest draft numbers ever given, and his only uniform was white Standard Stations, Inc. I asked if he had ever missed the bonding, the camaraderie, the adrenalin of fighting for a great cause. My father said he didn't. I had to admire his survival skills.

I joined the Navy when I was 17 and stayed in the Naval Reserve for the next 36 years, to the amazement of my peers at Officer Candidate School. I don't say that the Navy made a man out of me, but it pointed me in that direction.

In boot camp, the Navy taught me to swim by letting me jump into 10 feet of water from a high tower. When I spluttered to the surface, I was prodded back under with a very long pole until I got the idea. I got it. I also learned what a gas mask is for by being ordered into a large room filled with tear gas. We were then told to take off our masks and WALK to the exit. Those unlucky enough to run got to go back and try it again. I walked, but briskly.

Upon my graduation I received a commission, which came with clean sheets and far- flung destinations. Initially, I wanted no more than to be another Ensign Pulver. This officer avoided duty and responsibility with a dedication that became legendary. Look up *Mister Roberts* on Netflix. Jack Lemmon did a helluva job. I have a lobby card signed to me by him from the film *The Wackiest Ship in the Army* — "From one captain to another."

But I digress. I got by in my first few assignments by going to the leading chief and admitting that I knew absolutely nothing about absolutely anything. The chiefs and leading petty officers knew this already, of course, but it appealed to their fatherly or brotherly instincts, and I survived and was promoted accordingly.

I entered the service because I had to, but it did not take long to find out I was stirred by the sight of the flag being raised and lowered in far off places — the Western Pacific, North Atlantic, and in ports around the world. I had always been proud and grateful to be an American, but those feelings grew and deepened so far from home. Did we as a nation make mistakes? Sure we did and do. What country hasn't? Still we stood and stand for freedom and decency in a world where these qualities are often lacking. With our allies and a strong fair-weather friend, we defeated the most evil regimes in history. I witnessed this as a small boy but it must have left a deep impression. The good guys won, but with terrible sacrifices in blood and treasure — sacrifices that were shared by the nation, not just by those who fought the battle.

It was with this awareness that, in 1980, I was tasked to write a film for the 40th anniversary of Pearl Harbor. I was no longer on active duty but the Pentagon put me back in uniform for six weeks to go to Hawaii and come up with a script. I visited the USS *Arizona* and Punchbowl Cemetery. It was impossible not to be moved. Japanese visitors were present at both places, which I found upset me. My last stop was at the Pearl Harbor Memorial Center where I was allowed to interview a large number of survivors of the attack who now dedicate their time and energies to speak with and answer questions from visitors from all over the world. I still have tapes of those interviews — somewhere. While I currently do not have their names, I remember their stories, all of them. The one I remember most was a musician on USS *West Virginia*. He had just come out on deck to the sounds of action when he looked up to find a Japanese Zero headed right at him. Bullets flew over his head as he rushed to his general quarters station several decks below the main deck. He was the last man to report, "dogging the hatch" behind him. In less than a minute there was a huge explosion followed by total blackness in the compartment. The ship began to list and the water slowly to rise. Time lost its meaning. He was a small man and the water ultimately came just under his chin. He waited for the next explosion and death to free him from this horror. Minutes became hours, hours became years. In whispers from his mates and thoughts and in prayers unspoken they waited for help that they knew would never come in time. An eternity later a light shown from above, an emergency hatch had opened and eager hands reached to lift them to safety. An inspired and courageous Officer of the Deck had ordered counterflooding, righting the listed ship just as it settled to the bottom.

Other survivor stories were no less dramatic. There was no consensus among them about the events that led up to the attack and who may have known beforehand, if anyone. A few still despised the Japanese. Most did not. I was curious. Why in the world did they live so near to the Hell that they had passed through? One man in particular had flashbacks every day he came to work and saw the harbor below. In some spiritual, mystic way they were linked to those on the *Arizona* and at the Punchbowl. They agreed on only one thing — they would go through the ordeal again, for their country, for their shipmates. We must count ourselves fortunate that there were such men.

After finishing the script, I showed it to Glenn Ford and Jackie Cooper who would share the narration. They suggested minor changes, but it met with their approval overall. Back to Washington, D.C., it went and up the bureaucratic chain. I had been more interested in the heroism than assigning blame. I tried to be objective, but it was impossible to ignore the fact that, after all, the Japanese Empire had committed this act of war. After the usual delays, the word was passed down. I still have the comments on my copy of the script. "We do not wish to stigmatize or offend Japan at this time." Political correctness had come to the Pentagon, heroism and sacrifice be damned.

Mickey Rooney and Jackie Cooper

"MGM was a fairyland of talent and beauty.
Work was a pleasure.
What a wonderful place and time."

— Mickey Rooney, Actor/Performer/Author
Sugar Babies **— Backstage Pantages Theater**
Hollywood, California — 1984

"Bullshit!"

— Jackie Cooper, Actor/Director/Producer
Hollywood, California — 1984

This exchange took place on the same day, in the same city, but not at the same time, and most certainly not face-to-face. One of the benefits of tape over film is that you can see the results immediately. It does not have to be processed at a lab.

I was making a video about Jackie Cooper to be shown at a dinner in his honor. My crew and I had spent most of the afternoon backstage at the Pantages Theater where *Sugar Babies*, old vaudeville blackout humor, was

One of his managers once said that Mickey had "burned more bridges than Napoleon." But, what a talent.

being resurrected by Mickey, Ann Miller, and the ensemble. The business was "boffo" as *Variety* was want to say back in the day. I love that word, "boffo."

Well, Mickey Rooney was "boffo" too and a lot of other things. You have experienced nothing till you have experienced Rooney on a roll. He was promoting the next big things: Mickey vitamins and Mickey macaroni, which would be available all over the world next week. He had discovered the secret for beating the horses, and on and on and on. Mickey's manager, nose in *Variety* and/or the racing form, agreed with every word Mickey uttered. "That's great, Mick," "You're right, Mick." Mr. Manager had survived World War II, and he would survive Mickey, macaroni and all. He did look worn, though, as if life had handed him a series of shrewish, nagging wives, temperamental artists, and cars with bad transmissions. Mr. Manager was the background chorus, show time was approaching, and I watched Ann Miller through the open dressing-room door. She was warming up — tap-tap-tap-tap.

I decided to take Mr. Manager's approach. "That's just great Mickey, but we have to do the interview for the Jackie Cooper dinner."

"Yeah, Jack — great kid." (Cooper was two years younger than The Mick.)

"Tell us what it was like at MGM," I offered.

That was all Mickey needed. He made it sound like Oz, without the witches and with L. B. Mayer as an on-stage wizard. Rose-colored glasses were made for The Mick. MGM was special, no doubt, "more stars than there are in Heaven," and all that, but this was a bit much even for a movie lover like me. It was what we came for though, and I thanked my way out of the room, a minute or two before the curtain went up. The term "flop sweat" was obviously not in the Rooney vocabulary. As we were leaving, Mick had one more thing to say, "I know that Jack will agree with everything I said."

Two hours later I was in Cooper's office and showed him the tape. His critique after viewing it is shown above, but there were similar sentiments expressed throughout the screening. After he retired in 1989, Cooper refused to participate in any event that glorified the "good old days." Cooper and Mickey were at MGM at about the same time, but going in different directions. After a stint in *Our Gang* comedies, including a silent, Cooper soared to stardom in *Skippy*, a loan-out to Paramount which was a huge hit and brought him an Academy Award nomination for Best Actor. This was in 1931. At the same time, Mickey Rooney was appearing in over 70 Mickey McGuire shorts, a star but on a much smaller platform.

Cooper's child-star status continued for the next few years, including many films in which he costarred with MGM's "Big Galoot" Wallace Beery, a huge star at the time. Jackie Cooper despised his father figure, claiming Beery never talked to him off camera and was constantly doing bits of business designed to distract or steal scenes. Rooney, who later was in several films with Beery, professed to like the older man, perhaps the only person on the MGM lot who did. As Rooney climbed the ladder and Jackie was still popular, they did films together, including *The Devil Is a Sissy*.

Though Cooper and Rooney were never close, they shared many of the same interests including playing the drums, hot cars, and naturally, girls. Both of them dated Judy Garland, though Mickey's dates were for publicity and Jackie's were serious. Cooper complained to me that later when Judy was stuck in a Mexican hotel without funds, he paid her hotel bill, and that was the last he saw of his money. By the end of the decade, Mickey Rooney was the number-one box office star in the world, while Jackie, ushered off the Metro lot, was making films elsewhere, at Paramount, Universal, even at Monogram, the Siberia of Hollywood.

They both went to war. Mickey won a Bronze Star, and both had difficulties when they came back. The comebacks for both of them gladdened the hearts of their fans and supporters. Jackie Cooper had to go to Broadway and television to redefine himself as an actor and later as a director of countless quality television shows, besides turning up as Perry White in the *Superman* series of feature films. Jackie's one career regret was having only one chance at directing feature films (*Stand Up and Be Counted* in 1972), feeling that he had been typed by the industry as a television director.

Mickey's ups and downs and detours were too numerous to mention. His mood swings and pill addiction were not helpful and, often, he did not help himself. One of his many agents/managers said, wearily, "Mickey has burned more bridges than Napoleon." Somehow though, there would be an Academy Award nominated performance, or several, a *Sugar Babies,* and he would be back on top again. Jackie and Mickey both lived long lives. Mickey was 93, though in later years he must have wished not to have made it that far. Jackie Cooper, who was 88 at death, saved his money and had a pleasant retirement training horses, a longtime love, at Hollywood Park and Del Mar. Mickey Rooney didn't, and the $18,000 in his final estate was woefully short of paying off bills and taxes, not to mention funeral expenses. His last of eight marriages will not be examined here. I would rather recall one luncheon afternoon, and seeing his genius at full display. I was on of a team trying (vainly, as it turned out) to sell a special on Mickey's 75th anniversary in show business.

This would have been around 1978 or so. One of the meetings on this project took place in a fine Chinese restaurant in Brentwood, in a neighborhood that O. J. Simpson would make infamous a few years later. I can affirm that the restaurant was first rate, because the place was full, and we were the only Anglo faces in the place. Mickey was talking about how he got Walt Disney to change the name of his mouse from Mortimer to Mickey, and the fact that he had discovered Marilyn Monroe. This was old stuff. Mickey had told these stories countless times. He was even boring himself. Suddenly, he brightened. "Did you ever hear how Johnny Hyde died?" he asked, excitedly. Many of us had no idea who Johnny Hyde was. I only knew slightly. He was an agent at William Morris and had something to do with Marilyn Monroe's career — more than something actually.

Johnny Hyde was a Vice President at William Morris when he met Monroe in 1949. He signed her as a client and became her biggest supporter, talking up her attributes and talent at every studio in town. He also fell madly in love with Marilyn, left his wife, and asked her to marry him. Marilyn was grateful, even physically grateful, but she resisted his offers of matrimony, though she did live with him for a time. According to Mickey the stresses of his work and his love affair put such pressure on Hyde that he suffered a heart attack and was rushed to the hospital. On his return home, barely inside the front door, he pleaded for Monroe to have sex with him then and there. Concerned for his health, Marilyn begged him to remember he had just come from the hospital, till gratitude overwhelmed her and she consented.

Johnny Hyde died in the saddle, as it were, and Mickey Rooney took over the story from there. He played all the parts: Marilyn (if you closed your eyes you would swear it was Monroe), the maid, the two cops who showed up, the ambulance crew, a doctor — everybody. Mickey gave each of them a separate and distinct voice and style. It was worthy of both an Oscar and an Emmy. Nearby patrons looked our way as if they were witnessing a horrible accident. For you see, Mickey's voice chops were in full force. You could have heard him across the street. When The Mick finished his story, my tablemates and I rose and gave him a standing O. The reaction of the rest of the audience may have been mixed, but I was convinced that, as one of his directors at MGM had said, no doubt about it, Mickey Rooney was a genius. I have no idea whether the story of Johnny Hyde's death is true or not, but does it really matter?

Sir John Mills

The Man from Planet X?

— Sir John Mills, Actor
Studio City, California – 1999

Sportsman's Lodge has been a Hollywood hangout for celebrities for decades. Founded in the 1880s, once a trout farm, it eventually became a hotel and meeting place for many of the famous. Gable, Wayne, Hepburn, and Tracy stopped by frequently. It was no surprise then to discover that Sir John Mills, one of the great trio of English actors, including Ralph Richardson and Michael Redgrave, and whose talents lay just below Olivier and Gielgud, had booked a suite at the Lodge while in LA for his one-man show. This was all news to me, but I was having lunch there with my old business partner Herm Saunders, producer of *F Troop* and *Adam-12* and his good friend Robert Clarke.

Robert was an actor who had hitchhiked to Hollywood during WWII in search of fame and fortune. He found neither but had begun a long and varied career in the B feature depths of the "biz." Since most males were off to war and asthma had kept him out of it, Robert soon landed a contract with RKO and found work almost before he had unpacked. He was in *The Falcon in Hollywood* and two Val Lewton horror films, *The Body Snatcher* and *Bedlam*, which gave him a chance to work with such famous names as Boris Karloff and Bela Lugosi. Karloff signed a picture to Bob, "To Robert Clarke. Be as lucky as

I am." Handsome, with a pencil-thin mustache, Bob was often mistaken, in bad light, for Errol Flynn. This led to more work, in Tim Holt westerns and historical pics of the sword-swinging variety. The poor man's Flynn, he was called.

The sci-fi craze of the 1950s took Bob out of the ordinary and raised him to cult status. He emerged as a star in such vehicles as *The Astounding She Monster, The Incredible Petrified World, Beyond the Time Barrier, Frankenstein Island, The Man from Planet X,* and his own creation *The Hideous Sun Demon.* All of these films had budgets of less than a hundred grand, limited production values, and plots that featured lady scientists with big boobs, monsters, and special effects that could safely be called "cheesy." The actors were mostly tyros and faded veterans with minute, though recognizable, box-office appeal. In such settings Robert brought dignity and some professionalism to the proceedings. He was a bit wooden but always reliable. For his efforts in *The Man from Planet X,* where he was the top-billed star, he was paid $275, including overtime, for a one-week shoot. *X* was made on the proverbial shoestring, written, cast, and shot in six months. Haste was vital at the time to get it out before Howard Hawks' *The Thing from Another World* was released. *Thing* had trouble with its final scenes, which had to be shot in an Alaskan snow setting. It was a poor year for snow, as everywhere they went, the predicted white stuff failed to appear or melted on arrival. In a major upset, audiences starved for *The Thing* flocked to *The Man from Planet X* and made it a huge hit with grosses over a million on a budget of forty thousand. This inspired Robert Clarke to star, produce, direct, and finance his own sci-fi classic, *The Hideous Sun Demon.* The film is not bad, as these films go, but it wasn't all that good either. Robert could not find distribution, always a challenge for an indie; he lost most of his shirt and was left with a really impressive rubber monster suit and a stack of unpaid bills.

Television was the way out for Robert Clarke. He married one of the King Sisters, was a part of their television show, and did hundreds of guest shots over the next decades. What helped financially, in an unexpected way, was that the posters from the sci-fi films he had appeared in began to skyrocket in value. He should have been paid in posters. One-sheet posters from *The*

Man from Planet X sold for ten thousand and up. Robert was even able to sell a poster from *The Sorceress*, a film idea of his that was not only never made, there had never been a script or even a treatment attempted. Too costly.

The poster from *Sorceress*, which resembled the art from *The Astounding She Monster*, was one of the best I have ever seen — as good as those from American International Pictures, legendary in the field for combining sex, blood, and violence with snappy one-liners. A theater owner once counseled Sam Arkoff, the President of AIP, to figure a way to project the posters and forget the movies. This audacious suggestion was ignored, but Sam made money from both.

I realize that this has become the Robert Clarke show, but such longevity in a field that he had never conquered to his own satisfaction deserves a hearing, or reading.

FLASHBACK to our lunch at Sportsman's Lodge. As we were conversing, we were approached by someone at the next table. He was a Brit, a Robert Morley type, but better looking. He had been listening to our conversation, had discerned that we had something to do with the movie business, and wished to add to our knowledge. He was the manager of Sir John Mills, who was currently appearing in Los Angeles. Though knighted, Sir John had just turned down the opportunity to be Lord John, and would we like to meet him. I certainly did for, though I knew who he was, I was also quite certain he was dead. It turned out, at 90, Sir John was very much alive. And, yes sir, we would very much like to meet him. Herm and I did, at any rate — Robert Clarke much less so, as if he knew what was coming and would rather avoid it. He was a gamer though and we moved as a group to poolside where John Mills was reclining. Nut brown, quick as a cricket, Sir John bounced up and introduced himself and his nurse, a fetching blonde who could have been borrowed from the *Carry On* series of British comedies. Introductions all around, followed by small talk and the invariable, "And what do you do?" I looked at Robert who, as they say, had paled visibly.

Herman had produced shows that sparked recognition from Sir John. I had produced the "outtakes" show on television, had been involved in the production of some features, and had finished a screen play that Tom Cruise had interest in — the usual lies. Now it was Robert Clarke's turn. He said he was an actor, very softly. Mills showed some real interest. "Would you have appeared in anything I may have seen?" Sir John asked politely. Bob Clarke looked as if he had been kneed in the nuts. "*The Man from Planet X*," he finally whispered. John Mills repeated the title as if it were a question and then said something that lifted my esteem for this great artist, "Oh yes, I do remember that one — most enjoyable." How diplomatic. How wise. The three of us went away happy, heads held high. I was pleased further when, some five years later, Robert Clarke got a multi-column obituary in the LA times, citing his cult status and his extensive list of credits. Bob would not have believed it, but it would have made him very happy.

Bogart put it nicely, "If you are working, you are a good actor." Bob Clarke was always working, not always in what he wanted, but steadily employed — a good actor.

Studio Kids

MGM Studios

Culver City, California – 1995

"There's a horse in my hair."

— Ginger Rogers, Actress
Culver City, California – 1995

"Look Jackie, there's Uncle Miltie."

— Wife of Jackie Cooper
Culver City, California – 1995

"Keep moving."

— Jackie Cooper, Actor/Producer/Director
Culver City, California – 1995

"Well, you know Tony."

— Janet Leigh, Actress
Culver City, California — 1995

"My back is killing me."

— Shelley Winters, Actress
Culver City, California — 1995

"A little to the left, and harder."

— Douglas Fairbanks, Jr., Actor/Author/Diplomat
Culver City, California — 1995

"Well, you know Esther."

— Anonymous Voice
Culver City, California — 1995

In 1995 the magazine *Vanity Fair* began what would become an annual event — the Hollywood issue. Lavishly produced and promoted, it concentrated mainly on new Hollywood, with only a nod or two to Hollywood history. One of the latter was an article entitled "Studio Kids." Most of the major names of the studios were still around in 1995, but practically everything else had changed. No more stars, directors and producers under exclusive contracts with the majors — MGM, Fox, Paramount, Warners, Columbia, Universal,

Disney. No longer were there fully-stocked departments, everything from makeup and costume to set design and construction. Many studios had their own fire departments and police, their own barbershops and restaurants. The majors produced around fifty films a year, plus cartoons and short subjects. Many have called the period from the 1920s through the 1950s the Golden Age of cinema. For the moviegoer it was Entertainment Heaven, something for everyone. A lot of crap, to be sure, but *Gone with the Wind*, *Casablanca*, *Citizen Kane*, *Singing in the Rain*, *Maltese Falcon,* and dozens and dozens of others, make for wonderful memories. So nice that TCM brings this all back, even the dinkers, the cats, and the dogs.

In January 1995, after an ardent and prolonged courtship that consisted of gilded invitations, promises of five-star treatment and phone calls from silver-tongued promoters promising that all the biggest stars from the Golden time would be present, 38 veterans of the studio system agreed to be there for what would be a great and grand reunion. There would be limos, a catered luncheon from Hollywood's finest eatery, and a formal group portrait by famed photographer Annie Leibowitz. *Vanity Fair* made it sound too good to be true, which it was. Many of the surviving major stars did not make it. Among the absentees: Sinatra, Kirk Douglas, Glenn Ford, Loretta Young, Lana Turner, Debbie Reynolds, Esther Williams, June Allyson, Jimmy Stewart, and others. The shoot was held on a stage on the old MGM lot in Culver City, a studio then

After the death of Robert Young's beloved wife Betty, Gayle Frederick was Bob's principal caregiver. She did a great job. Bob loved her. I did too.

owned by the Japanese company Sony. The mighty had fallen, or retreated anyway, and the whole place looked a little shabby. I should not complain. I was lucky to be there.

My wife, Gayle, was then a caregiver, with an assist from me whenever needed, for Robert Young, the actor. Gayle had started as a driver for Bob and Betty Young, and in Betty's last days in Good Samaritan Hospital, she asked Gayle to help take care of the man who had been her constant companion since Lincoln High School, for nearly 70 years when Betty passed. Many thought that Robert would not survive the blow.

There were indeed dark days at the Enchanted Cottage on Saddletree Drive in Westlake Village, until one evening when dinner was served by my wife, the caregiver, dressed in a black and white cow suit, complete with udders. The bovine imitation lifted Robert's mood and spirits, and life became worth living again on Saddletree Drive. Peace, serenity, and boredom reigned until multiple invitations arrived from *Vanity Fair* to attend their "gala event." Robert, in his eighties, had seen enough of such nonsense and

Van Johnson, Gayle, and Milton Berle at the Vanity Fair Studio Kids event at old MGM studios. Nearly forty stars from Hollywood's Golden Age were there. It was like old home week.

refused to participate. Gayle, as movie and star struck as the most faithful TCM viewer, begged and pleaded and worked her woman's magic till Robert finally agreed to attend, on the condition he would never have to do anything like it ever again.

Thus we were delivered by limo to what had been MGM's famous Stage 7 to take part in a blast from the past, one that few who attended would ever forget.

The whole thing turned out to be a love fest, a glorified high school or college reunion where everyone met on equal terms. Status and ego were absent, and friendship and fond memo-

Gayle "borrows" Gene Autry's Cowboy hat at the Studio Kids shoot.

ries ruled. This is a partial list of the attendees: Ginger Rogers, Gene Autry, Tony Curtis, Janet Leigh, Richard Widmark, Jane Powell, Howard Keel, Ann Blyth, Ernest Borgnine, Douglas Fairbanks, Jr., Shelley Winters, Eva Marie Saint, Van Johnson, Lassie, Eddie Albert, Sylvia Sidney, Sid Caesar, Robert Stack, Roddy McDowell, Virginia Mayo, Burgess Meredith, Celeste Holm, Rod Taylor, Jane Wyatt, Anne Francis, Carroll Baker, Kathryn Grayson, Jackie Cooper, Max Schell, and Milton Berle — an autograph seeker's delight.

Wife Gayle got her picture taken with everyone, including Lassie. I got to mix and mingle like Woody Allen in the Hollywood party in *Annie Hall*. In Allen's Best Picture film, he walked through the party collecting such gems as "All the Best Meetings Are Taken" and a frantic "What's my sign?" I was so busy eavesdropping that I missed the opportunities to pose with the friendly and willing famous, but I heard a few things that still bring a smile. Go back to the previous page and you can share my snoopery. Ginger Rogers' comment about someone messing with her hairdo referred to Gene Autry's Champion,

III, her immediate neighbor in the photo, who had an immediate reaction to the actress' lacquered tresses. Then, there was Barbara Cooper's excitement on seeing Milton Berle. Husband Jackie, it appears, had already met the comic. Janet Leigh was observing the arrival of ex-husband Tony with a gorgeous twenty-something blonde. Shelley Winters remark was an excuse for preempting the couch in Robert Young's dressing room.

Doug Fairbanks, Ernest Borgnine, Robert Young, and Richard Widmark were a chatty group sharing anecdotes of days past, friends lost and, best of all, some of the most embarrassing experiences of their movie careers. Young and Widmark, not known for socializing, were yucking it up, seeming to be having the time of their lives when the call came to report to the stage for the photo shoot. As his old friend Fairbanks passed him, Robert Young whacked him on the ass with a small pillow with the words "Screw the

With Burgess Meredith in his memorabilia-filled office at his beachfront home in Malibu.

Gold Years" embossed in gold. Fairbanks' response reflected his sophisticated, urbane personality.

Many of the comments I overheard that day were regrets that Frank and Kirk, Esther and all the others had not made the event. They would have enjoyed it also. Sadly, just a handful of those who did make it are still with us. Still, as long as there are movies shown, they live — young, handsome, beautiful, and talented, bonded forever in a unique place and time, members of an exclusive club that will never again meet.

John Wayne

*"So, we couldn't get the church, but Pappy Ford
had a better idea."*

**— John Wayne, Actor
Newport Beach, California – 1977**

John Wayne was never afraid to mix it up with his enemies, and not just on screen. In the middle of the Vietnam War, Wayne accepted an invitation from the Harvard Lampoon to "show some guts" and come to Harvard to debate the issues, including Vietnam. Mister Wayne (I always called him that) showed up riding in an APC, an Armored Personnel Carrier. Once in the arena he may have faced hostility, but his responses to questions brought friendly laughs, i.e., Q: "Is your hair real?" A: "Yeah, it's real — it's not mine but it's real hair." Q: "Does President Nixon advise you on the making of your movies?" A: "No, all my movies have been successful so far." Wayne left the scene and an audience prepared to scorn him instead had shown affection and respect. John Wayne was always more than a manly man, a symbol of a He-Man.

I always liked John Wayne; virtually all boys and young men my age did, but it was working with him that produced a real sense of respect. His opinions were thoughtful and wide ranging. In talking about his many years in the motion picture business, he opposed the straight-laced censorship so prominent through the 1950s. "The Code — God, yes it was dumb — twin beds and one foot on the floor, all of that. But I wonder if we haven't gone too far — sweaty,

119

On the set for *Home for the Seabees* with the Duke, September, 1977. I always called him Mister Wayne.

matted hair, and flesh — that's not sex to me. If you want to see real sex, sexual tension, go screen *The Quiet Man* with Maureen, and I never took my shirt off."

I screened *The Quiet Man*, and it was still beautiful, an adult Irish fairy tale. John Ford is said to have bought the rights to the Colliers story for ten bucks and held it in reserve till he was able to film it his way, in Ireland. It is a beautiful film, the eye-popping green of the Emerald Isle as big a star as the caricatures and stereotyped characters in the picture. The obvious interiors and process shots diminish its impact; and the Duke's lighting, deeply inhaling, and angrily flipping away coffin nails are troubling, besides giving Smoky the Bear fits. It all works, though, even though in any Irish film things are not always what they sem. Barry Fitzgerald, the archetypical priest and his real-life brother Arthur Shields, though ardent Eire nationalists, were also Protestants. Victor McLaglen was English, and it seldom seemed to rain in John Ford's Ireland. But the chemistry, the animal magnetism between the Wayne and O'Hara lovers, that was all of what the Duke said it was. In their embraces, which were quite few, they seemed ready to devour one another and, as he said, they remained fully clothed. Even the scene where Wayne drags O'Hara up a grassy hillside, she — bouncing, sliding, falling, being dragged to her feet — has a sexuality about it. Feminists be damned. John Ford lingered on this film, taking far longer to shoot it than usual. It was surely his happiest film, and his artistry was on constant, if unheralded, display.

When the local hierarchy refused permission to film in the parish church, which was in the script, Ford penned a scene whereby O'Hara meets her priest (Ward Bond) as he is trying to snag a salmon he has been stalking for years. The priest is sympathetic as she pours out her marital problem in Gaelic, until the salmon strikes and all Hell breaks loose. The salmon quest is also introduced later in the midst of the final showdown fight between Wayne (Sean Thornton) and Squire "Red" Will Danaher (McLaglen). They are some of the funniest scenes in the film. *The Quiet Man* was a John Wayne favorite. Mine too, but my all-time favorite movie is still *Abbott and Costello Meet Frankenstein*, which was also Jerry Garcia's favorite picture. Make of that what you will.

Anthony Hopkins and Rod Serling

"I don't want them to."

— **Anthony Hopkins, Actor**
Hollywood, California — 1982

"Just like that, there was gold in my closet."

— **Rod Serling, Writer**
Brentwood, California — 1973

I must be rigorously honest about this. Anthony Hopkins did not invite me to lunch. His publicist and close advisor, Bob Palmer, a good friend of mine, did and as a bonus brought the famed actor with him. We met at Musso & Frank Grill in Hollywood. Musso's had been around since 1919, which in Hollywood-land is practically prehistoric. For decades it had been a regular meeting place for the Hollywood elite, especially writers, who were allowed to run tabs. Hemingway, Fitzgerald, and Faulkner could be found within its clubby walls. Actor Paul Douglas observed that the place was "just like a New York bar." To Douglas this was a great compliment. The newer crowd, not tradition bound, has gone elsewhere to more trendy places. Bob and I and, as it turned out, Tony, are fans of old movies and the history of Hollywood. The food isn't bad either, and if the uniformed waiters can be intimidating, they are also competent.

We ate on the bar side, which was less crowded. I cannot claim to be a friend of Anthony Hopkins. To say he is reserved and is a loner is an under-statement. Still, when he is engaged he is a fascinating conversationalist. It did not take long to realize we had at least two things in common. I was an abominable student, finishing in the bottom third of my high-school class. He was no better. In my school days I immersed myself in books, movies, and the wonderfully imaginative radio of the time. He did too. When he prepares for a role, Hopkins is apt to read the script through up to a hundred times, or more, till he is word perfect. When producing a film I had written, I looked at every scene that had been shot, endlessly, until I had committed it to memory. I would work out where I wanted each cut, only after I knew exactly what it looked and sounded like — all of them, even obvious outtakes. This was bonding. As the Brits would say, "We got on."

The Brits also got me in a spot of trouble.

Tony (he wants people to call him that — a reality check perhaps) had been working both in films and television. His progress as a star had been steady, but a year or two before he had been cast in a romantic comedy, which was not his forte. The movie was not a happy experience, nor a success for that matter. He was now contemplating a return to the stage, to London, for a new play called *Pravda*. 1982 was still a time when there were movie actors and television actors, and seldom would the twain meet. And Tony wanted to throw in plays as well. "What is it about English actors that they can go back and forth between movies and TV and go on the stage for little...?" He stopped me in mid-sentence, reaching across the table and grabbing my wrist — firmly — very firmly. "Welsh!" he demanded, with a smile that would one day belong to Hannibal Lecter. I got it.

My maternal grandmother was Caroline Hedgpeth, originally Hudson's Path, and you can't get more Welsh than that.

The rest of the lunch went nicely, and afterward Tony and I wandered down Hollywood Boulevard and across the street to Larry Edmunds Bookshop, another hallowed spot in Hollywood history. Bob Palmer had an interview with another of his clients, Dick Van Dyke, and did not accompany us. As Tony and I walked, I noticed something very peculiar. No one had spotted him. No one had the slightest idea who he was. Hollywood stars have for eons been conflicted about being recognized out and about. Many have resorted to devices such as dark glasses with frames the size of hockey pucks and donning orange wigs. These stars would be unmasked, as it were, and then moan and groan about it to the press. All the rest of the day, even in Larry Edmunds, where Hollywood history is all over the bookshelves and everywhere else, no one caught on to Tony. I complimented him on his performance. I asked him how he did it. His answer made it sound simple, but I think it was one of his better performances. Anthony Hopkins the Invisible Star.

Rod Serling WAS black-and-white TV for me. I never missed a *Twilight Zone*, and when the director and editor of a documentary of mine said he thought he could get Serling as the narrator, I was "over the moon," as a cousin of mine liked to say. We went to Serling's Hollywood home in Brentwood — English manor in style, flagstone and slate roofs, with a pool. We recorded in his living room.

In 1973, Serling was ending his association with *Night Gallery*, which though no *Twilight Zone*, had done okay in the ratings. Serling was not happy with the show, citing interference from many quarters. He was a small man, no more than five-four in height. It seemed so odd — on TV he filled the frame. He was also very intense.

Serling was a chain smoker and coughed a lot. That voice, though, was money in the bank. It did not bother me that we would have to chop the tape up like spaghetti to get what we needed. These pieces were all there and we would worry about that later. Between the coughing and some outside noise interference, we had to take several breaks. I asked Serling about his career. I was a novice and an old one at that. Like most writers, he was very generous with advice from his own history. "Don't be discouraged by rejection," he said. The first fifty odd scripts of his had been rejected. His first major success came on the *Kraft Television Playhouse*. It was a drama called "Patterns," a story of in-fighting in a major corporation. It was a great success and many of his early rejections were suddenly salable. Though happy to get the money, Serling would regret the decision to take it, as many of these stories he felt were not up to his best work. The film he narrated for me was called *Wings of Eagles, Wings of Gold* and was a history of Naval Aviation. The WWII scenes interested him greatly, as he had been an Army paratrooper and had participated in the campaign in the Philippines. Serling praised my work and was good enough to put his opinion on my copy of the script.

Serling left Hollywood soon after, for writing and teaching. I devoured every bit of information I could find about Rod Serling after that. He had written all, or almost all, of the first year *Twilight Zone* scripts, forty-four of them. He was fifty when he died of heart failure. I feel he was screwed to death by executives with a talent bypass and the creative instincts of a turd. None of them could carry Serling's jock, much less his typewriter.

William Shatner

"My tits and toes are killing me."

**— William Shatner, Actor/Director/Producer, etc.
Manhattan Beach, California — 2005**

William Shatner has been around as long as anybody and is still going. His website (https://williamshatner.com/ws/) reveals all his upcoming personal appearances here and abroad. He came to us from Canada in 1956, trained in Shakespeare at the National Repertory Company and the Stratford Festival, destined for stardom either on stage or in film.

Bill did finally climb the heights, but it was television and Captain Kirk that put him up there, where he has remained ever since, with a year or two off as a cult legend was building. Back on top, Bill also decided to sell us a few things while he was at it. He may not have been the best actor of his time, but he has been, far and away, the best actor/salesman.

In the beginning, and come to think of it now, Bill Shatner was known as an actor who would play any part, or rather take any role, offered to him. This can lead to a busy and productive career, but it can also work against you. My old business partner Herm Saunders used to say that in show business, it never hurts to say "No." Shatner is above such thinking, and it seems that the more he gets into, the more popular he gets. For his many fans, his willingness to try anything, singing for example, is one of his most winning and endearing traits.

Along the way he has learned to laugh at himself, kidding his own persona on a regular basis. On the set of *Boston Legal*, I found him to be affable and charming. I found his costar, James Spader, to be neither though, fine actor who he is, I am sure he could perform both roles.

After *Star Trek*, many producers thought Bill Shatner to be typecast in the manner of George Reeves as Superman, and we know what happened to him. So little had turned up for Bill at that time that he was doing an ABC radio show for, I believe, $500 a week. My high school friend, James Drury, was closing out his starring role as The *Virginian* and asked me to go along to see his friend. Shatner was on the air at the time, and off mike he and Jim talked about their mutual interest in archery and other outdoor activities of which I knew little. So, I just listened and observed. Shatner was shorter than I thought he would be — a normal reaction when meeting the famous. On the other hand, he had the heft and build of a weight lifter. He exuded power. He was both dynamic and positive, even though his career was temporarily in the dumper, and his attitude gave no indication that he had lost his house and was living in a camper. I was in a slump myself, having proved to be unemployable after a blizzard of my resumes and appointments went nowhere. At least Shatner had a radio gig.

I didn't see Bill again for 25 years. By then conditions for both of us had vastly improved. Out of sheer necessity I had taken a low-paying civil service job with the Navy Alcohol Rehabilitation Unit in San Diego. If being humbled is good for you as many claim, I was wallowing in goodness, having to commute 150 miles on weekends and sleeping on the floor in my office for the first month or so. Humility aside, I was tasked to make a docudrama about a Navy pilot entering recovery. As I was doing this, I was also hoping that my fictional character would have better luck than I was having.

Making that movie was, like its title, *Turning Point*, the most positive experience that I had ever gone through, pointing the way to a new career for me. Dick Van Dyke was the narrator of the picture, and working with a star of that magnitude gave me some of the confidence I sorely needed. William Shatner

In a recording session with Dick Van Dyke for the Navy film,
"Turning Point." The story of an alcoholic Naval aviator,
who found recovery and returned to the cockpit.

was doing a bit better, starring and directing feature films in the *Star Trek* series
and in a popular TV series *T. J. Hooker*.

During the making of *Turning Point* I was approached by a young woman
named Janet Knutsen. She was temporary summer hire, working in a dull, clerical job. She had a college degree and had studied in France. If granted permission, could she work with us on the picture? Well, this woman had studied
at the Sorbonne; besides, chauvinist who I was (and am) she was quite attractive. Janet proved to be a talented and indispensable production coordinator, a
thankless job in the smallest of movies and one which required diplomacy and
an unflappable temperament. Ms. Knutsen filled the bill in every regard, and
director Harry Flynn and I were so pleased that we gave her assistant director
billing in the final credits.

A few years later, when we had both moved on, I saw Janet Knutsen occasionally in Hollywood. The *Turning Point* experience had inspired her to give filmdom a try. She was just beginning and having the usual rough going. I had gone a few steps up the ladder by then, had cofounded a small company which had success coming out of the gate, and I vowed to help her again when an opportunity arose. I needn't have bothered. She decided to help herself. She got a great job for contacts as the assistant to the legendary Dolly Parton and had moved on and up the ranks. By 2005, she was the production manager of the highly successful David Kelley show, *Boston Legal*. Harry Flynn, a Hollywood publicist of note as well as a Commander, U.S. Naval Reserve, had gotten in touch with her to express congratulations on her success. The upshot of that call was an invitation to come to Manhattan Beach's new Raleigh Studios to visit the set of *Boston Legal*. Janet gave us, Harry and me, and my wife Gayle, the VIP treatment. She introduced us to everyone who was anybody. We watched the taping of the show from behind the camera, and it was a great time and episode to watch. It was the Halloween party sequence whereby Shatner/Denny Crane and Spader/Alan Shore go to the event dressed as pink flamingoes. (Are there any other kind?) After a long take or three, a visibly pained Shatner passed by me to announce his discomfort in the costume. Exiting from that take, he had bumped into my daughter Elisabeth, who, thanks to Janet, had gotten a part as an extra. Liz was dressed as an alien, and when Shatner passed her, he gave her a long look and another quote, "Haven't I seen you someplace before?"

Taping was no place for great conversation, but it was a damn good time. Before we left, Gayle and I posed for pictures on the balcony set, smoking cigars, à la Crane and Shore. The balcony set was an illusion, set firmly on the ground floor, with a painted backdrop of the Boston skyline at night at the ready when needed.

Ms. Knutsen's thoughtfulness had not ended. A few weeks later, Gayle and I were invited to another *Boston Legal* shoot, this time on location in Hidden Valley, less than a mile from our home in Lake Sherwood. Hidden Valley has long been a movie location, and if you have ever seen a car commercial that features white picket fences, it was probably filmed in Hidden Valley. The Valley is also the home of the expansive, expensive Murdock ranch, David Murdock being the lesser known of the Murdock billionaires. David does not own newspapers, but the last time I looked, he had title to the Hawaiian island of Lanai. Murdock's lush green pastures would be background to scenes that fitted William Shatner nicely. These sequences would feature a romantic interest for Denny Crane, as well as a love interest for Shatner — a horse.

Bill loves horses and has charities that take care of them. He got to ride horses and inspect cattle. The lengths that a good show will go for authenticity were dramatized for me that day. The Murdock ranch is especially proud of its Arabian horses and costly Australian beef. These animals were too good for *Boston Legal*, which brought in good old American steeds and stock. This was a second unit shoot with only an assistant director present, which suited Shatner nicely.

Back at the studio, there had been a few testy discussions between star and director, nothing major, but Bill usually got his way. The young assistant would be well satisfied if Bill was. So it was a lovely time as we all sat around the camera truck between changes of scene. Bill Shatner could not have been more pleasant. He spoke of horses, his charities, and even mentioned his favorite restaurant in nearby Moorpark, which I am going to visit one of these days, if and when I remember the name of the place. Again, Janet had set it all up.

While I am not and will never be a Trekkie, I am forever a devoted William Shatner fan. One other feel-good part to this story: Good things happen to nice people, even in Hollywood. Janet Knutsen has gone upward in the Hollywood firmament, a great Lina Lamont line from *Singin' in the Rain*. She ended a full producer of *Boston Legal* and has moved on to produce *Rizzoli and Isles* and currently the cable smash *Game of Thrones*.

James Drury

*"Come on over to the set today;
I get to kill six guys."*

— **James Drury, Actor** *The Virginian*
Studio City, California — 1970

What I remember about the sixties is violence, Vietnam, riots and violent non-violence, peace now, the Weathermen, and Charlie Manson. I could be said to be a contributor to violence, as I spent a year in the Pentagon as a very junior officer. Generals and senior officers were and are a dime a dozen at the Pentagon, but an Ensign or a Second Lieutenant always got stares. We junior officers did not usually put up signs on our desks that said, "Vietnam Not Much of a War, Just the Only One We've Got." It was much more war than any of us needed. I remember passing my few peers in the catacombs, and we would whisper to each other. "There is no plan," to which the response would be, "You're right; there is no plan." Though I did get to see the smoke and fire of the Washington, D.C., riots after the death of MLK, I completely missed the March on the Pentagon, as I was in Los Angeles on hardship duty at Armed Forces Radio. I heard from a friend who was there that Saturday, and he looked at the gathering and heard someone near him say, "God, look at all those fucking Indians," a recall of the 7th Cavalry at Little Big Horn. Protestors who crossed the line were brought into the building and were beaten, not by the troops, but by civil service security. Fear of the mob will do that to you. I hope it was punished, but I doubt it.

My only contribution to the Vietnam War was to design a certificate/proclamation of LBJ's last visit there. The request came from the Big Man himself to Secretary McNamara, on down to an Assistant Secretary of Defense, Something-Something, then to the office of Information for the Armed Forces... and finally to me. I was given a two-day deadline to come up with something significant. I spent a sleepless weekend on a design, which featured a map of Vietnam, Air Force One, some words from Johnson's speech to the troops, trying to make him sound like Churchill, and not one of the Foggy Bottom Boys. I presented it on Monday and off it went through the chop chain, initialed by almost everybody above me, with suggestions for improvement. It arrived at the White House where it got chopped some more, and on to the President's desk where it was approved, with some more suggestions. All this was in a matter of days. Some graphic artists improved it from my stick figure drawings, but, sure enough, I recognized it.

The project moved forward, without me, fortunately. Five hundred fifty thousand copies of this document were printed on expensive parchment paper. GPO, the Government Printing Office, worked on nothing else for days. These were to be given out to every soldier, sailor, and airman in-country, save those who were in the brig (this last, a Presidential order).

Since all military aircraft were committed, nothing less than a commercial charter would do, and a multi-ship convoy was soon on its way to Dulles. The whole evolution took less than a week, which shows, when the government really wants something done, no matter how useless and idiotic, it can be done — and then undone. The air convoy was wheels down and locked on their approach to Tan Son Nhut in Saigon, when the Tet offensive struck. The planes were re-routed to Bangkok where they remained, gone and forgotten.

As Tet raged on, there they remained until some Thai in authority, most probably a General, realized he might have a goldmine on his hands.

As best I can tell, the proclamations were confiscated (read stolen). Whoever opened the boxes was in for quite a surprise, a blizzard of paper that could not even be used as toilet tissue without injury. Just another loss in what was to become a lost cause despite all the blood and bravery on both sides.

During the early hours of Tet, many of us gathered around the KO-6 voice scrambler, listening to the far-off sounds of battle — mortar rounds, machine gun, and small arms fire at MAAG, Military Assistance Command Vietnam Headquarters. Through the din, I was told a voice was heard calling out, "Where the Hell are our goddamn certificates?" This comment is known as a prime example of a failure to prioritize.

There was always violence in the movies and on television. It was usually pretty bloodless stuff. In black and white, as a matter of fact, the blood was chocolate syrup. In Technicolor, blood and gore were rare. Fifties horror and sci-fi violence was mostly laughable. Even in Hitchcock films, violent, frightening moments took up barely a few minutes in overall running time. In the sixties, it all began to change. Almost anything went. Sex and violence meant motion picture box office. Television was slow, cautious at first, but eventually it too came along. There were numerous Westerns to be had with brawls and shootouts aplenty. The murders of Martin Luther King and Robert Kennedy produced some responsive action in both film and television — violence was in, especially by the gun.

At this moment in time I met Jim Drury. I should have met him years before, because we went to the same high school, Salem High in Salem, the capitol of the state of Oregon. Jim was a few years ahead of me, in life and in living. Jim was born in New York City, where his father was a professor at New York University. His mom was from Oregon, and shortly after his birth, she took him there for the first time to meet the grandparents. He would go back and forth every year for the next two decades.

In the West, Grandpa told stories of the Old West, taught young Jim to ride and shoot, hunt, and fish. In New York, he pursued more creative activities. At age 12, he was in a road company of *Life with Father*. By high school, most of his time was spent in Oregon. Jim identified with the West, and in the lives of the Western pioneers he found values and beliefs that struck a chord with him. All his life he has been a passionate defender of the Second Amendment and a believer in the American Legend and the American Dream. He finished his degree at UCLA in 1954 and almost immediately found work in films, first at MGM and then at Fox. He did some solid work at Disney, in *Toby Tyler* and other films. His best role was a présager of what was to come, a prospector in the lovely Sam Peckinpah Western, *Ride the High Country*, which also provided a final capstone for the long and successful Western careers of Randolph Scott and Joel McCrea.

We'll get back to Peckinpah later, but under his tutelage and that of such mentors as Scott and McCrea, Jim was ready for his big break.

Jim was cast in the groundbreaking 90-minute Universal Western, *The Virginian*. Jim WAS The Virginian, and from 1972 to 1981, the show was a ratings and critical success. I met Jim around this time and our high school connection fostered a casual friendship. I visited the set on a few occasions and saw first-hand the difficulties of a ninety-minute weekly show. Jim and others in the cast were rushed about from set to set, a few lines here, a few lines there. It worked, but it was tough on all concerned. This was a time when the Universal tour had few attractions but consisted of sending the tour buses to witness shooting on the various shows working on the lot.

On *McHale's Navy*, Ernie Borgnine, Tim Conway, Bob Hastings, and others welcomed visitors and often posed for pictures. Other buses would be driven by buildings said to be occupied by the likes of Alfred Hitchcock and told that the Master was planning at that very moment scenes for his latest picture. In fact, Hitchcock was probably at home in Bel Air having lunch, a few drinks, snacking, or snoozing. One bus, visiting the stage where the Western *Laredo* was normally filmed, paused outside the building, the tour guide explaining that the show was today shooting on location. Not all of the cast, however. One of the stars of *Laredo* was Neville Brand, a decorated WWII vet and one of the meanest- looking villains ever. Neville was also an epic drinker in the Aldo Ray/

Broderick Crawford mode. His erratic behavior and occasional disappearances led the producers to stern and restrictive measures. On this day, with shooting going on elsewhere, they had locked Neville in the building and momentarily thrown away the key. No matter, as the tour guide went on about Laredo, Neville kicked out a door and made an appearance. He was nude, save for cowboy boots. He strode calmly but purposefully to the bus and proceeded to pee on a tire. "The star of the show is Mr. Neville Brand... and there's Neville now... oh Jesus!"

Jim Drury once had a problem with a lady tourist who snapped a flash in his face as he was vainly trying to remember a line. It was rumored that he left the set, went straight to the Black Tower to Lew Wasserman's desk and pounded on it with his .44, while the Great Man blanched and cowered. This was perhaps the reason that Jim's career did not go on to greater heights. I don't believe that story, but doing that 90-minute show was a killer, and sometimes tempers grew short.

In mid-1968, after the political assassinations, an antiviolence epidemic eventually reached commercial television. Jim was bothered by this, as he felt it would hurt the realism of the show, and negotiating with bad guys and even occasionally shooting a gun out of their hands was a bow to political correctness and meant a loss of credibility.

The Virginian with its great cast, Jim, Doug McClure, Lee J. Cobb, and guest stars of the quality of Robert Redford, Lee Marvin, George C. Scott, Myrna Loy, Rhonda Fleming, and others, stayed on top, but Jim wasn't happy. He and his friend and costar Doug McClure practiced bow-and-arrow shooting between takes and planned trips to Alaska to hunt big game with these weapons as their skills progressed.

One night I was invited to Jim's home on stilts in the Hollywood Hills, which looked out over lights like a bed of stars draped over the San Fernando Valley. It was my first visit there; and when Jim met me at the door, in civilian clothes and wearing horn-rimmed glasses, he looked much more like a college professor than a Western star. He was neither tall nor short, though he had seemed taller on the Western street at Universal. I learned later that the buildings in Western Town were 7/8 normal size, like Main Street in Disneyland, so that heroes would look more heroic and big men like John Wayne, Jim Arness, and others would look like André the Giant.

Jim Drury played big and, with his stylish hairpiece, was close to six feet. We talked about his narrating a film for me, my first effort as a civilian, though it would be about the history of Naval Aviation, made for the planned Naval Aviation Museum in Pensacola. The film was in final editing and Jim agreed to do it. He had a great voice, a Wellesian, Bill Conrad voice, and I always wondered why he didn't do more voice work. Then Doug McClure showed up, friendly, happy, and very drunk. I had gotten lost on those narrow, winding, badly-lit streets, and I wondered how he had made it, drunk as he was. Doug later sobered up, remained popular, and worked steadily; but like so many of his peers and earlier idols, cigarettes got him before he was sixty.

Jim Drury did narrate that film for me. It was called *Flight from Yesterday*, and he did a great job. He would later narrate another for me called *Quest*. He was better than the movie. Jim had gone to Vietnam for the USO. He was very supportive of the military. He eventually got a commission in the Naval Reserve. I helped some. He later retired as a Commander. All that was far in the future, when in late 1969, he invited me to the Universal lot to watch him dispose of six heavies. A lot had changed, time had gone by for one thing, and there was *The Wild Bunch*. Sam Peckinpah had gone from lovely to carnage in his Western world, and *The Virginian* followed along. Jim shot bad guys off horses, off a balcony, and into an airbag-prepared wagon. It was fun to watch.

I don't want you to think that Jim Drury was a violent man. He was actually thoughtful and sensitive. The only time I saw him get angry was when Pete Duel died. Pete was the star of a show called *Alias Smith and Jones*, on which Jim had guest starred. Duel had a serious drinking problem and had picked up a number of DUIs. He was a very troubled young man, but the show was a hit and the studio wanted to keep him working. Instead of treatment and counseling, he got medication. He was at his place one evening with his girlfriend. They

On location in Pensacola, FL, on the film, *Flight from Yesterday* for the Naval Aviation Museum. James Drury did a great job on the narration. I am "flying" a restored Corsair, showing the 34 victories of Captain David McCampbell, the Navy's leading WWII Ace.

were just talking and making out when he stepped away into the next room and shot himself in the head. Drury was mad as hell about it, as he should have been — as we all should have been. It may have taken something out of him. He left Hollywood after that and moved to Texas. He returned occasionally, if the part was a good one, but mostly he did dinner theater, a chance to show his versatility. They loved him in Texas. He was a Western hero, after all.

It's funny, or maybe it isn't, that actors in Westerns almost always lean to the right politically. Some lean way far; Chill Wills and Walter Brennan voted for George Wallace. That was not Jim. I think the Code of the West, the independent, self-reliant frontiersman, well, he/they believed in that. They had lived it, vicariously I know, but it became a part of them. They were believers. Jim was and is loved and respected in Texas, where he dabbled in oil and gas, like everybody in the Lone Star state. He appeared in Western-themed events until his death April 6, 2020. See his great website (https://www.thevirginian.net).

Jim Drury lived a long life and was a good man. I should know. I watched him stand for good against evil with his six gun, on a dusty Western street in Universal City, California, on a warm autumn day in 1969. His website says the following:

He lived by the "Cowboy Way."
If it's not true, don't say it.
If it's not yours, don't take it.
If it's not right, don't do it.

Humphrey Bogart

"Is that your bike, kid?"

— Humphrey Bogart, Actor
Warner Brothers Studios
Burbank, California – 1947

I got this one from a good friend, Bob Palmer, who had a long and successful career as a publicist in Hollywood.

In 1947, Bob, still in his teens, was trying to break into the movies. He had the advantage over wannabes from the Corn Belt, because he was born within sight of the Hollywood sign. He got extra work in pictures.

There were quite a few films made that year that featured teenagers. One of them was called *That Hagen Girl* and featured future President Ronald Reagan and a newly grown-up Shirley Temple. The film itself was a tedious waste of your time, save for the curious pairing of the President and the child star.

One of the sequences was a teen dance, what would later be called a "hop." Between takes, the young folk hung out, smoking cigarettes and talking. This group included Bob Palmer and Shirley Temple. Shirley complimented Bob and his dancing technique in the scene that had just been shot. She fished in her purse and then said something that must seem very unlike the Shirley Temple we knew and loved. "Damn," she said, "I'm out of cigarettes." Bob was happy to help. He offered to go across the street from the Burbank studio and buy her a pack of Pall Mall's. Shirley offered a dimpled thank you and away Bob went, bolting out of the sound stage. The Rexall Drug store was some two blocks away, and he had to hurry to get back for the next shot. He spotted a bike in the bike rack next to an adjoining stage and was just reaching for it when a nearby door burst open, revealing a quickly indignant Humphrey Bogart. When asked if it was his bike, Bob admitted hurriedly that it wasn't. "Damn right it isn't," Bogart snarled, an authentic Bogart snarl. The movie's favorite bad guy turned good guy then asked, "Where the hell do you think you're going?" There was nothing for it but for Bob to confess the truth. He told the irate actor that he was just going over to the drugstore to buy Shirley Temple a pack of smokes. Bob might have thought that this would satisfy the chain-smoking Bogart. It didn't. Bogart's eyes narrowed, the famed Bogart squint. "Sure you are!" he growled. Palmer put the bike back and ran like hell to the drugstore. He ran back the same way and got there as the set was being lit. For that day, Bob Palmer was a cigarette-bearing Prince Charming.

Shirley's nicotine habit did not last, nor did stardom as an adult. In real life, after a Hollywood marriage to fellow performer John Agar, an admitted alcoholic, Shirley Temple made significant contributions to her community, her party (Republican), and even became a US Ambassador to Ghana. She had a long and happy second marriage to Charles Black. Her fellow smokers among the stars did not fare so well.

Everyone, it seemed, smoked in those days. We may gossip about deaths from alcohol and drugs, but the roster of - drawer talent who died from smok- ing would fill a small book, or at least a pamphlet from the American Cancer Society. Reagan, who never smoked was spared, but Robert Taylor, Clark Gable, Tyrone Power, Betty Grable, Steve McQueen, Vincent Price, and Nat King Cole were not. Smoking contributed to the deaths of John Wayne and Alan Ladd, among many others. Many of them did not make it to their sixties.

Jonathan Winters

"How are we going to get these stiffs off my property?"

— **Jonathan Winters, Comedian/Actor**
The Loved One – 1965

The Santa Barbara Writers Conference was founded in 1964 by Barnaby Conrad and his wife, Mary. Barnaby was a writer, painter, sculptor, and bullfighter. He also owned a great bar in San Francisco, El Matador. The bar was named after Barnaby's successful first novel, which was going to be made into a movie, but never was, time passing it by as time will do.

I realize there has been an enormous amount of name dropping in what you have read so far, and that has been my purpose. If you weren't interested in legends, eccentrics, icons, and characters from the Golden Age, you wouldn't be here. I am you, you see, just a fan fascinated by old movies and those who appeared in them, sports stars who played more for the love of the game than for money, and men and women who went to war because their country needed them. I don't know if tourists come to Hollywood today looking for stars, but if they do, they are shit out of luck. There are no more stars, but what passes for stars today live in places like Antigua, Switzerland or Marin County, and they are not worth bothering with anyway. You could, however, have seen stars at the Santa Barbara Writers Conference, even into this century. The writers alone who appeared there make a truly celestial body — Maya

Angelou, Ray Bradbury, William F. Buckley, Erskine Caldwell, Jackie Collins, Clive Cussler, Joan Didion, Dominick Dunne, Elmore Leonard, Ross Macdonald, James Michener, Budd Schulberg, William Styron, Artie and Irwin Shaw, Charles Schultz, Jonathan Winters, and several hundred others. You might see in the audience Bob Mitchum, Jane Russell, Richard Widmark, and a large part of the Douglas family.

Have to pause here for Kirk Douglas. I was present when Douglas and one of his sons (not Michael) made an entrance in the middle of a presentation. Douglas appeared not to notice that he had become the focus of attention, robbing the speaker of his audience. Douglas oozed both unconcern and arrogance. It was his MO in those days. This was 35 years ago. Since then, Kirk Douglas suffered severe injuries in a helicopter crash and a terrible stroke. These were turning points in his life. He underwent what can only be called a spiritual experience and transformation. Robbed of the power of speech by the latter event, he fought back to regain it. He embraced anew his Jewish faith. Clawing his way up from poverty to the slippery ladder of stardom, he had been angry, difficult, and demanding. Determined to stay on top, he had succeeded. The traits that had propelled him suddenly seemed meaningless and faded away. Almost overnight, he became the kind, gentle, and generous soul who had always been at his very core. He became a successful author, writing about the new direction his life had taken. He and his wife, Anne, became generous donors of time and money to various worthwhile causes — tens of millions of dollars' worth. The most notable may be the dozens of playgrounds they sponsored in schools, mostly in minority areas where such recreation was most needed. In his new and best role, Kirk Douglas has been a benefactor to many and an inspiration to all. Sorry about the op-ed, but I thought it was important.

Back to the Writers Conference. Attending one of the many sessions or strolling the grounds of the beautiful and historic Montecito Inn, you were apt to bump into Ray Bradbury, Charles Schultz, or Jonathan Winters, whose attendance and participation could be counted on year after year. On a lucky day, Jonathan might also give you five minutes of hilarious improv. Jonathan Winters was also one of those "out of the box" talents who could never find a permanent home in motion pictures. He was at his best unscripted. *The Loved One*, a 1965 film based on a book by Evelyn Waugh, was probably his best. *Loved One* was a satire on the funeral industry in general, and Forest Lawn in particular. Winters played two brothers, one who was a comically inspired Reverend Glenworthy, who wanted to turn his mortuary and cemetery complex, Whispering Glades, into a Sun City retirement community. In what I thought was the funniest scene in the picture, Glenworthy strides into a boardroom, divesting himself of his clerical robes, revealing a business suit as he does so. He then gets right to the point, "First order of business. How are we going to get these stiffs off my property?" I love that line. I literally bumped into Jonathan on campus one morning and addressed him as Reverend Glenworthy. He fired that line right back at me. At the lunch break, I rushed out to buy a poster from the movie and caught up with Winters later that day. He signed the poster with the full quote and his real and Episcopal names. A blessing from Whispering Glades.

Hal Ashby

"Paranoid man, really paranoid."

— Hal Ashby, Director/Editor
Hollywood Hills – 1972

Successful songwriters and movie directors of the 20th Century shared a facet of their careers that is rare today. They had longevity. Music styles remained more or less the same until rock and roll arrived and artists wrote and sang their own stuff. Irving Berlin, Cole Porter, Johnny Mercer, and many others had been on top for decades, but they became passé overnight. The great Golden Age movie directors had their names on films, some above the title, from silent to sound, color and beyond. Some were typed like Hitchcock and DeMille, but most worked in all genres, and usually until Forest Lawn came calling. You knew their names — Hawks, Capra, Wellman, Ford, Wyler, Stevens. The New Wave of directors, not household words, but well-known to purists, are dying off, and what is left is mostly anonymous, many of them one- and two-shot wonders, and others whose careers die decades before they do. Spielberg, Lucas, and Ron Howard are exceptions. The latter is a poster child for nepotism, Lucas is *Star Wars*, and Spielberg is also a movie studio. Enough of them; let's get back to me.

In 1972, I had left the Navy for unemployment, not planned that way, but that's how it worked out. Looking for work in Hollywood in the business is like nowhere and nothing else. I have pointed out elsewhere the joys of nepotism for those who possess it. For the rest of us it can be a long and crazy ordeal, bad for men and worse for women. Among those in charge of these charades were and are found predators and idiots and idiot predators. Thankfully, that breed is being hunted down, but dummies will always be with us. Usually, they are young and stupid.

Johnny Winters, in his later years, told of being auditioned by a twenty-something who asked what kind of experience he had and "what had he been in." I wish I had been there to hear Winters' reply, which he wouldn't tell me because women were present. In my case, I was thirty-something with no experience, save college, the Navy, and the pitching rubber. This led to very few jobs. I had a few ideas for film and television projects. I had no agent. An agent will only talk to you if you are in the Writer's Guild, and the Guild will only take you if you have done something that has been exhibited in a theater or shown on television. In other words, getting in the Guild is impossible, and I advise you not to even try, even though I have been a vested member for thirty years and counting. I guess it is possible at that, but it is hard. As a budding writer I booked my own appointments, which were few and far between.

In 1972, one of these appointments took me to the top of Laurel Canyon Boulevard, just a block or so from famed Mulholland Drive. The house was a rambling Spanish one-story, which served as residence and office for an authentic Wunderkind. His name was Chuck Braverman, and he had been employed by the Smothers Brothers, who had an innovative and irreverent variety show on CBS. Evidently, it and they had been too irreverent. President Nixon had been after them for their anti-Vietnam material, federal agencies were hounding CBS and William Paley, and the upshot was that the Smothers Brothers got canned and their show was dropped — a tempest on a TV tray at the time.

I had been to CBS a few months after the banishment. As I left CBS TV City, near the Farmer's Market, I noticed that the Smothers had rented a billboard across the street. It showed a giant, bloodshot eye, and under it were the words, "The Smothers Brothers are Watching You." CBS, though properly threatened managed to stay in business, as did the Smothers Brothers, albeit on a smaller platform. Chuck Braverman was an experimental film maker whose work was shown on the Smothers Brothers show. One of his efforts was called *An American Time Capsule*. It was the history of the United States in three minutes. The process was not new — it was called kinestasis, but Braverman revolutionized it with quick cuts and well-known historical images, timed perfectly to a drum beat.

Chuck was a hot property, though, and I was lucky to get in to see him. I seem to recall that he was trying to get in the Naval Reserve to beat the draft, and I may have offered some help there.

The place had a large number of rooms. I was asked to wait in the living room. On the way, I noticed several interns, probably working for experience, laboring on the old-fashioned, chattering, one-screen Moviolas of the time. Reels of film spilled into large baskets as the interns worked away through the raw footage. When these editors saw a scene they wanted, they would string the film up on one of a series of hooks to be assembled later for Braverman's approval.

The young genius was not in the house. He was out by the pool talking on a phone with the longest extension cord I had ever seen. I sat and waited... and waited. I had the place to myself save for a middle-aged man who looked and dressed like Hollywood's version of a hippie, with requisite beard, shorts, and Roman sandals. We sat in silence, staring at each other across 25 feet of empty space. Braverman was still on that damn phone.

The silence began to get to me. I am impatient by nature, and when I began to believe I would be spending eternity in this room with a strange man, I suddenly heard myself saying, "Well, how's showbiz?" It was surely one of the most inane conversation starters of my life. The man looked to his right, then his left, at nothing, finally returning my gaze and whispering just loud enough for me to hear, "Paranoid, man, really paranoid." I thought for a moment that he was joking, but he could not have been more serious. That was the extent of our conversation. The rest was silence.

I didn't get the job, and neither did the stranger. In his case, it hardly mattered. His name was Hal Ashby and he had just directed his first two features.

The first was called *The Landlord*, and it starred Beau Bridges, Lee Grant, Pearl Bailey, and Lou Gossett, among others. Few people saw it, but those who did loved the film. Critics seemed to like it as well. The other picture was *Harold and Maude* with Bud Cort and Ruth Gordon. It had not been released yet, and when it was, it would become a surprise hit and has remained a cult favorite over decades. This propelled Hal Ashby, a former award-winning editor, to the top rank of film directors. In fact, he was probably the most famous and highly regarded director of the 1970s. He helmed such winners as *The Last Detail*, *Shampoo*, *Coming Home*, *Bound for Glory,* and *Being There*. I regarded his rise with envy, mixed with jealousy, followed by more envy. I was doing fairly well in a comfortable little niche I had discovered, but a few of the seven deadly sins still held me.

Without intending to, I had advanced both the careers of Ashby and actor Jack Nicholson. While on temporary duty at the Navy's Los Angeles Public Affairs Office, I had been approached by Gerald Ayers, the producer of *The Last Detail*. He had given me a copy of the book, written by someone who had been in the Navy and knew a lot about sailors and what they were all about. The writer's name was Darryl Ponicson, and he soon would write another Navy story. This one was called *Cinderella Liberty*, and the success of *Last Detail* would get it made. It too was a hit, and, in fact, Ponicson is still selling stories about the Navy. More power to him. I love to see films about the Navy being made.

Back to *The Last Detail*, the book. I loved it — the real feel of it, the colorful characters. It was a winner. I also knew that the Navy brass would hate it and would not in any way support the book being made into a film. Therefore, I told Ayers how he could make the film, as most Navy bases were open to visitors in those days, and many such bases, such as the 32nd Street base in San Diego, could be filmed literally from across the street. No ships or planes or other types of hardware were needed. It was a people story, and all that was required was building exteriors and interiors that looked Navy and could be copied and filmed in a studio. The film was made without Navy cooperation and became a huge hit, more so in the "white hat" enlisted Navy than anywhere else. The Navy brass even banned the film on its ships and military bases, until the outcry from Naval personnel became so loud and concerted that the powers that be finally caved in, and it became the most popular film ever exhibited therein. Jack Nicholson gave what many, including me, thought to be his finest performance as rough and tumble Petty Officer Second Class "Badass" Buddusky.

While Hal Ashby was busy soaring upward, I, or rather my company, gave him another small boost. My business partner at FMS, Rick Miner, a gifted editor/director of documentaries on his own, but with our facilities, began to create a film about Jeff Minnebraker, who had become a paraplegic after a motorcycle accident. The movie was a story of Minnebraker's comeback and was called *Get It Together*. The title was mine, stolen from The Beatles. The film got some worldwide acclaim, and Rick somehow was able to get it screened for Hal Ashby who was making *Coming Home*, which dealt in part with paraplegia.

The *Coming Home* script was altered to reflect some of the scenes in Rick Miner's picture. Neither my company nor I benefitted in any way from our modest contribution to *Coming Home's* success. Rick did better. Rick was given a sniff, or a snort, of Hollywood high life. He was invited to Hal Ashby's place in Malibu, where they smoked a lot of dope and discussed the possibilities of their collaboration. It turned out that there wasn't any, which turned out to be a break for Rick in the long run, for after 1979's *Being There*, one of Ashby's best, his career went only one way — down. Rick, in the meantime, got divorced, sold his home in Bel Air, moved to Seattle, where in the 70s, housing was still relatively cheap. Rick bought three properties on Lake Union with his half of the house. These properties would eventually make him a millionaire. Rick Miner is today the most successful seller of prime waterfront properties in the area, and Seattle does not lack for water or property. Another of my favorite Hollywood success stories.

Hal Ashby never produced a work of any quality after 1979. The drug stories turned out to be more than rumors. His behavior became more erratic, as did the quality and number of his films. He was hired and fired, hired and replaced. Nothing he touched garnered much interest. He shot over 800,000 feet of film on one project, and his editorial control of the material took endless time and produced poor results. Hal Ashby even tried shaving his beard and wearing a suit. Nothing worked, nothing good ever happened again, and he didn't live to see sixty.

And me? Well, I learned to be content in my little niche. I also learned that envy and jealousy are luxuries that I could simply not afford. Not bad lessons, and they didn't cost me a dime.

Maureen

*The rosary in his hand, the Bible in his lap —
it just wasn't him."*

**— Maureen, USO Person
Pacific Palisades, California – 1970**

O nly diehard fans of old movies remember Ed Begley. There is still an Ed Begley, an actor/environmentalist/activist, Ed Begley, Jr. Junior is a character actor like his father. He in no way resembles his old man physically, though perhaps there are emotional genetic ties. I did meet the son in an airport when we were both waiting for planes.

Ed Begley's father I met only after he was dead.

It was in 1970 when I was serving in the Navy, in Hollywood of all places, as a motion picture and television officer. We did a lot of work with Bob Hope and the United Services Organization, which in Hollywood was almost the same thing. I was not surprised one morning to get a call from Irish Maureen, our liaison with the USO, with a request for Navy cooperation. The request itself was unusual though. She asked if I would come to a memorial service for Ed Begley, who had just passed, and would I please come in uniform. We normally wore civvies in the office. The Vietnam War was still raging, and antiwar protesters from nearby UCLA were a disruptive problem. I had just made Lieutenant Commander and was more than happy to wear my dress blues.

I brushed up on what I could find out about Ed Begley, though of course I knew who he was. He had left home while not yet a teenager to find his way in the world. He held a series of odd jobs, and one of them was a hitch in the US Navy. Begley had recently gone to Vietnam, unannounced and unheralded, to speak directly to the troops. He went out in the boonies to see them and offer some support from the people back home. I was impressed. He had worked as an actor since his teens, first on the stage in vaudeville and in the New York Theater. He was a prominent voice on radio, his most famous role that of Charlie Chan.

In the late 1940s Ed Begley made a move to films where he had been visible, if not prominent. He was the prototypical believable character actor, usually playing hard-edged authority figures — cops, military officers, heads of corporations, and the like. He had won a Tony on Broadway and an Academy Award for Best Supporting Actor in *Sweet Bird of Youth*. He was a rarity — the feature player who became a star. The upward arc of his career came, not from his looks, but from his talent, which was considerable.

I told Maureen that I would be more than happy to show the flag, but I had just come to LA. I, did, however, know a bar in that area. We agreed to meet there an hour before the service, which was to be in a Catholic church a few blocks away. I had learned promptness in the Navy. When a ship's departure time is 0700, one had best be on board. I had arrived at the bar fifteen minutes early and had knocked down a martini and a half. When Maureen arrived, the fine Irish lass she was, ordered a double and almost immediately caught up with me. We had another, then another, but made it to the church on time.

I was, along with Maureen, to escort the widow to the front of the church just beside the casket, as it turned out. Seeing my uniform, the grieving spouse expressed her gratitude to me and the Navy for coming. The Navy had always been close to Ed's heart, she said. She seemed sad and reflective, suitable emotions for the occasion. She turned out to be wife number 3, quite attractive and about half of her late husband's age of 69. No matter, I gave her my arm, Maureen the other, and though I had been consuming breath mints, was careful to exhale in a forward direction. We seated ourselves and bowed our heads, endlessly it seemed, till the service began. I could hear the church filling up behind us, and I fought an urge to doze.

Most church services make me drowsy, even when totally sober, but this one was an exception. The service was quite beautiful, even to Congregationalist's ears. I may not have understood it, but I was moved. At its conclusion, the casket, which had been closed, was opened for viewing. The three of us were the first viewers.

Ed looked quite peaceful lying there in his blue suit. "Of course he looks peaceful, you dumb shit," I thought to myself. "He's dead and you can't get more peaceful than that."

We were there a long moment when out of nowhere I heard the scream of a banshee. Maureen was howling like the Irish legend come to life. I had never heard such wailing. I grabbed her arm, the arm of the widow, and pulled them both gently but firmly toward the exit. I glanced up to view a sea of faces, all of them recognizable to me, though I didn't know any of them. The whole lot of mourners was directly from central casting. Every character actor in town was in this holy place, and the whole group of them was staring at me — Carroll O'Connor, Iris Adrian, Elisha Cook, Jr. and Beulah Bondi, William Demarest, Grady Sutton, and Marjorie Main — all could have been there, a 200+ cast list. My heart pounded. Was it the DTs or was I starring in my own whacked-out, surreal movie?

The movies saved me again. I thought of a Mantan Moreland line in an old Charlie Chan film. It was racist but appropriate, "Feet don't fail me now!" An eternity or two later we made it outside to beautiful smog-filled air. Maureen had composed herself by now. The family arrived to escort Mrs. Begley, who thanked me for coming. When she was out of earshot, I hissed at Maureen, "What the hell was that all about?" Her answer can be found above the opening paragraph. I have no idea what she meant. I did not ask her.

We went back to the bar and drank for another hour in total silence. I still have nightmares about the experience, and on these times, my feet won't move and I awake in a cold sweat.

Danny Trejo

*"For this money,
he could hit me with a baseball bat."*

**— Danny Trejo, Actor/Inmate
Los Angeles, California — 1985**

Danny Trejo, California born of Mexican heritage, is a throwback to the actors of the 1930s and 40s. He has appeared in over three hundred films, TV shows, video games, music videos — you name it, he has appeared in it. Amazing for a man who got his start at age 40, give or take a little. He was occupied for much of his early adult life as a thief, armed robber, and gang member. In those relatively peaceful days, gangs or lone-wolf gangsters did not have a habit of spraying automatic weapons fire

Danny Trejo, the convict who became a movie star.
His face was his fortune.

indiscriminately around neighborhoods and wounding and killing innocent noncombatants.

Danny was a smalltime version of Willie Sutton, the infamous bank robber of the 1920s and 30s. He showed the weapon and got the money or the drugs. That was it. Of course, he spent most of those early years in and out of jails and prisons. He was a certified badass, certainly looking the part. It was said that Danny made Charles Bronson look like Paul Newman. After a riot that followed Cinco de Mayo, Danny found himself in the "hole" at Soledad Prison, one of the toughest venues of its kind in the country. This was around the end of the sixties.

The thought that life could be better than this blossomed when he entered a 12-step program while in prison. He has been clean and sober since that time. One of his mentors in the program was a friend of mine, Sam Hardy. Six-five and 270 pounds, Sam had been a football player at Auburn, a Marine in Korea, a convict, and a killer since his teens.

Sam Hardy had turned his life around and was working with troubled youth and others with addiction problems and issues. He was one of the few men tough enough to handle Danny Trejo.

Sam's conversion to the right side of the law was so complete that, in his last years, he was granted a pardon for murder. This, friends, is a rarity, as was Sam himself. Even at 12-step meetings, Danny would get into fights. He talked about it with Sam, who told him frankly, "Danny, you are a bad man. What's worse, you look like a bad man. You have to take the extra mile and make nice with others." Danny claimed in a movie we made, *They Call Me Mr. Trejo*, that Sam suggested he brush his teeth in the morning in his cell, look in the mirror, and sing "Zip-a-Dee-Doo-Dah" from the Disney film *Song of the South*. One can imagine how this may have played in the prison yard.

After release, while attending meetings and working with others, Danny Trejo worked odd jobs in construction and as a gardener. More would be in store. As the years passed and his sobriety lengthened, Danny was a popular speaker at 12-step meetings around the LA area. At one such meeting in upscale Brentwood, before an audience of mostly "professionals — doctors and lawyers — just the kind of people I used to rob," he was approached by a young man who asked Danny to be his sponsor, saying that he was a victim of the "pitiful and incomprehensible demoralization" that is part and parcel of addiction. The young man was also wearing a Rolex watch, Trejo noted objectively, thinking, "If I get this kid outside, I can boost this watch." Recovering addicts and alcoholics may have the same thoughts they used to have. They just don't act on them.

Danny agreed to be the young man's sponsor. Six months later, Danny was watching Johnny Carson, when his young friend called. It was near midnight and there was trouble at his work. Drugs were present and being passed around. He was on shaky ground. Grumbling all the way, yet willing to answer the call, Danny dressed quickly and headed for downtown Los Angeles. The next several hours would change Danny Trejo's life forever.

The workplace turned out to be a location for the filming of a movie, *Runaway Train*, which featured, among others, Jon Voight and Eric Roberts. After meeting with his sponsee and cleansing the area around the young man of potential dangers, Danny assured his charge that he would stick around to "keep an eye on things." The "cleansing" was verbal only, but was reinforced by his appearance and the fact that Danny had been a boxing champion of every prison he was in. Having never been on a movie set, Danny observed the proceedings with a jaundiced eye.

Runaway Train was about a prison escape and the LA locations featured prison scenes and interiors of the train. There were countless "prisoners" milling about "the yard, trying to look tough." As Danny put it, "They wouldn't have lasted five minutes in the real deal." Danny, whose chest featured a large tattoo of a woman wearing a sombrero, was the real deal, and he was noticed immediately by an alert assistant director. Asked if he wanted to be an extra, Danny displayed his knowledge of movie lingo by asking, "An extra what?" It was an opportunity to pick up some extra bucks and still keep an eye on his 12-step charge. Danny signed up. He soon caught the eye of the director, Andre Konchalovsky, and co-writer, Eddie Bunker, a former prison mate of Danny's in San Quentin.

A character was developed just for Danny, that of a prisoner/boxing trainer who would prepare Eric Roberts for a bout.

In practicing for a fight scene, Roberts accidentally tagged Danny on the chin. "He hit you... he hit you!" cried out the excitable director, who immediately called, "Cut!" Danny shrugged the incident off with the quote that preceded this story, "For this money, he could hit me with a baseball bat." He was in the money now, over $300 a day. The film and Danny's appearance in it may not have been earthshaking, but they certainly caught the eye of casting directors throughout the industry.

Over the next several years, Danny Trejo menaced, manhandled, and died in many a violent epic, mostly as what John Wayne used to call a "dog heavy," one of the disposable underlings of the "brain heavy" who seldom sullied his hands or fought. Most of Danny's movies had a hawser-sized streak of violence running through them, especially in films directed by his cousin, Robert Rodriguez, a popular, economical filmmaker, who also was shrewd enough to cast Danny in a sympathetic role in his *Spy Kids* series.

By this time, Danny Trejo had also appeared in three documentary films of ours, the aforementioned *Mr. Trejo*, *Rage and Recidivism* and *A Better Way*, which to this day are staples in many correctional facilities' substance abuse programs.

During these shoots, I had immediately noticed that, contrary to his image, Danny was quick to laugh, even at himself, and had a great sense of humor. I had hoped to see the actor cast against type, and I was pleased when it happened. I also noted with pleasure that, at this stage of his career, Danny retained an attitude of gratitude and had not lost touch with his roots or the neighborhood in which he was raised.

A sense of humility and awe at the good breaks that have come your way are rare in any business, *and* a definite rara avis in the entertainment field.

The high point of awe may have happened in 1995 when Danny Trejo was cast in *Heat* with major players Robert De Niro, Al Pacino, and Val Kilmer. He had to remind himself verbally of where he was and how much recovery had contributed to his new role in life. His fellow players had more than a little curiosity, and perhaps even a little awe themselves, in this living proof of the rehabilitation of a "Bad Guy." Danny claimed that he had been asked to join them in "packing heat" as they entered a bank, a kind of joke that could really go wrong. "I did that before and I ain't doing it again," Danny said, kidding them out of the idea.

Back in the real world, Danny Trejo found himself with a large and ever-growing fan base. He never ignores them, is always willing to shake hands, answer questions, or pose for a picture. He also tries to keep up with a small mountain of fan mail, a chore in itself. He has also kept his commitment to the recovery program that saved his life.

I know personally that he has passed the message on to countless others. I attended an event in 2009 honoring his forty years of sobriety. My wife Gayle and I were part of a small Anglo minority who was invited, but everyone in the place was welcomed with open arms and hugs. I sat at a table with two Hispanic men of early middle age who appeared to be the business executives they had become after starting life following a path of gangs and drugs, until Danny Trejo showed them a better way. One of the men owned three restaurants in the Palm Springs area, while the other headed up an entertainment union. Many speakers that night lauded Danny Trejo's contributions to their sobriety. I thought then, with everything working for him, that this had to be the pinnacle. I was wrong. The totally unbelievable and unexpected now occurred.

Danny Trejo became a movie star.

The film was *Machete*, a character first introduced in *Spy Kids*, now spun out on Danny's own. This modestly-budgeted ($10 million or so) film grossed over a $100 million, a result that came, in part, from a two-months long publicity tour of Europe that demonstrated Danny's appeal far beyond the United States.

Today Danny Trejo is into restaurants and other commercial ventures, while still making action films at age 70 plus. The latter is made possible only because of a rigorous exercise program that maintains his physique as that of a man 25 or 30 years younger. His face is ageless and still menacing.

For all the fame Danny Trejo has achieved, I believe that it is all the good that he has done means more to him personally. He has kept the faith and passed it on. This is his real legacy. Don't ever screw with him though — you will find he still has an edge. Danny has spurned Beverly Hills, Bel Air, and Malibu and still lives in the San Fernando Valley, where he was born and raised in much improved circumstances.

I must admit, it could not happen to a nicer guy, but a man with an edge.

The Incredible Dr. Pursch

"The recovering addict or alcoholic must be on guard against a well-meaning but ill-informed doctor from harming him/her with his prescription pad."

— Joseph A. Pursch, M.D.
On numerous Occasions, at Numerous Locations

"Alcoholism is not a valium deficiency."

— Joseph A. Pursch, M.D.
On numerous Occasions, at Numerous Locations – 1970s

"It's the 3-2-1 Syndrome."

— Joseph A. Pursch, M.D.
On numerous Occasions, at Numerous Locations

"One Option is that I will go and tell the ladies that they must move."

**— Joseph A. Pursch, M.D.
Long Beach, California – 1978**

Among these stories of the famous and fascinating to me is a name that may not be familiar to you. If you have enjoyed what you have read so far, you may want to discover the incredible Doctor Pursch. Doctor Joseph A. Pursch was born in Chicago in 1930, assuring him of American citizenship, which his parents lacked, because they had emigrated illegally from Canada in 1926. Originally, the Pursch family had fled from the newly cobbled-together country of Yugoslavia. The Treaty of Versailles had created this mixed nation, which managed to bring four ethnic groups together that had hated one another for centuries. They were united in only one way — not one of them could never forget a slight. Joe's father was of German origin. The family came from Germany to the Balkans in 1700, and his mother's people from Croatia around 1800. This made them virtual newcomers and not particularly welcomed. Although welcomed in Canada, Joe's parents had always wanted to come to America, which they regarded as a land of unlimited opportunity. Both of them sought and found employment almost immediately.

They worked hard and, when little Joe came along, it seemed their life was complete. Their past caught up with them, however, and they were detained and finally deported to Yugoslavia in 1932. They took with themselves their savings of $3,000, which made them both wealthy and welcomed émigrés. The Pursches purchased a slaughter house, two butcher shops, 40 acres of land, and a large, comfortable home. Money went a little further in those days.

Times were good but the Pursches and millions of others would be affected by the death and destruction of World War II. The Germans invaded Yugoslavia in 1941.

There were two groups of Yugoslav partisans. They fought the Germans and one another. When the war turned against the Axis powers and the Russians invaded the benighted nation in 1944, young Joe Pursch was put into a refugee camp for children by the retreating German army. Joe was told that the Russians had killed his parents and nationalized their land and property. Marshal Tito's communist government had by then controlled large parts of the country that they would soon rule totally, with Russian aid and support. This was a sign of the Cold War to come.

With nowhere to go and nothing to lose, young Joe Pursch escaped, crossed the border into Austria, and hid in the bombed-out ruins of a railway station near Vienna. He did what he needed to survive, scrounging what food and secondhand coffee grounds he could find from US Army garbage dumps to sell on the black market. Placed in a Displaced Persons camp in Germany, Joe Pursch, at age 15, found himself homeless with no family and few friends. There was one thing still going for him, however. He was a citizen of the United States of America.

In 1947, with the aid of the American Consulate in Stuttgart, Germany, Joe Pursch was able to obtain sponsorship to the states from a Detroit business-man, the owner of a high-rise window washing company. Joe arrived in Detroit with $2.73 in his pocket. The very next day, Joe was cleaning windows on the ground floor soon to work his way up, hoping that the flimsy scaffolding would keep him safe.

Ambitious from an early age, Joe soon owned his own window-washing business. He learned English by watching Western movies and Humphrey Bogart gangster films. Sunday was movie day at the Riviera Theater on Grand River Avenue. From the time the theater opened till the time it closed, Joe Pursch was there, adding to his improving English language capabilities. Often, the next day he would question his window-washing friends on such arcane expressions as, "They went that-a-way!" "We'll head em off at the pass." and "Step on it!"

Joe Pursch met Irene, a pastor's daughter who would be his wife, and responsibility was added to his burning ambition. At this point he lacked the prerequisite high-school diploma so he could further his education. In fact, he had barely attended high school, the fog of war again standing in his way. Joe offered a believable explanation that his diploma had been buried under a pile of rubble in the devastation of his homeland.

Once back in school, the years flew by and events began moving in Joe Pursch's favor. He graduated from college, learned to fly, became a licensed multi-engine pilot, and entered and graduated from the Indiana University School of Medicine. With his European background, a military career was a positive and offered the most promise. After a 7-year stint in the Michigan National Guard, when it came time to select an officer program, Joe chose the United States Navy to avoid the draft. His first duty was in Pensacola, Florida, the home of Naval Aviation, where he was qualified as a flight surgeon. After this, he was assigned to super carrier USS *Forrestal*, where he participated in a study that involved naval personnel who were being separated from the Navy. This was Dr. Pursch's first real look at the role of alcohol and alcohol abuse in these cases. His was the final word as to who would be retained and who would be discharged. This experience changed the course of his life.

In 1963 after the *Forrestal*, Joe Pursch entered a Psychiatric Residency at the Naval Hospital in Bethesda, Maryland, the home of Navy medicine, continuing his interest in alcoholism in the Navy. There may have been Admiral's stars in his future, but around this time he was quietly informed by senior officers that if he chose a career to work with alcoholics, it would harm his chances. In the face of this warning, Joe nevertheless persisted in his work.

In 1972, our paths crossed. I heard Dr. Pursch speak in a conference in Washington, D.C., and was impressed. He approached this serious problem with both insight and humor. In his talk, he spoke of the pervasive nature of alcohol in the Navy, and specifically in Naval Aviation. "We drink at happy hour. We drink to celebrate a good flight or to forget a bad one. We drink to celebrate a promotion or in sadness or self-pity if passed over. We drink if it's a sunny day or if it is raining. We drink if our team won or lost the pennant."

I had been working in alcoholism recovery for about a year. All the films I had seen were the *Lost Weekend* variety, focusing on the problem itself, and here was someone willing to look at it in a different way, one that would offer hope and recovery.

I congratulated Dr. Pursch on his talk and expressed the hope that we might work together someday. It happened sooner than either one of us would have imagined. By then, Dr. Pursch was Medical Director of the Alcohol Rehabilitation Center at Long Beach Naval Hospital. I met him there and we discussed making films of his presentations on the positive solutions for alcoholism and not just the problems of the disease. My company, FMS Productions, had established itself in the alcoholism treatment field, and Joe and I agreed to work together. It is a relationship that has continued to this day.

All of Doctor Pursch's films would have "Recovery" in the title. T*he Life, Death and Recovery of an Alcoholic*; *Alcohol, Pills and Recovery*; and *Romance to Recovery* soon became audiovisual staples in treatment centers all around the country and beyond, helping to establish Dr. Pursch's growing reputation worldwide.

In this process I was able to hear more of Joe's amazing story. In 1944, he got word that his parents had been executed by communists. Actually, his parents were not dead but were incarcerated in Yugoslavia as political prisoners. Thus began a four-year struggle to obtain their release. His mother and father had been separated, by the war — his father as a laborer in a copper mine, and his mother in a camp on the other side of the country. Through the Camp Commandant's secretary, Joe obtained the address of a Jewish lady who had been a family friend of Joe's parents through WWII and was now, in 1945, free. Dr. Pursch began to send shipments of clothing materials, including two bolts of Thai silk, to the Jewish friend. She, in turn, passed them to the Commandant's secretary who passed them on to the Commandant, who passed them to his wife, who ultimately became the most fashionable woman at the communist party's official gatherings.

Joe's mother's release was soon followed by his father's, and Joe brought them both to America in 1951, where they became US citizens and lived the rest of their lives in comfort, peace, and security.

Since my relationship with the good doctor has been a long one, there were many quotes to choose from. From the beginning, Joe Pursch wished to explain and clarify what alcoholics and alcoholism are all about, but to put them in the vernacular that lay people could understand. This meant addressing the general public and not just the health-care field of doctors and nurses and others who are involved in treating patients. Too often physicians, frustrated by patients who will refuse to discuss their problems with alcohol honestly or even deny there is a problem, will treat the symptoms of the disease, rather than the disease itself.

It is not the physicians' fault necessarily, as in three years of clinical medicine they receive only two hours of study in the most preventable and treatable diseases in the United States, namely alcoholism and drug abuse. Doctor Pursch was forty years ahead of the opioid crisis in describing the dangers of overprescribing pills that, when abused, may double the problem of addiction. As an aside, if Dr. Pursch was prescient in regards to dual addiction, he could also have given American foreign policy a "heads up."

In 1981 between takes on a film, I asked Dr. Pursch what would happen in Yugoslavia when Tito, the strongman leader of his country since the end of WWII, died. Joe drew his finger across his throat, "Yugoslav haircut!" he said.

Dr. Joe Pursch was fifteen years ahead of our State Department on that one.

The event that made Joe Pursch famous is when he led the intervention team that brought former First Lady Betty Ford into treatment for her addiction to pills and later to alcohol. Betty Ford describes beautifully in her book, *The Times of My Life*, her admission to Long Beach Naval Hospital and other aspects of her recovery. "Captain Pursch met me and took me down the hall to what I expected would be a private room... Now we came to a room with four

Betty Ford, a strong and courageous woman, and a pleasure to work with. We did some good work, had fun, and it shows.

beds... and it was obvious other people lived here. I balked. I was not going to sign in... Captain Pursch was used to this kind of thing... 'If you insist on a private room, I will have these ladies move out,' he said." Betty Ford assured Dr. Pursch that this would not be necessary, which he regarded as a positive sign and a good prognosis.

Betty Ford could be a poster person for the opioid crisis of today. The overuse of prescription drugs has led many to dependency. The former First Lady fit right in at Long Beach. She drank coffee with the sailors around the coffee bar. The sailors loved her — they called her Aunt Betty.

After two weeks, in a meeting which President Ford also attended, the delicate subject of alcoholism was breached by Dr. Pursch. Again quoting *The Times of My Life*, Betty Ford said, "Up to that point I had been talking about medications while everyone nodded respectfully... Now these doctors wanted me to admit I was an alcoholic... I refused. 'I don't want to embarrass my husband.' I started to cry and Jerry took my hand. 'There will be no embarrassment to me. You go ahead and say what should be said.'"

President Ford's response was a gift of love and reassurance for his wife and humanity itself, especially among the many women and men who sought treatment in the next few weeks and months for the same disease Betty Ford had and so bravely discussed in many public forums thereafter.

I asked Dr. Pursch if, as he became widely known, it was putting too much pressure on the former First Lady. "For her, it will be a challenge to be met. It will save many thousands of lives and contribute to her staying sober." Betty Ford died in 2011, a much- beloved, sober lady.

In the midst of my good fortune and my company's during this period, Joe Pursch gave me a precious gift. I had known fear and anxiety in my alcoholism, but by starting a business and contributing to society, I had become what many, including me, could call a successful human being. In the midst of this positive thrust of fortune and a bit of fame, I suffered the worst spell of anxiety in my life. For days and weeks I could not sleep, I could not eat, and I certainly could not relax. There was not a moment's peace. I went to work and tried to soldier on. I went to doctor after doctor. They could find nothing.

In desperation, I called Joe Pursch. I knew that he could have me locked up in a rubber room where I could be safe and do no harm to myself or others. I unburdened myself to Joe over the phone. "Doc, I have this feeling of impending doom. I just know something is going to happen to me."

After a long pause he, in an accent that I thought of as Viennese in honor of Freud, spoke the magic words, "Yah, yah, it is going to happen many times and it's going to be VUNDERFUL!" The thought had never occurred to me. What do you know? He was right. The symptoms disappeared overnight, and I haven't had a panic attack since. Since then I have expected the VUNDERFUL and have seldom been disappointed.

You may have seen or heard in the media of the famous individuals Dr. Pursch had treated with success. They include Senator Herman Talmadge from a famous Georgia political family, astronaut Buzz Aldrin, and the first brother of President Jimmy Carter, among scores of political, entertainment, literary, and sports figures he has shown the path to recovery. He is proudest of his work with hundreds of naval aviators. For me, on behalf of the thousands of Navy men and women, Admirals and sailors, I would like to say "Thanks Joe, you magic healer you."

I don't want to forget the lawyers, pilots, police officers, and countless ordinary men and women of all occupations whose lives you have touched. One such lovely lady came up to Joe and me at an alcoholism conference in Las Vegas, "Oh, Doctor Pursch, you are so wonderful. You have saved my life with those fabulous films of yours." Joe asked politely if she wanted to meet the producer of these films, the one who discovered Joe Pursch. "Oh, I don't care about him. Doctor Pursch, I just want to talk to you."

Well, humility is a good thing. I asked Dr. Pursch once why, of all the possibilities in the medical field, did he come to focus on alcoholism. "Easy," he said. "Look at an oncologist. The percentage of people he may treat successfully is quite small, and with the tools at hand, even the survivors may be diminished. With alcoholism and the recovery from it, anything is possible."

Prisoner

"You're somebody, ain't cha?"

**— Prisoner, Lincoln Heights Jail
Los Angeles, California – 1950s**

J ack Warden was a New Jersey-born character actor who had two Academy nominations for Best Supporting Actor and an Emmy to his credit. He had played many types of characters, and it may have been easy for him because he was quite a character himself. He had been a boxer, bouncer, and deckhand before he joined the Navy for a three-year hitch in 1938. He got out just before Pearl Harbor, and when we declared war, he volunteered for the Merchant Marines. That was too dull, and he ended up a paratrooper in the 101st Airborne Division. In a run up to D-Day, he was injured in a night parachute exercise and spent eight months in a hospital. While there, he read a play, probably *Waiting for Lefty* by Clifford Odets, and decided to become an actor.

Warden appeared with success on the stage and in early television shows. In the early fifties he found himself in Hollywood. Soon after that, he found himself in the Lincoln Heights jail in LA for drunk driving. Lincoln heights was a notorious lockup that had hosted celebrities before, as well as a cast of many thousands of ordinary folks and others. In a cell with a scruffy band of miscreants, Warden was both embarrassed and remorseful. His characterization was one of anonymity; he tried to blend into a wall. Jack Warden spent a downcast hour, and when he happened to look up he found a disheveled looking soul, badly dressed even for the circumstances, approaching him. The man was eyeing him closely. "Jesus, don't recognize me," Jack Warden thought. The man moved toward him unsteadily but purposefully. He looked like a creature from a Eugene O'Neill barroom. He was unshaven and had one tooth, on the right side, and from five feet away his breath was pure Night Train. Warden knew the man had one tooth because he started smiling at Jack halfway across the cell. He got right in Jack's face and said, "You're somebody, ain't cha?" Warden shook his head, his back to the cell bars. "No, no, no, no," he muttered. "Ah, ya can't fool me. I know you're somebody." Warden was cornered in more ways than one. "I have been in a few movies," he finally offered. The fellow prisoner nodded vigorously. Oddly, Warden's only thought was that he hoped the man's good tooth would not fall out. It didn't. "You know Maria Montez?"

"Huh?" Warden managed.

"Maria Montez the actress — you know her?"

Jack quickly reviewed his Hollywood history. Maria Montez was an exotic actress at Universal, who specialized in what were called "tits and sand" movies in the trade. They were in Technicolor, with titles like *Arabian Nights* and *Cobra Woman*. They were quite successful. Miss Montez died in her bathtub in Paris at age 39. These fleeting thoughts did not help Jack Warden with his dialog — he was temporarily wordless. "I think I may have met her once or twice," he said, after a pregnant pause. His new friend's one-tooth smile broadened. "Well... I fucked her maid," he announced to the whole cell.

Jack vowed then and there not to take another drink as long as he lived. He kept that promise for nearly three weeks, and he never went back to Lincoln Heights.

I must thank my trusted friend and partner Herm Saunders for the Jack Warden story.

(Herm's Hollywood career, beginning as a big band pianist, and ending as a respected producer, could be a book in itself. He always said that if he wrote a book, its title would be *Actors Aren't People*.)

President John F. Kennedy

"Admiral I don't suppose the Russians would give us that second pass?"

— John F. Kennedy, President of the United States USS *Enterprise* (CVN-65), Atlantic Ocean – April 1962

I got this one, not second, but third-hand from a friend of a friend. It sure sounds like Jack Kennedy though — the love of the Navy, the Irish wit. The event was a Presidential visit to the Fleet, followed by a firepower demo. Naval air is the greatest show on the water and all hands were looking forward to it. There were speed-of-sound flybys, bombing and strafing runs, the works. The catapult launches were high drama in themselves. There was also to be a guided missile shoot with one of the newly reconfigured Cruisers. I was on one myself a few years later, USS *Springfield* (CLG-7). The *Springfield* had been just an ordinary light cruiser till the missiles were added. It was obsolete very soon thereafter and was turned into a Fleet Flagship, which it served with dignity and honor. And it didn't have to fire missiles very often, thank God.

Back to Kennedy on the Enterprise. The announcement was made over the 1MC that a drone would be passing along the port side. Chairs were shifted to port. There it was. The drone was flying straight and level at 10,000 feet so that the President and his group would be able to see its destruction. To set the stage better, the ship firing the missiles was equipped with two types of these new weapons. One was called the Talos, which was big, and the Terrier, which wasn't. They were very menacing looking. There was one problem with both of them, still in their early stages of use. Often, they didn't launch. Whether it was the system or the missiles themselves, the drone flew by unhampered and unscathed. The missiles did not fire. It was then that the President made his observation. The drone was eventually sent around again, and this time it was splashed. I have to add that the trouble with the Terriers was eventually licked. The Talos went into the dustbin of history.

We can only imagine what the President would add to the story when he returned to the White House to talk about his day. One thing though, JFK looked great in the leather flight jacket that they had made up for him. Kennedy was always close to the Navy as President, and he made sure that his old PT skipper, John Bulkeley, was promoted to Admiral, which was not going to happen till the Presidential intervention. That was the scuttlebutt anyway, a wonderful Navy word that sounds much better than gossip.

Borden Chase

"Did you spot it Bill — did you see it?"

— Borden Chase, Author/Screenwriter
Hollywood, California — 1948

I n the intro to this book, I promised that you would meet some strangers whom you would want to know. Here then are two men whom you have probably never heard of, but whose works you may have seen and enjoyed. I will fill in the blanks.

Borden Chase, born Frank Foster in 1908, was a writer of stories, novels, and films. His non de plume was derived from a milk carton and the name on the side of a bank. He was married three times, had a daughter named Barrie, an actress/dancer, who appeared in four TV specials with Fred Astaire. Borden's literary and film works had various themes initially, but he ended up almost exclusively writing Western movies. He was a major contributor to what is called the "adult Western," which featured multi-dimensional creations — heroes with flaws and villains with positives. He helped James Stewart remake his film persona from the boyish, idealistic, simple Mr. Smith, and George Bailey to more complex characters, often with a dark side or life view in such films as *Winchester 73*, *Bend of the River*, *The Far Country,* and *Night Passage*. Borden is also the author of the quote above which referred to his greatest success, *Red River*, based on his magazine story, directed by Howard Hawks and starring John Wayne and Montgomery Clift.

As a special bonus to the reader, I will now reveal a little known fact about one of your favorite movies. Let's hear from John Wayne and then put him off to one side — as if that were possible. Speaking of *Red River*, Wayne told me that one of the most difficult things was "making it look like Monty Clift or Randy could lick me in a fight." Randy was Randolph Scott, who appeared in three films with Wayne during WWII, which also featured Marlene Dietrich, a fan of Wayne and vice versa. Now Montgomery Clift was known for his sensitive, often neurotic but appealing romantic leads, not for his physical gifts or prowess. Randolph Scott, on the other hand, was a Western hero of longstanding, later hailed by Mel Brooks in *Blazing Saddles*. Randy Scott had also been a football star in college. Randy, as the Duke explained, was a good friend, but his fighting technique required doubles and some creative editing, plus some help from his cinematic opponent in at least three cases, John Wayne. "He kinda' fought like a girl," the Duke concluded sheepishly. Another film legend blown to hell. I don't care. I love Randolph Scott and his movies.

The "Bill" referred to above was William Bowers, a friend of a friend, who became a friend of mine. Bill Bowers was a prolific screenwriter with nearly fifty feature credits to his resume — an impossibility today. Bill had been in the Army Air Corps in World War II, with my business partner Herm Saunders, who had "flown a Steinway," in the West Coast version of the Glenn Miller Air Force Orchestra. Bill was not only a screenwriter; he was a helluva good screenwriter, with two Academy nominations, one for the seminal Western, *The Gunfighter*, and another, a lesser effort, *The Sheepman*, which starred Glenn Ford, then at the peak of his career.

Later, Bill Bowers would satirize the brand in such comedies as *Support Your Local Sheriff* and *The Wild Wild West*. Herm, Bill, and I often ate lunch at the executive dining room at Universal, and he dropped in on us occasionally at our offices at General Service and later at our new digs across the street from Capitol Records on Vine. Besides being a great writer, with a whimsical sense of humor, Bowers was also a wonderful storyteller, especially about Hollywood's Golden Age.

Writers were not highly thought of then, and there was a writer's building on most every major lot, where its occupants were required to punch a time clock. Bill was at Columbia then under the tyrannical rule of Harry Cohn. Cohn was known to have bugged the sound stages at Columbia in search of gossip and disloyalty. He approached his writers searching for treason by sneaking around to their enclave and waiting till there was silence, then screaming out, "You lousy bums; you're stealing my money," whereupon 12 or so Underwoods would come alive with the rat-a-tat-tat of full employment. "Liars, liars!" Cohn would respond.

What Bill Bowers didn't know about screenwriting was hardly worth knowing, but he could be surprised or, on occasion, fooled. One of his close friends was Borden Chase, and in early 1948, Chase arranged for a screening for Bill of a film he had written two years before but had not yet released. That film was *Red River*. Bowers loved the film, which he said was, "one of the great ones," and was otherwise effusive in his praise. Chase ignored the compliments; he was enthused about something else. "Didn't you see it Bill, what I did there?" Bill honestly didn't. Laughing, Chase explained, "Remember, I told you several years ago that *Mutiny on the Bounty* would make a great Western." Think about the film: the obsessed, driven leader, Fletcher Christian/Matt Dunston, the Mutiny, the threat of revenge, the survival against all odds of Bligh/Dunston, the resolution, all of it. In the story Tom Dunston gets killed; in the movie, there was a happy ending, the expected Hollywood finale in those days. The whole experience with Bill Bowers was an insight that there is nothing new under the Hollywood sun, that any plot can be re-jiggered to fit any other genre, and when I think that I have come up with something new and original, I am only fooling myself, which has been known to happen.

Jimmy Stewart, Charles Durning, Ernest Borgnine, and Jackie Cooper

"All the heroes are dead."

— Jimmy Stewart, Actor
Hollywood, California — 1946

"They were real heroes."

— Charles Durning, Actor
Studio City, California — 2001

---

*"The Navy owes me nothing.
I feel I owe the Navy something."*

— Ernest Borgnine, Actor
Hollywood Hills, California — 1997

"The Navy made a man of me."

— Jackie Cooper, Actor/Director
Beverly Hills, California — 1980

T his is not a story. It is a tribute. I was three years old when America entered the war after the Japanese attack on Pearl Harbor. My memories of World War II are few, but they are vivid. In my hometown, Salem, Oregon, there was a real fear of invasion. The Japanese were expected on the next tide. To buck up morale, a firepower demonstration was held just weeks into the New Year. I remember it as the first fireworks display I ever saw. I guess it did boost morale. As time passed and more neighborhoods were affected, gold star flags appeared in too many windows. People would speak to one another in whispers as they passed by. I was taken to the train depot to watch troop trains pass through. If they stopped, a host of volunteers met them on the platform with free coffee and donuts. Uniforms were everywhere where there had been none. In the nearby fields, German and Italian prisoners worked, picking hops and beans. They wore uniforms too — blue ones with POW on their backs. I was told we were winning, but what we were winning I did not know. If a soldier or sailor was seen hitchhiking on a local street or road, they always got a ride; a thumb was hardly necessary. My mom and dad always stopped for them. The day the war ended, I was walking around the neighborhood near Dad's service station. A soldier grabbed me, kissed me, and threw me into the air. Dad came over in his white Standard Stations uniform, I thought to rescue me. Instead, Dad set me down carefully and hugged the soldier. Today the soldier would have been arrested. Then, it meant that he would live. That meant everything!

When I went to California in 1969, I was still on active duty with the Navy. My work then and later put me into contact with many of these World War II vets.

The quotes that head this piece represent just a few of them. Save for Jimmy Stewart, I heard these words from each of these men. I have no doubt that Stewart's words ring true, though I got them second or third hand. James Stewart enlisted before Pearl Harbor and in four years became one of few men to rise from the rank of Private to Colonel. As a squadron leader and staff officer, he had flown combat missions far into Nazi Germany. Twenty in all were authorized, but there were many more that were not. He went along anyway.

To say that James Stewart had a distinguished career in the service does not do him and his service justice. When he returned to Hollywood and films, he had it stipulated in each contract that there was to be no publicity concerning his military career. It was then that the first question was posed to him, probably in the form of a compliment. "But why not, Jimmy? You were a hero." And his answer in familiar but different words would always be the same.

Stewart stayed in the Air Force Reserves, qualifying as a pilot in the B-36, the B-47, and the B-52 Stratofortress. He even flew on a B-52 mission over North Vietnam. You did not hear about it because he would not allow it. I spoke to Stewart once or twice over the phone and met him at a dinner honoring Frank Capra. He was... Jimmy Stewart... what else? Upon his retirement he received the Presidential Medal of Freedom and a promotion to Major General. They were honors richly deserved.

I met Charles Durning at a Pacific Pioneer Broadcaster luncheon. I had a book with me, *Stars in Khaki*, and I asked him to sign it. He noticed the photos of Audie Murphy and James Stewart on the cover. "They were real heroes," he said. He underplayed his role in WWII.

If you were casting for a hero-type, Charles Durning would not have made the cut. But he was one — was he ever. He landed on Omaha Beach on D-day and was wounded a few days later. His recovery took six months, just time to put him back on the front line for the German offensive in the Battle of the Bulge, where he was wounded again. More recovery, back to the front line, only to be hurt again, his third Purple Heart. Along the way Charles Durning won the Bronze and Silver stars, the nation's third and second highest military awards for bravery. Durning had PTSD before they gave it a name. There would be flashbacks, nights of terror and horror. Still, he said he was no hero.

The war experiences of Ernie Borgnine and Jackie Cooper were less dramatic but no less meaningful. Ernie spent 10 years on active duty, the longest lasting tour of duty of any of the performers on my list of honor. He left the service as a Gunner's Mate First Class. Jackie Cooper was Navy enlisted as well, but his experience so touched him that while doing *Hennesey*, a TV series about a Navy doctor, he accepted a commission in the Naval Reserve. He retired many years later as a Captain. In a way, he never left the service. My bad, I found out later that George Kennedy had put in 17 years in the Army. Sorry Ernie.

Captain Jackie Cooper, USNR, is buried at Arlington National Cemetery. Both Borgnine and Cooper, one in uniform, one not, lent their time and talents to numerous ceremonies and events, Navy recruiting films, and programs for almost as long as they lived. Upon his Navy retirement, Jackie Cooper was awarded the Legion of Merit. Ernie Borgnine got a promotion to Honorary Chief Petty Officer.

I must add two Navy memories to this list, Captain Glenn Ford, USNR, and Captain Douglas Fairbanks, Jr., USNR. Glenn Ford was a Marine in WWII, rising to the rank of Sergeant. In 1958 Ford accepted a commission in the Naval Reserve. He was at the height of his stardom, number one at the box office. For the next several years Ford appeared in countless Navy-themed broadcasts, TV shows, and films (including one of mine). He had a tour in Vietnam in 1967 and continued to support the war in spite of its growing unpopularity.

With President Ford at a luncheon
benefitting the Betty Ford Center.
President Ford served as a naval officer in WWII.

For Doug Fairbanks WWII was a long one. He received a commission before Pearl Harbor and was sent on a diplomatic/military mission to South America by President Franklin Roosevelt. Once in the war, Lt. Fairbanks was assigned to commando training under British Admiral Louis Mountbatten. He planned and participated in commando raids, served on many fronts and was awarded numerous medals and citations, including the Bronze Star with Combat V, the Silver Star, and the French Croix de Guerre, all for bravery.

Demobilized in 1946, Fairbanks stayed in the Reserves and served as an envoy to NATO, finally retiring in 1984. I first met Captain Fairbanks at a "Studio Kids" photo shoot for Vanity Fair in 1995. By this time, I was a Captain myself. We had something to talk about. I found him to be a gentleman's gentleman — charming, witty, and self-effacing. We continued a correspondence until his death at age 90. There were others whose lives I touched, and who touched mine.

As I do today, I never met WWII vets without thanking them for their service. I served for 35 years in the Navy and never heard a shot fired in anger. It is to them and their brothers and sisters that this is so, and I remain grateful. They now are nearly gone. Those who came from Hollywood came from a world of privilege. Yet, few if any asked for special treatment or favors. Clark Gable, the King of Hollywood himself, flew combat missions over occupied Europe, age 40 plus.

There is no ranking from me in the names that follow. Having met them and thanked them, I honor them all: Burgess Meredith - Army; Mickey Rooney - Army; George Kennedy - Army; Larry Storch - Navy; Jack Lemmon - Navy; Tony Curtis - Navy; Robert Stack - Navy; Jason Robards - Navy; Dennis Weaver - Navy; Buddy Rogers - Navy; Frank Coghlan - Navy (a career officer after the war); Jonathan Winters - Marine; Rod Steiger - Navy; Charlton Heston - Army Air Corps; Gene Autry - Army Air Corps; Gordon MacRae - Army Air Corps; Donald O'Connor - Army Air Corps; Peter Graves - Army Air Corps; Mel Brooks - Army; Karl Malden - Army Air Corps; James Whitmore - Marines.

I fully realize we have only looked at only Hollywood, a microscopic part of the fight for freedom that was World War II. Even there we have looked at

My wife Gayle and I pose after a dinner with
Academy Award winner Rod Steiger.
Rod Steiger was a WWII Navy Veteran.

My wife Gayle and I having some laughs with Carl Reiner and
Mel Brooks at a book signing for *2000 Year Old Man.*
Both Carl Reiner and Mel Brooks served in the US Army in WWII.

only performers, exclusively male. There were countless others, artists and artisans in entertainment, most anonymously, in all services and in all theaters of war. Special mention to directors like Frank Capra - Army (*Why We Fight* series); Anatole Litvak - Army (not well remembered today but a true hero);

John Huston - Army (Battle of San Pietro/Report from the Aleutians); John Ford - Navy (wounded during the Japanese attack on Midway, directed filming footage of the D-Day invasion); William Wyler (flew over Germany to record the story of the Memphis Belle).

When you see documentary footage of D-Day and Iwo Jima, think long and hard of the brave cameramen and photographers who took those dramatic images while under fire themselves. Bless them all. Hooray for Hollywood. A special shout out to Bob Hope who went everywhere for the troops; his only weapons were humor, commitment, and love of freedom; to the men and women of the USO who traveled far and wide to every front to provide entertainment and a few bright moments to the dark world of combat; finally, to Carole Lombard, who gave her all, and to Martha (Colonel Maggie) Raye, an honorary Green Beret and Marine, who not only entertained but worked in field hospitals as a Licensed Practical Nurse in Vietnam. She lies today with her boys in the military cemetery at Fort Bragg, North Carolina.

Thanks to you all. I will not forget you, and I ask everyone to remember as well. The price of freedom is paid by a relatively few, but it benefits us all. REMEMBER! These individuals came from diverse backgrounds and politics that varied from liberal Democrats to rock-ribbed Republican conservatives. They left their politics at the induction center door and worked together for a great and noble cause. And we sure as hell should remember THAT!

Short Takes and Incidental Contact

Nick Nolte and Liza Minnelli

— Nick Nolte/Liza Minnelli, Actor/Actress
Hollywood, California/Rancho Mirage, California — 1994

The above incidental meetings were more in the nature of avoiding serious casting problems. A shorter title would be "Bus Accidents Avoided." The idea I felt was a good one. In order to add to our company's recovery films for treatment facilities, mental health units, and correctional institutions, we would provide recovery works of Jack Weiner and his wife, Sandy.

Jack was an excellent writer who had written a fine book called *The Morning After*, which had been made into an award-winning television movie starring Dick Van Dyke. The Weiner husband and wife team paired up, without credits, for a series of motivational/inspirational recovery books of daily meditations. My company obtained the audio rights to two of them, *A New Day* and *A Time to Be Free*. We eventually secured an excellent cast which included Julie Harris, Dick Van Dyke, Louis Gossett, Jr., and Ali McGraw. I am, however, getting too far ahead of myself. Our search for talent led us to two big names, Nick Nolte and Liza Minnelli. How to get, or how to get to them, apart from an agent whose financial requests would put us out of business before we got started?

The four previously mentioned stars contributed their talents without compensation, a virtual necessity to a financially underfunded media company such as ours. They believed in our mission and what it could do, and for that I am as grateful as one can be after piloting a beloved failure.

But how to get to Nolte and Minnelli? Nick was hot, just a few years after *Prince of Tides*. I called a friend, Bob Case, who was a man about the sports and Malibu movie communities who knew Nolte and had been to his house several times. I offered Bob a nonpaying producer credit, and he agreed to help. We were driving around LA. I think we went to Dodger Stadium to watch batting practice. Bob Case knew everyone in the place, players and all, and could get in with just a wave. After that, we drove around talking about making the approach to Nolte.

What happened next is right out of a Hollywood storybook. We were just west of Universal on the Ventura freeway in the number 2 lane in medium, rush-hour traffic when a limo pulls up along the driver's side, the tinted glass slides down, and it's Nick Nolte.

"Bob, how ya' doin'?" Nick knew Bob's car. After a short period of disbelief, a discussion ensued and we ended up passing the script to him at 30 miles an hour.

What a break! What a God shot! If we had been boozers, we would have gotten shit-faced then and there. As it was, we just hooted and hollered. A week went by. Nolte never got back to us. And a good thing too, because not long after this his mug shot was in the papers on a drunk driving or drunk-in-public rap. It remains to this day, the number 1 celebrity mug shot of all time. Saved by the incomplete pass.

And what happened to Nick Nolte? He went into a picture called *I'll Do Anything*. It was a kind of musical in which he and his costar Albert Brooks and a few other poor sods were required to sing. It was a cinematic disaster of San Francisco earthquake proportions, did no box office, and got lousy reviews. It was one of the few — perhaps the only — misstep by famed director James L. Brooks. We must have put the curse on him.

Brooks was far from being alone in the directorial flop department.

A few years before, Peter Bogdanovich, one of the hot new-wave directors decided to make a Cole Porter-themed 30s kind of musical. It starred Burt Reynolds, then very hot, and Cybill Shepherd, ditto. They had to sing also, to their eternal shame. There was said to have been a black-tie preview at 20th Century Fox with all the finest food and drink one could wish for. It was held, not in a theater on the lot, but on a giant stage with banners and blown up photos of the stars. The lights dimmed and *At Long Last Love* was finally shown to the general public for the first time. After the film, the credits rolled and the lights came up. There was no one there. They had all gone home.

Burt Reynolds was on a talk show a short time later and told this story. "There was a little bird who decided to fly South all on his own. It was a songbird, a perky, happy creature. As he flew high, it grew colder and colder, till his wings could carry him no more. He glided to earth and landed in a cow pie. The bovine's excretion was soft and warm and soon the bird regained his strength and began to sing. Then a cat came along and ate him. The moral of this tale," Burt Reynolds explained, "was, if you find yourself in a piece of shit, don't sing."

This is an awkward place to introduce Judy Garland's multi-talented daughter, Liza, but this was promised, so here she is.

The meeting was arranged by friends at the Betty Ford Center. I had played a small role in the formation of the Center and Ms. Minnelli was a well-known alumna. She was performing, I believe, a benefit concert for BFC at the time. We met backstage and she could not have been more pleasant or charming. She would be honored to do whatever was asked of her, as soon as she read the script, which had not been written yet. She gave us her private number, introduced us to her assistant who gave us her number, and we were set to go, as soon as I wrote the narration for *A Time to Be Free*, the work we had chosen for her.

The word "free" has a haunting quality for me, since of her own free will, and being an alcoholic and addict, Liza relapsed, more than once. There went our dreams of landing super stars. We had to use plain old, everyday stars, and Julie, Dick, Lou, and Ali came to the fair and were wonderful. To end this, we must unfortunately talk about failure. This is painful but instructive. If you are going to create something, you better know how to sell it — the who, the when, the where, and the how. We had a great product, we all knew that, but we never licked the problem of distribution. It was and is timeless material that just never happened, never came together. *A New Day* and *A Time to Be Free* remain my proudest regret.

Keystone Kop

— Keystone Kop
Salem, Oregon – 1947

I wasn't sure how far to go back on this section, but I finally decided, what the hell, go back as far as you can remember. I was just eight or nine when I met my first and only Keystone Kop. I was waiting for a bus. The buses in Salem, Oregon, were called Cherriots, because Salem was the Cherry City. Don't ask. Most often I would walk to town, alone or with a friend. It was safe, even at night. If I had a dime though, I could ride the city bus to within a block of my house on Liberty Street.

A ragged old man approached me at the bus stop. My father had told me about them. They were called hoboes or tramps and they lived in a jungle by the railroad tracks. I was not afraid. There were many people about, and if I had to, I could run very fast. He reached in his pocket to show me something. His wallet held, not money, but news clippings, yellow and fragile. It was a story about the Keystone Kops. I don't remember what the story was about. He told me his name, but I can't remember that either. He told me that he was one of the original Kops. If this were true, their retirement system was faulty, for he had seen better days. I told my dad about it, and he said he had seen movies of the Keystone Kops before sound came in. He reminded me to be careful around strangers. It was not a lecture. He said I would know what to do. He trusted my judgment. I had never felt so proud. If this were to happen today, the stranger

187

would lie about being a Kop. He would be a registered sex offender whose file had been mislaid by the authorities. I would be molested and sliced into little pieces and would be dumped on my grandparents' grave. But I could not have been dumped on my parents' grave because they were cremated and I have the urn. This would be 21st century progress — for sexual predators.

Rock Hudson

— Rock Hudson
Salem, Oregon — 1952

I n 1952, Universal made a movie called *Bend of the River*. It was shot in Oregon. Jimmy Stewart was the star, and Arthur Kennedy and Julie Adams were in it too. The studio decided to hold previews of the picture all over the Northwest. Though it was filmed in Oregon, Washington and Idaho got previews too, because they shared the Columbia River. Seattle, Portland, and maybe Boise got the big stars, and we Salemites got some minor players, Lori Nelson and Rock Hudson.

It was at the end of the studio system, when contract players were given seven-year contracts, which required them to attend events such as previews, supermarket openings, and the like. There was a small turnout for this event, held at the Elsinore Theater, an old-fashioned movie palace with loges and opera boxes and a giant organ that had not been used since the twenties.

Television was taking its toll on moving pictures, and even the slogan "Movies are Better than Ever" had not moved audiences from their living room black-and-white TVs. I lusted for Lori Nelson, a winsome blonde. Puberty had me in its grasp. Rock Hudson was a handsome young hunk. He made a pat little speech about being from Winnetka, Illinois, citing a song, "Big Noise from Winnetka," which hasn't been heard before or since, at least not by me. I had no idea that here was a star in the making and certainly could not conceive of the tragic turn his life would take. I must add here that everything I later heard in Hollywood about Rock Hudson was positive. Everyone who worked with him liked him. He was easily one of the most popular stars in the film community.

Lori Nelson never made it big, but my lust for her lasted till I was out of high school and started reading *Playboy*.

Burt Lancaster and Charles Bronson

— Burt Lancaster and Charles Bronson
Los Angeles, California — 1956

In November 1955, I joined the Naval Reserve to avoid being drafted in the Army. Other options such as shooting off a few toes or eating a pound and a half of sugar before going to the induction center never occurred to me. The idea of Canada was a decade away, but I wouldn't have done that either. I liked being an American in America. The next year I had to go to Navy boot camp in San Diego. Inspired by the movie *It Happened One Night* with Gable and Colbert, I decided to take "The Long Dog," a Greyhound bus to California. The movie featured a happy bus ride with passengers group singing "The Daring Young Man on the Flying Trapeze." I did not expect that kind of entertainment, but a long bus ride seemed like an adventure for someone like me — and it certainly was. My seatmate at the beginning of my journey was a Mr. Everyman, in his late thirties or early forties. He was a talker, and I was a listener, so it seemed a good fit. He had just been released from a Seattle jail and had a clipping or two that he wanted to show me. The newspaper articles dealt with a death in the last few days that had occurred in the drunk tank of said lockup. A brief investigation had ruled the incident an accident. No charges were pressed. "I killed him," the man confided. He seemed quite pleased about it. I remained awake and alert for the next several hours. Fortunately, he got off in Sacramento.

After that, boot camp seemed a breeze. On the way home, Mom and Dad had arranged to have me stay a few days with my only rich relatives, Uncle Art and Aunt Helen, who lived in Studio City in a nice neighborhood on Radford, directly behind Republic Studios. On the way to being picked up, my bus traveled along Hollywood Boulevard.

Still thinking in nautical terms, I sat on the port window side of the bus. I was looking idly out when a white Cadillac convertible, top down, came into view. Burt Lancaster was driving, smiling it up, his white teeth gleaming as brightly as the Caddy grille. He looked like he had just come from a tanning salon. While I was still digesting this minor miracle, on a street corner I beheld Moses, wearing a grey robe and clutching a staff that went up to his shoulders waiting for a bus. No one but I was paying the slightest bit of attention to him. Both these visions seemed perfectly natural to me. We were in Hollywood, after all. After Uncle Art and Aunt Helen picked me up in their Cadillac, they showed me around Republic Studios. Clark Gable was supposed to be on the lot, but the most I got to see was the standing set of *Dragnet*, which was shooting there then. It was an exact duplicate of LAPD headquarters, down to the cigarette burns on the beat-up desks. For Jack Webb, the LAPD had surveyed a bunch of their old furniture to give the Dragnet show its authentic aura.

Later, I smoked cigars and drank whisky with Uncle Art. He was a big shot at Consolidated Labs which owned Republic. I felt very grown-up. Aunt Helen, a good and kind lady, took me to the May Company in Westwood Village (really a village then), to buy me a shirt or two. While we were shopping, I saw a familiar face and physique. It was Charles Bronson, and he had on a white T-shirt and blue jeans. He had biceps like Virginia hams. He was not yet a movie star but had his own black-and-white TV series — something about a *Man with a Camera*. I left LA very grateful for my only rich relatives. I thought they would live forever and vowed to see them again when I returned to Hollywood. I did get back, fourteen years later. I phoned Uncle Art, hoping he would ask me over to the house. He was drunk, and he died two days later, naked in his living room. He never got over Aunt Helen's death, and after he retired he wasn't a big shot anymore.

All Uncle Art had was money, and it wasn't enough.

Dean Martin and Lena Horne

— **Dean Martin and Lena Horne**
Los Angeles, California — 1990s

When the Dean Martin/Jerry Lewis partnership broke up, almost everyone thought that Lewis would go sailing on from success to success. Lewis did have a few early hits as a single, but as he took himself more and more seriously, his act began to wane.

Dean Martin started slowly with a bomb of a movie, *Ten Thousand Bedrooms*, and he was written off by many, when, in fact, he was just getting started. His singing career got bigger and better, and in his movie career with such movies as *Some Came Running*, he gained respect as a serious actor, and then he became a movie star, till he Matt Helmed himself out of that part of the business, only to reinvent himself as the host of a wildly successful variety show.

All the while, Martin was running a kind of con, as a kind of smooth, relaxed, loveable drunk. He was anything but an alcoholic then. Of course he drank, perhaps heavily, but no real alcoholic could have maintained that busy schedule of films, recording dates, night club performances, television, and personal appearances if he were bombed all the time. Only after the death of his son in a military air crash in 1987 did his world begin to turn dark. Alcohol did not kill Dean Martin, though it is a poor recipe for grief, but cigarettes surely did.

StarCatcher

People always wondered, "What was Dean Martin really like? Was there a façade behind the façade?" Jeanne, the longest lasting of his three wives, married 24 years and the love of Dean's life, was probably closest to the mark when she said something like, "I was only with him for 20 plus years, and I'd still like to know what he was really like."

It must be very difficult for a celebrity to know whom to trust and what to believe. Except for Dean's TV shows, I saw him only once. It was on the first tee at the Riviera Country Club.

Besides his foursome, Dean was engulfed by well-wishers and hangers on, what a friend of mine calls "green flies," well-dressed maggots who cling to the famous until they die or lose their popularity. Dean was set to tee off, but at the last minute he was called away to take a call from wife number 3. He got hoots and catcalls and a ration of shit from his following about being pussy-whipped, the usual crap. There was a smile on his face as he returned to the tee, and I got closer to him, but he was not happy. His eyes spoke volumes. He didn't want to hear the bullshit from his phony friends; he didn't want to have to be Dean Martin now. All he wanted was to play golf and get the hell away from everybody and everything.

Phoniness does drag you down, even if you're Dean Martin. He hit a good drive down the right side of the fairway, quickly jumped into his cart, and was gone.

I am going to put Lena Horne on the *Dean Martin Show*, because we just talked about Dean. But Flip Wilson was hot then. Both his show and Dean's were at NBC, and I sat in the same seat, far right in the front row, and I can't remember which show it was. I remember the lady and the scene though, and can't forget it. Lena Horne, in a beautiful white outfit was just back stage out of public view, except from me, and was getting ready to go on, but it looked as if she wanted to go anywhere else. She was shivering and shaking, her arms crossed clutching herself as if to hold it all together. At first, I thought she was having a seizure. Performing in public seemed to be sheer agony for her. But she came on stage as if she did not have a care in the world. She embraced her host (Dean, Flip?) and went right into her number.

Lena Horne was wonderful!

Robert Young's Luncheon Companion

"Where is your star?"

**— Robert Young's Luncheon Companion
at The Brown Derby
Hollywood, California – 1950s**

Most people of a certain age remember Robert Young from television, either in *Father Knows Best* or *Marcus Welby*. It is not widely known, but with Robert's blessing, the radio version of the show, which pre-dated TV, was titled *Father Knows Best?* Their TV sponsor demanded that the question mark be removed. Reluctantly, Young agreed to this. Before all that, starting in 1931, he had appeared in 100 films. He was never nominated for a major award in film, but he did win an Emmy for

The "Father Knows Best" couple, Robert Young and Jane Wyatt with my wife, Gayle Frederick

196

comedy, another for drama, and a Golden Globe for his work in television. He was a very underrated actor. His costars, especially ladies, loved him because he did not try to steal scenes from them. Hedy Lamarr, who had been paired with the best — Gable and Tracy for starters — said Young was her favorite leading man. She was not alone.

The Hollywood Chamber of Commerce did recognize Robert Young with three stars on their Walk of Fame, one each for radio, television, and movies. In those days, merit was the only entry.

You did not have to buy your star.

By the time this story took place, Robert was working on *Father Knows Best* on the Columbia lot on Gower Street. Gower was just a few blocks from the Brown Derby on Vine, and it was one of Young's favorite spots for lunch. He was having lunch that day with a friend who will be nameless, because I have no idea who he was. They had finished their meal and were waiting for the valet to bring up their cars, when Luncheon Companion posed the question above. "I haven't the slightest idea," Robert Young said. The man gave him an odd look, got in his car, and drove away. Before Young entered his vehicle, he happened to glance down at his shoe, which had been pinching him slightly. Robert Young was standing in the very center of his Star.

Robert Young told me this one on himself.

Henry King

— Henry King, Director
Toluca Lake, California — 1978

Henry King was a well-known director, but not as well-known as he should have been, because he was one of the great ones. He worked primarily at 20th Century Fox, which was famous for its story quality, not so much for its directors and producers, and not even for its stable of stars, though Tyrone Power, Gregory Peck, and Betty Grable fans would argue the point. I only exchanged a few words with Henry King. I did not, at the time, even know of him, though I had been a movie buff since childhood.

I was playing at Lakeside in a foursome of friends. On the 10th hole, I shoved my drive to the right, still in play, but along the row of homes that line the fairway. A man I judged to be in his late 70s or early 80s was leaning against his back gate watching the play as golfers came by. There was a wheelchair and a caregiver nearby, but he did not seem to need them. He stood erect and strong as I came up to him. "How are you playing?" he asked. I was one over par at that point, one of my better rounds, and I told him so. "Shot 71 out there one day," he said. And that was it. I hit my shot and moved on. "Who was that?" I asked one of my foursome. I knew it had to be somebody special.

No Wikipedia in those days, and I had to do a bit of research to find out who Henry King was. He directed his first film in 1916 and his last in 1962. He flew his own plane to scout movie locations. Seven of his pictures were nominated for

Best Picture. You should look him up. The range of his movies will surprise you. It was quite a moment after the fact.

I had come to Hollywood in 1969, and I was lucky enough to meet a few men and women who were there when Hollywood movies were born. Henry King was one of these pioneers. For me it was like walking in to the Museum of Natural History and talking to an amiable dinosaur who chats with you about his day.

William Conrad

*"You don't expect me to
remember that shit, do you?"*

**— William Conrad, Actor/Fighter Pilot
Burbank, California — 1981**

William Conrad's voice was money in his bank. Bill did over 7,500 radio shows, plus countless commercials on both radio and TV over the years. He had a movie career too, but also a weight problem, which made it somewhat ironic that he often played "heavies," villains of the piece.

I was fortunate enough to get to work with Conrad on a few occasions. By this time he was late in his career and had moved to hero roles, a very unusual switch. He was the lead in two successful shows, *Cannon* and *Jake and the Fat Man*. While we were working on one of our projects, I asked him if it was true that he read all his lines off large cue cards. It WAS true, he affirmed, and not only that, he also had no idea what the particular show was about that week and who his co-stars would be other than the regulars. He almost never looked at a script, except to check on whether any exertion would be involved. He would then attempt to keep his participation in such scenes to a minimum. He had no idea what he was going to say until he said it. Only someone who had been radio-trained to the max could get away with it. As George Burns said,

"The first thing an actor has to project is sincerity. When you can fake that, you're home free."

But Bill Conrad wasn't faking. He was acting as only he knew how, and it never seemed to fail him.

Sean Connery

"I am Sean Connery."

— Sean Connery
New York City, New York – 2000

I never thought of myself as being mature — even today I have a problem with that description, though in my short-lived acting career, I always played fathers. I was the father in *Wilbur Minds the Baby* in the 8th grade and again in *The Purification*, a Tennessee Williams loser in my junior year in college. I was verbally linked to actors occasionally.

A so-called friend told me that I resembled a mature Henry Fonda. This was hardly a compliment, because the actor was some thirty years older. As Sean Connery and I grew old together, as our facial hair grew gray, and he had no further need to hide under a toupee, there were occasional comparisons. He was THE James Bond after all. We both ended up in New York City in the year 2000. He was making a movie, *Finding Forrester*, and I was taking my wife Gayle to plays, her favorite entertainment. Now a visiting celebrity in New York is as common as a General in the Pentagon, and anything short of an English monarch or a Pope, attracts little or no attention. As to the former and forever James Bond, well nearly everyone knew he was in town, including me.

Gayle and I were standing on a street corner, waiting to cross the street to see a play I have forgotten completely, when a tour bus pulled up across the street. The bus, in fact, had virtually screeched to a stop; and the driver, a middle-aged black gentleman, rushed around to the front of his transporter, waving his arms. I thought it must be some kind of medical emergency. He was looking in my direction, and I turned to see what was going on behind me. Nothing going on. Then the driver began to scream above the noise of New York traffic, "Sean Connery, Sean Connery!" he was yelling. "Where, where?" I thought.

There was not a sign of the famous Scot. Gayle grasped the situation immediately, and never one to ignore a spotlight, began pointing — at ME. By now the driver was waving, everyone on my side of the bus was waving, and hands and faces soon appeared above the wavers, filling each and every window with my adoring fans. What could I do? I waved back, what else? Gayle was pointing, I kept waving, in a modest royal kind of way, till the light changed. I decided to stay where I was, while other pedestrians streamed by.

I thought Sean would have kept his distance, and besides, I did not want to destroy the illusion.

This was my last acting gig, and my favorite by far. I kept on waving, modestly, until the driver returned to his rig and headed on uptown, downtown, or wherever. My last image was of hands still waving from the back of the bus. They looked like a small flock of birds in flight.

Roy Rogers and Dale Evans

— **Roy Rogers and Dale Evans**
Victorville, California – 1986

Victorville, California, was and is not well known as a tourist destination, except perhaps as a rest stop on the road to Vegas from LA. I made it a point to go there twice in the 1980s for one reason only, to see Roy Rogers and visit the Roy Rogers Museum. I must confess though, that I was not a real fan of the singing Western, exemplified by Gene Autry and Roy Rogers. The genre was almost destroyed when John Wayne, then slaving in B movies, was required to lend his musical gifts to a character call "Singin' Sandy" in a film that, in its own awful way, is a classic of its kind. It was rumored that Wayne, after he had become famous, wished to buy the negative and destroy it and all known copies. I have seen the picture, and the Duke had the right idea.

Singing aside, and Roy Rogers had a very pleasant voice, Rogers and most every hero on the Western movie range stood for values of honesty, chivalry, bravery, modesty, humility, and honor. Those words seem almost out of place today, but thank God there are men and women to whom these virtues still have meaning.

But back to the King of the Cowboys and his museum. After pausing for a picture or two of Trigger rearing on his hind legs and towering over the front entrance, I went inside to find a collection of the colorful, the bizarre, the historical, and the endlessly trivial. Rogers must never have discarded anything he saw, liked, bought, or was given — they all had a space or a place in the Roy Rogers Museum. Every animal with a screen credit was there, resplendently stuffed. Most everything he drove was in evidence, including a family car that went back to the days when he was Leonard Slye from Cincinnati, Ohio. Every shirt, saddle, shooting iron, suit, sock, snakeskin belt, sales slip, if not in view, was around

With the King of the Cowboys, Roy Rogers, at his museum in Victorville, California

somewhere. Roy Rogers and his wife, Dale, were there that day, and they could not have been nicer. They willingly posed for pictures. Perhaps there was a slight fee involved. I don't remember, but I doubt it.

In 1986, after a six-year trial run that both of us survived, my high school sweetheart, Gayle LaBranche, and I were married. The wedding took place at our home in Lake Sherwood, a bit of the Northwest set in Southern California. The setting was our patio, overlooking the pool. Our parents, numerous friends and relatives witnessed the ceremony, which had been planned for 30 years before, but had been derailed by my failure to commit to a date and the fact that she dumped me. In the midst of the nondenominational service, our two dogs, Creature and Gizmo, both females, staged a make-believe orgy next to

The dog-friendly Frederick family

the nearly newlyweds. This was the only time this ever happened. Don't tell me that dogs lack a sense of humor.

I had promised Gayle a European honeymoon, but we were in production at the time, and it proved to be impossible. So I promised her a big surprise instead. My surprise turned out to be a visit to Victorville and the Roy Rogers Museum.

I have always thought of myself as being an amusing person with a great sense of humor. Gayle was not amused. I tried to make up for it that evening by a night at the Apple Valley Inn, which since 1948 had had a great reputation as a celebrity getaway.

The inn had a Western theme; there were midnight hay rides and square dancing. Unfortunately, we were twenty years late for these events. The place was now a ghost town, with all the charm and warmth of the snowbound lodge in *The Shining*.

By this time my wife was not speaking to me, and I could tell she was reconsidering her decision to spend the rest of her life with an idiot. Not even the rest of the honeymoon in Vegas, where she could indulge her addiction to losing on the slot machines, was enough to break the ice.

The joke, for sure, was on me. And what of Roy Rogers and Dale Evans? This happy couple relocated themselves and their museum to the welcoming old-timers who have made visiting Branson, Missouri, a rural success story. The Museum closed its doors in 2010. By this time, both Roy and his lovely bride were riding Happy Trails in the Hereafter. What they left behind made a ton of money, three million bucks, to be less than precise. Trigger went for $260 grand and Roy's prize saddle went for sixty thousand dollars more than that. There were new homes for all the deceased animals, and the cars as well. It was a sunset to remember.

Don't tell me nostalgia doesn't sell. Come to think of it, we need a lot more nostalgia these days — and a lot less reality.

Happy trails, "pardners!"

Jack Lemmon, Dick Van Dyke, and Carol Burnett

**— Jack Lemmon, Dick Van Dyke, Carol Burnett
Southern California — 1970s — 1990s**

This book is about quotes, yet I don't have any to share from these well-beloved performers. Besides, I must face it — this is also about name dropping. I dislike it in others, but I'm going to do it anyway.

I love this trio — Jack Lemmon, Dick Van Dyke, and Carol Burnett — and if you have come this far, I believe that you do too. I played golf in a foursome with Jack Lemmon in a tournament that benefitted the Pasadena Council on Alcoholism and Drug abuse.

Jack was as warm and friendly as you would expect him to be. I identified with his love of golf and our mutual willingness to be uplifted, disappointed, hopeful, and baffled by this addictive, vexing sport. As a team, we were well back in the pack. We talked about nothing but golf, and to non-golfers, nothing can be more boring. I knew that Jack had quit drinking many years before, and I wondered if playing in *Days of Wine and Roses* had anything to do with this decision. But I muffed my chance to ask him about it because I was thinking of only the next shot, or grieving over the most recent errant blow. Years later, I attended an event honoring director Blake Edwards, whom most people identify with the *Pink Panther* and comedy. Actually, Blake Edwards also directed *Days of Wine and Roses*, *Breakfast at Tiffany's*, a great underrated suspense film *Experiment in Terror,* and many others across all genres. It was at lunch during the making of *Wine* that Edwards looked mistily at his star and observed, "You know, Jack, we're drinking just like the guy in the movie." Having made this observation, Edwards took it to heart and never had another drink for the rest of his life. That he was tested by the immensely talented but horribly erratic Peter Sellers and survived without falling off the wagon or committing mayhem on the comic genius is a tribute to his disciplined nature. Lemmon eventually followed him into the sober life.

Jack Lemmon was much loved by many, including me, and everybody loves Dick Van Dyke. There was a great outpouring of grief following the death of Lucille Ball, the beloved Lucy. As he watched the tributes on television, the man who created the Van Dyke persona on *The Dick Van Dyke Show*, Carl Reiner, remarked to his wife, "Just wait till Dick dies, if he ever does." Dick is over ninety now and gives no sign of slowing down.

My business partner, Herm, and I were fortunate to obtain Dick's talents on several projects. Dick appeared in and narrated a Navy film called *The Turning Point* about a naval aviator's recovery from alcoholism. He co-narrated with Julie Harris *A New Day: Meditations for Personal and Spiritual Growth*.

Dick also appeared in our film on celebrity recovery, *Hollywood and Vine*. We shot some of the sequences on his sailboat, cruising off San Diego. He was a fine sailor, one of many talents. He can sing, dance, do comedy and drama — everything it seems but an English accent in *Mary Poppins*.

All of Dick Van Dyke's contributions were made possible by our mutual friend, publicist Bob Palmer. Bob also took me to the set of *Diagnosis Murder*, a Van Dyke starring vehicle that ran successfully several years longer than the original *Dick Van Dyke Show*.

I was around him more than a little bit. And what is Dick Van Dyke really like? I haven't a clue, and I am not sure anyone else does either. Many of his passions are solitary. He works with all manner of computers and electronic gizmos, on only God knows what. His public persona is that of a friendly extrovert, but he is extremely private. And why not? Dick Van Dyke should be entitled to all the privacy he wants.

Bogart said it years ago, "All the public is entitled to is a good performance."

Carol Burnett was wounded by a tabloid that accused her of being drunk in public. Her parents had been alcoholic, and her daughter Carrie fought and won her battle with addiction. Burnett sued the tabloid, and won. Among her other charitable interests, Carol Burnett had given her talents and energy in support of those who deal with addiction and its many consequences. She opened her home to my company when we filmed an interview with Betty Ford for the National Council on Alcoholism. At the same time, we were preparing to make a film on the subject of women and alcoholism. I had done quite a bit of research on the subject with experts in the field, mostly men, and found that none of the males felt they had a real grasp on the subject. I include myself, though not a physician, and I was by this time living with my high-school sweetheart Gayle, who was a recovering alcoholic and drug addict.

I decided to turn to her and to approach the subject with a production and postproduction team entirely composed of women. This was in 1980. My very good friend Dr. Jokichi (Joe) Takamine was a personal physician to Carol Burnett, and with his help she agreed to host the film. I went to the set a few times, met Miss Burnett, but mostly I stayed away and let the women handle it.

The film was a success, even though it was not exactly what I wanted, and I saw to it that key members of the crew received points directly from gross profits on the picture. Perhaps I should have tried to publicize what we had done, with a female publicist. I am still proud of the film and the reaction it received, even though my name appeared nowhere in the credits. No men period.

As an aside, the director came to me in the middle of postproduction editing. My business partners, Herm and Rick, had been sitting in on editing sessions and had offered a host of opinions. The director was conflicted and confused and wanted my help. "Don't listen to them," I said. "And for that matter, don't listen to me either. You'll figure it out."

She did.

Audrey Totter, Dorothy McGuire, and Jane Wyatt

— Audrey Totter, Dorothy McGuire, and Jane Wyatt
Los Angeles, California -— 1980s/90s

Richard Brautigan once described his youthful home in the Great Northwest as a "dark and haunted place." I won't go that far, but I lived in Oregon for the first 22 years of my life and I can say one thing with absolute certainty — it was wet. As a young boy, I can remember splashing around in mud puddles in my rubber boots. Fun. In college, as a baseball pitcher, I always took with me to the mound a Popsicle stick, the better to clean the mud off my spikes after practically every pitch. Not fun. I went to California in 1969 and I remember standing on the first tee on December 26th of that year. The temperature was in the mid-80s. There was not a cloud in the sky. I thought to myself, "How long has this been going on?" I am still here, over fifty years later.

I do return to Oregon from time to time. One such occasion was for a 50th wedding anniversary for two friends of my wife, Gayle. Joyce and Bill Scott, he an educator, she a housewife, were two very nice people. They had very nice children and a very nice, new home in Bend, a Mecca for restless Californians who wished to experience the joys of snow and the change of seasons. Then, as now, I pass. I was struck by the number of Golden Wedding couples in attendance. There were many others who volunteered that they had forty years of wedded bliss. I had to get in the act. I rose and announced, "Does two twenties and a ten count?" This did not get the laughs I felt it deserved. I did a considerable amount of checking while visiting my old home town of Salem, the state capitol. I found that nearly all of my high school classmates who had stayed in Salem had remained married and to one person.

Irene and I enjoyed Paris.

In my group of close friends in Southern California, there is one who has been married six times. The last one has lasted. The other wives got houses, the first more than one. This guy was complaining about it one day and I told him, "Just look at it this way, Phil. You're just solving the homeless problem one wife at a time." He was not amused. Two other guys had four brides, another three, and I am one of the two's. This is not funny either, and I have no idea why all this happened, but it is California.

Irene Robertson and Gayle and Edd Byrnes

Those who left home tended to be more like me. I actually have been married only twice. I am now very happily entwined with lovely Irene.

Irene Robertson, Edd Byrnes, and Gayle are on the set of my film, *I Really Don't Want To Know*. Edd Byrnes was the star. The movie was based on the lyrics of a Number One hit written by my good friend, Country Music Hall of Fame pianist and composer, Don Robertson, who was also featured in the picture. Irene was Don's wife and Gayle Frederick's best friend. Don and Gayle passed away within a year of each other—Gayle in June, 2014 and Don in January, 2015. Irene and I became an item a year later and have been happily together ever since.

When I tell my Oregon friends I live near Los Angeles, they look at me as if I were reporting a death in the family. "You poor soul," is their wordless message. My long-time California home in Ventura County features a lovely body of water, ducks and geese that refuse to fly to Canada, and a broad spectrum of wildlife that includes cranes, raccoons, deer, and even an occasional mountain lion. Yes, my new home state has

Here I am with Irene in Liverpool, England. The Beatles from Liverpool released the song "Penny Lane" giving it international fame.

fires, earthquakes, traffic problems, and all the rest, but as that great philosopher W.C. Fields once said, "You can't beat the weather."

My friends back home and outliers all over the country somehow regard Hollywood as Sodom and Gomorrah. I have not noticed sin running amuck here more than anywhere else. Yes, we have Harvey Weinstein, drug use, gerbils as sex objects and other oddities, as well as a cinematic crowd, the most vocal of who rail and resist anyone to the right of Trotsky, but this is not the complete picture. There are nice people here in the entertainment business, good folks who live relatively normal lives in a fishbowl. There are stable people aplenty at the very top of La La Land. I have met many of them.

I would like to focus on the three women noted above — Audrey Totter, Dorothy McGuire, and Jane Wyatt. They had much in common. They were suburb professionals who gave back and were honored by their communities. Not a hint of scandal touched any of them. Jane Wyatt was blacklisted, but that should be considered a badge of honor. They had one husband apiece. Their children have never made the headlines. Audrey Totter was the epitome of the film noir "bad girl." She loved to play them. They were more fun, she said, and she gave up the good girl roles to her friend Jane Greer and others. In real life, she could not have been nicer. The same could be said of Dorothy McGuire, who was as wholesome at home as she nearly always was on the screen. Her friend, Roddy McDowell, always called her "Mrs. Swope." Her husband, John, was a professional news photographer from a famous family. Jane Wyatt was politically active. She was a Catholic and a liberal, a combination not so common back in the day. She was a real-life Margaret Anderson in *Father Knows Best*, and was, in fact, a second mother to Elinore Donahue, Billy Gray, and Lauren Chapin and they often sought her counsel and support.

Speaking of Jim Anderson, a.k.a. Robert Young, he married his high school sweetheart, Betty, and they were together for 70 years. Then there were Jimmy and Gloria Stewart, Alexis Smith and Craig Stevens, George and Gracie...

That's enough nice for now. Hope it wasn't boring. Hooray for happy, *normal* Hollywood.

John Frederick

"I made this picture in spite of the opposition from small and willful people; I owe absolutely nothing to anyone. I did it all myself."

— John Frederick, Writer
IFPA CINDY Awards
Los Angeles, California – 1985

Yes, this is a quote, my quote, but it certainly doesn't belong with movie stars and such, so here it is in Short Takes. IFPA was the Information Producers of America, and the CINDYs were their Academy Awards. There were actually three kinds of awards — bronze, silver, and gold — and almost too many categories to keep track of. It was nice that documentary and educational filmmakers got some notice. My company FMS (for famous) Productions was a winner at IFPA for several years. The truth of it is that now, today, there are too many damn awards shows, rendering such honors almost meaningless — Academy Awards, Grammy Awards, Country Music Awards, Emmy Awards, Golden Globes, SAG Awards, BAFTA Awards, People's Choice Awards, awards for every ethnic, racial, or any other group, not forgetting the porn industry.

The Academy Awards, now a super spectacle, started as a simple little dinner affair in 1927 at the Roosevelt Hotel on Hollywood Boulevard. Now it is a mostly boring extravaganza, except when they get the Best Picture names

I was the co-founder of FMS Productions, a company that has won numerous awards over the years for film and video excellence.

mixed up. I was and am down on award shows, even as a winner.

In 1985, at IFPA, we won in several categories. The program took place at, I believe, the Westin Hotel near LAX. That year it seemed to me to be an affair longer and duller than ever before. The acceptance speeches dragged on and on and people thanked everyone and everything helping them on their way, from the doctor who delivered them, to teachers, parents, grandparents, cousins, uncles, aunts, coworkers, religious figures, including a faith healer, and those who put up the money. Since I put up the money on my film, I decided if I won that I would thank myself. It must have been after midnight when my name was called. I decided on the way up to the podium to broaden my remarks in such a way that I took credit for everything in the film.

Actually, my son Randall and our Marketing Director Yvonne Parsons had brought a little book to me called *The Cat Who Drank Too Much*. I dismissed the idea out of hand, as everyone knows that films with animals or children always go way over budget, a killer for a small, poorly funded, new company. *The Cat Who Drank and Used Too Much,* narrated by Julie Harris and Carmen Zapata, became a huge hit for us, in spite of me, though I was the co-writer and executive producer, the one who puts up or finds the money. My acceptance speech began, and probably should have ended, with the words listed on the top of the preceding page. The five or six hundred people in the ballroom who were still awake were stunned by my remarks.

The word agape is fascinating, as it has two meanings. This group was not thinking of the Greek definition of love. No, they were all agape. You never saw so many slack-jawed souls in your life. There was a total silence in the room till I said, "Now, don't you all wish you had said something like that, and we could have gone home sooner?" I then paid tribute to Randall, Yvonne, Tim Armstrong the director and others, including Dr. Claire Bissell, who wrote the book and the wonderful Julie and Carmen, who gave such meaning to the words. I did not have the guts to take it all the way, and to this day I wish I had. Whoever was there that night, would never have forgotten it.

Obviously, I didn't either.

As a sidebar, and since I can't think of any other place to put it, Donald Trump said something once that I absolutely agreed with, when referring to Alec Baldwin I believe, he stated that "there are no movie stars today."

There are good actors and actresses around, I guess, but none of them can compete with the mystique, the aura, of Wayne, Gable, Tracy, Cooper, Flynn, Crawford, Davis, Turner, Hepburn, and Marilyn Monroe. I met only one of them, Wayne, and boy was he larger than life. Today's stars are nothing but shadows on film, a line I stole from my second favorite movie, *Singin' in the Rain*. I believe it was Hemingway who stated once that "all writing is organized plagiarism."

I stole his line too.

Hemingway, Rex Allen, and the Smothers Brothers

"Only if he was cleaning it with his teeth."

— Deputy Sheriff
Ketchum, Idaho – 1962

In 1962, I was assigned to the Navy Recruiting station in Portland, Oregon, near my birthplace in Salem. I bought a brand-new home in Lake Grove, a nice Portland suburb, for $13,900, nothing down to vets. Because of Oregon's wet weather, I asked the builder to run a heating duct into the garage so my son, Randall, could play out of the rain. The builder did so, at no charge.

That spring, a fellow Lieutenant (jg), Bill Cochran, and I went on a recruiting trip to Idaho looking for Navy officer prospects. The draft was still on, Vietnam hadn't happened yet, and we had some success. Over a long weekend, we stayed in Ketchum, Twin Falls, and Pocatello, great names from the Old West. In Ketchum we went to see Hemingway's grave and ran into a deputy sheriff in town who was the first on the scene that July morning in 1961.

The deputy was an interesting character. He had just come in from rounding up some cattle rustlers. The rustling business had changed a bit, since the cattle thieves used an empty semi to make off with the beef. That part of Idaho is not noted for the quality of its roads, and the truck was no match for a posse full of cop cars. No gunplay required.

Back to Papa.

Mary Hemingway, Papa's wife, was still clinging to the fiction that Ernest had died cleaning his gun. I asked the deputy about it. Western lawmen are laconic. His answer is shown in full above. I haven't been back to the Sun Valley/Ketchum area since. It is very beautiful there. Think I will put it on my bucket list.

A few final words about Hemingway. Here was a man who won the Nobel Prize by writing in sentences of fewer than three words, who sniped, carped, and back bit all his male literary peers plus Gertrude Stein, who screwed around on all his wives until he could not get it up, and perhaps worst of all, gave masculinity a bad name. Of course, since I am inept at fishing, boxing, and hunting, plus screwing around and writing, it may be sheer jealousy.

On Saturday morning we drove to Twin Falls, got on Highway 93, and headed south for forty miles of uninterrupted rangeland devoid of almost every living creature. We did see a sheep or two. Coming over a rise we looked down at the bright lights of a micro Las Vegas called Jackpot, Nevada. Jackpot consisted of two casinos, a gas station, and an air strip. It was invented so that Jack Mormons from Idaho or nearby Utah could drink relatively guilt free.

We checked in at Cactus Pete's and got a room that gave Best Western a run for its money. The rate was two bucks a night, plus two miniatures of Jim Beam and an ashtray. Now that is my idea of progress.

After an excellent dinner, and dropping a small fortune, fifty bucks between us, we resigned ourselves to an early sleep, things to do in Jackpot after 6 p.m. being so few that they were written on after-dinner toothpicks in print so small I could not read them. So imagine our surprise when we discovered that Cactus Pete's had a showroom.

Actually, the dining room *was* the showroom. Patti Page had just played there. Our star for the evening was Rex Allen, "the Arizona Cowboy." Rex was the last of the singing cowboys, a breed that deserved to become extinct. He was also, save for Monte Hale, the last of the great Western stars. One cannot feel sorry for the breed. Nearly all of them bought land on or near the locations where their films were made. Joel McCrea picked up 10,000 acres of prime

California real estate for three bucks an acre. The rest of them, including Rex Allen, did nicely too. They all made such fortunes on skyrocketing land values that they could nearly afford the skyrocketing property taxes, as government really got greedy.

Our table seats were in the first row, and we could hear Rex tuning up backstage. The curtain parted to a round of applause, revealing Rex in colorful Western movie attire. He was sitting on a stool and strumming, temporarily. Rex was drunk, as drunk as a... cowboy.

Suddenly, everything fell apart.

The stool went skittering across the stage. Rex fell straight down and landed on his guitar. After an attempt to sing without musical accompaniment and a few incoherent stories, the rest of the program was dispensed with. Our evening's entertainment was shot to hell, but not quite.

Rex Allen was a gamer. If he couldn't perform, he could play blackjack. We watched him the rest of the night. He had great staying power. I could not believe, after what he had been doing, that Rex looked so good, tanned and youthful. Chill Wills later described it better than I when I complimented him on his rosy face. "That's my Jack Daniels flush, Cousin," he explained. Rex had it too.

That night at the card table, Rex could not make out the cards he was dealt. He was playing two hands at a minimum of a hundred bucks each. He had to ask the dealer what he had. "What have I got, darlin'?" he would say.

The serious drinker often sees double. If this had been true, Rex Allen would have lost four times as much instead of just two.

Everybody loved Rex. He bought drinks for most of the house. All I can say about this is that I am glad that I did not witness this display when I was an impressionable young boy. My faith in Western stars would have taken a mighty beating. As it was, Rex put on a better show than anything he could have done on stage.

Meeting the Smothers Brothers in a hotel bar in Pocatello could not top this. They were then hitting their stride on the college circuit. Tom was funny.

Dick was quiet. It was that way on stage too. Within a few years they would be network stars — and then they weren't. CBS dumped them for being too controversial. Our standards in controversy have changed, and not for the better. The Brothers are still around.

For nostalgia buffs like me, signed picture of the Brothers can be found on eBay sites starting at ten bucks. Signed pictures of Abraham Lincoln can also probably be found on eBay. They cost more.

Disney Studios Gate Guard

"Walt wants it that way."

— Disney Studios Gate Guard
Burbank, California — 1970

During my time in Hollywood, I have been able to visit every major studio lot. If you were not known or recognized, you were treated as if you were a commie or a possible terrorist. This may be considered understandable for many reasons, but I always thought there must be a better way to handle things. The exception was Disney. Every employee on the gate the Mouse built treated you as a welcome visitor.

We were invited there, since the Navy was cooperating with a Disney film called *Bedknobs and Broomsticks*. E. Cardon Walker, a top executive, had served in the Navy during WWII, and in return for the Navy's cooperation on the film, we got a tour of the studio version of the Magic Kingdom.

Walker's office, as I recall, was on the corner of Mickey and Dopey Drives. We swabbies were treated in every way as if we were minor royalty. It was the gatekeepers though that I could not get out of my mind. As we drove out of the gates, I could not resist going out and coming back in to ask the man on duty, "Why are you so damn nice when every other studio in town is so nasty?" His answer is above. Walt had been dead for five years, but this is just an example of how his influence remained.

Disney had some rocky times after Walt's death. The studio's animated offerings were few and not of the quality of *Bambi* and *Cinderella*. *Jungle Book* was the last animated film Walt had a hand in.

Today things are better, and Walt's cockles would surely be warmed by Disney being Number One again in Animation. I am not as convinced that Walt would be happy about pricing at the many Disney Parks around the world. Walt sought to create a unique, nostalgic, and affordable Disney experience for everyone. Today, the common man or woman, or family is being screwed. Walt wouldn't like it.

Dana Andrews, Rod Cameron, Jan Clayton, and Gary Crosby

These names may not mean a great deal to most of you, but they mean a great deal to me, and I would like you to get to know them better. They were a part of a small group of celebrities who appeared in a 1976 movie my business partner Herm and I made called *Hollywood and Vine*, discussing alcoholics and their journey to recovery. Save for Dana Andrews, who was a major star during the war years, and a decade or so after that, none of them were what you would term A-list performers.

Announcing you were an alcoholic, a drug addict, or both was placing you somewhere between a social disease and animal cruelty. It took guts for these folks to come forward, and many, who would not appear, feared a blacklist — a distinct possibility. Hollywood stars who were gay, for example, were almost always forced to hide or deny their life choices.

Dana Andrews was in such major films as *The Best Years of Our Lives*, *Laura*, and *The Ox-Bow Incident*. He also was top billed in one of the very best films on WWII, *A Walk in the Sun*. It was about a platoon that landed in Italy, and while moving forward, captured a farmhouse. It was a great character study of men in combat. There were quick cuts of each of the soldiers as they waited for the whistle that would lead them on a charge across open space under fire to capture the objective. Andrews looked pale and sweaty as he waited. It was small wonder, as he was hung over out of his mind and having to make that charge over and over, he became violently ill. It not only looked realistic, it *was* realistic!

Dana, the shakes notwithstanding, was a shrewd investor in real estate and watched his money closely. After our one-day shoot, Dana filed for unemployment, to which he was entitled. Small wonder he had money and I don't. Years before, right-wing Republican actor Adolphe Menjou, a fervent anti-New Dealer, used to be driven to the unemployment office in his Rolls Royce to collect his check. It was practically a meeting place for performers.

Rod Cameron was also a star, mainly in serials and adventure films, mostly Westerns, at Republic and Universal. He had retired by the time he did our film, and he had nothing to lose professionally by labeling himself an alcoholic in recovery. Still, it took some courage to stand up and be counted.

The social media microscope was not present back in the day, though Rod had made the papers on a few occasions for driving under the influence. We shot our sequence at Rod's home, which unexpectedly had the look of a Chinese museum. Dorothy Cameron, Rod's second wife, had spent much of her childhood in China where her father was a highly placed American diplomat. Dorothy had also been Rod's mother-in-law, which should have made for some fascinating family gatherings. Rod did have a man-cave workshop, and as we filmed he was creating metallic works of art with a welding torch. Although he was a rugged six feet five, he was very much a gentle giant.

Jan Clayton was just a doll. She had made her mark on Broadway in *Carousel* and other musicals such as *Showboat* and *Annie Get Your Gun*. She had little success in movies however, and was best known as Tommy Rettig's super sweet mother in the long running *Lassie* series on television. Jan made an effort to recruit more actresses for our film. Many of these ladies were in recovery but very reluctant to talk about it in public. Jan also did a wonderful job as a board member of the Los Angeles Council on Alcoholism and in working with many facilities treating women with addiction. Jan had done so much for us, in fact, that I promised her if we ever did a film for women, she would produce and narrate it.

A couple of years later, we decided to make a picture, *Women and Alcohol: Through the Drinking Glass*, and I called Jan to tell her we were going ahead.

Just about then a good friend, Dr. Joe Takamine, a heavyweight in the addiction field who had heard of our project, called to say that he thought Carol Burnett would be interested in doing the film. Burnett was a super star, and Joe Takamine was treating Carol's daughter Carrie and the family for their substance abuse problem. What happened after that still makes me cringe. Burnett did the film. Jan Clayton did not. I did not have the courtesy, or the balls, to call Jan to tell her she was being replaced. I felt like a shit, which I was, and the film's success made it seem even worse. Jan Clayton deserved better from me — and she didn't get it.

Gary Crosby was an unusual story in that he had given up alcohol on his own and had been sober for over 20 years. My business partner Herm Saunders had given a recurring part to Gary as the producer of the Jack Webb show *Adam-12,* and Gary had returned the favor. Being the famous son of a famous father like Bing can mean problems, but there were other difficulties with the family dynamic that haunted both Gary and his three brothers. There were some successes in this quartet, but marital and career failures were the norm. Gary had the most talent, but alcohol and anger had caused some severe problems in the areas just mentioned. He stated in the film that, as often as he was able, he would play three sets of tennis every morning, whacking away at that white ball, just to keep his rage at bay. Having the time, and the tennis court, to be able to utilize this type of therapy did not relate to our audience.

Thankfully, Gary found his way into a 12-step program after this and could put his intense, white-knuckling, solitary sobriety behind him. Friends described the new Gary as having mellowed and enjoying his new life.

But Gary had not put the past completely behind him.

In 1963, Gary authored a memoir, *Going My Own Way,* about Bing and the family. Though stressing his improved relationship and love for his father, he had not forgotten the bitter memories of the past. All four brothers became alcoholics, but only Gary found a way out. The twins, Lindsey and Dennis, killed themselves with long guns. Phillip, alone among them, bitterly fought with and disowned Gary Crosby for opening the window to family secrets.

Phillip claimed the book was written only for money and revenge. I believe it was part of Gary's therapy and recovery. None of the four made it to their 70s, including Gary who, the exception among them, had cleaned up his act.

Sadly, as it did so many others of his generation, lung cancer struck Gary Crosby down. He was just 62 years of age.

Fast Cutting

Fast cutting: An editing device that uses a series of quick takes designed to clarify a theme or the character of a player in a short period of time. I cannot vouch for every one of these, as I heard some of them second hand.

Tom Hanks

"That will kill you, pal."

— Tom Hanks, Actor
Hollywood, California — 2017

Tom Hanks said this to my son Richard on a movie set. Richard was eating a piece of catering chocolate cake on his lunch break. Hanks had recently found out he had type 2 diabetes. Tom Hanks wins the John Frederick, recently established, Jimmy Stewart Award, which goes to the most polite, noncontroversial, well-spoken, well-liked, relatively modest, sane leading man in Hollywood.

Jackie Cooper

***"And the old bastard didn't die
for another 25 years."***

**— Jackie Cooper, Actor/Director/Producer
Beverly Hills, California — 1980**

Jackie Cooper, age ten, was nominated for Best Actor in 1931 for his performance in *Skippy*. He attended the informal ceremony, held that year at the Biltmore Hotel. He was accompanied by his mother but somehow ended up in Marie Dressler's lap. Dressler was a wonderful character actress who had made an Irving Thalberg-inspired comeback.

Early in the evening of acceptance speeches, many long even then, young Jackie dozed off. He was rescued from Marie's ample bosom by his mom, about the time Dressler won for Best Actress in *Min and Bill*, with Wallace Beery. Back to sleep until the end of the evening, the youngster was shaken from his slumber by fellow competitor Lionel Barrymore, who had won as Best Supporting Actor for *A Free Soul*. Lionel was still mobile then, and he handed over the golden statue, which not yet named but would be shortly by Bette Davis.

I was told this story by Captain Jack while visiting him on Navy business at his then home south of Sunset.

I had just admired the leather-bound scripts of films Jackie had appeared in and noticed *Skippy* was the first. Jackie mentioned the fact that the film was directed by his uncle Norman Taurog, whom he mentioned was an asshole.

Then Jackie told me, as he had many others, the story of Academy Award night, ending with Barrymore handing the statue and saying, "Young man, this really belongs to you, but they gave it to me because I am an old man and I'm going to die soon."

Jackie Cooper paused and considered the past thoughtfully. "You know," he said, "the old bastard didn't die for another twenty-five years."

Shecky Greene

"Wayne Newton just went off."

— Shecky Greene, Comedian
Las Vegas, Nevada — 1980s

Another great Shecky Greene's quote was, "No spray wax," which goes back to Shecky's drinking days. He was tooling down the Vegas Strip in his sports car at one a.m. when he lost control and ended up in the fountain at Caesar's Palace. No one was hurt and the fountain was not injured badly. Only the car was totaled.

Shecky stuck his head out of the window of the wreck and gave the above quote to the first arriving authority figure. Many think Buddy Hackett, Shecky's good friend, tacked on the line later. Whatever, the next one is absolutely new and fresh.

It was around 1980, and I was paired with Shecky in Vegas in a golf tournament that bore his name. We were held up on a par three by a group that was malingering in the area of the green. There was a large gallery of Shecky lovers who had been following us, and Shecky and individuals in the crowd had been going back and forth. It was great — and then a long delay. Shecky finally looked at his watch and announced, "Wayne Newton just went off." His casino and theater-wise audience broke up. I didn't get it at all until it was explained to me later.

Wayne Newton was famous for his thirst for applause and audience approval. He was King of the Strip in those days. What Shecky was saying was that Newton had finally closed his midnight show from the night before — it now being about ten a.m. Well, it was funny at the time.

Groucho Marx always said that Shecky was the funniest man in the world. Groucho should know.

Peng Meng-ji

*"Charlie, why aren't we going
to get those airplanes?"*

**— Peng Meng-ji, Chief of ROC Army Staff
Taipei, Taiwan – 1962**

---

merica has always been naive about intelligence gathering, that is, until sometime in the last century. In 1925, a stiff-backed aristocrat named Henry Stimson was Hoover's Secretary of State. When someone went to him and announced that we had broken the Japanese diplomatic code, Stimson was not excited but incensed. "Gentlemen," he announced, "do not read one another's mail."

In 1962, the Republic of China on Taiwan was our only China, and I was stationed there. Chiang Kai-shek and the Nationalists ruled with a mild form of martial law. The danger to the United States was Chiang's insistence that he was "going back to the mainland," which would have been okay, but he had just been thrown off of that property by Mao and his Red hordes. Even with massive support from us, he would have had little or no chance. We had already amply supplied the ROC armed forces with ships, planes, tanks — the whole enchilada. This was for defense of the island. Chiang wanted more, like F-4 Phantom jets. There was still a powerful China lobby, but JFK, who had already had problems with abortive invasions, wasn't looking for more. This was all very hush-hush. "Top Secret NOFORN," was the designation of the messages I broke in the Taiwan Defense Command Headquarters — NOFORN for No Foreign Distribution.

Now the headquarters had been given to us by the Nationalist government. It had been a Japanese hostel during their occupation of the island. Classy building. When the word went down that the word was "NO," General Worden, our Chief of Staff, was delegated to break the news to Peng Meng-ji, Chief of the ROC General Staff.

Peng was really a political General. He spoke perfect English and was called The Grand Eunuch. I haven't the slightest idea why. When Peng met his counterpart, General Worden, his first words are seen above.

Worden kept his temper, but on the way back to headquarters he got very red in the face. He stormed into the Comm Center in a rage and scapegoats and traitors were sought all over the place.

The truth was, the place was bugged. Every place we had people was bugged. We were all very incensed. These were our allies, after all. What was the name on Mark Twain's book? *Innocents Abroad?* I'll say, but looking back, there was something sweet and innocent about it all. Dumb too, of course.

Short Takes and Incidental Contact Sports

Gallery Marshal

"Just stay here; he'll come up for you."

**— Gallery Marshal – Bob Hope Classic
Bermuda Dunes, California – 2009**

Two icons, Bob Hope and Arnold Palmer, met and became friends in the 1950s. Palmer was a star attraction in the annual Bob Hope Desert Classic. Arnie played with Hope, with presidents and celebs, and with common every-day millionaires. As Hope got into his nineties and could no longer appear at his own event, loyal Arnie still showed up. In 2009 Palmer agreed to host the Classic, which had been losing celebrities and top-level golfers due to the pros' dislike of the five-day tournament, the only such event on the PGA tour. Hope had passed, but Arnie was still committed to keeping the event going.

Years before, I had followed The King around the Indian Wells track. I was not alone. Arnold Palmer, especially in a Pro Am, was perhaps the most approachable golfer who ever lived.

Arnie's game had gone downhill and he suffered, not always silently, but the fans still came, and he interacted wonderfully with them. Attractive ladies of a mature age seemed drawn to him. They may have been old friends. Hearing him complain about his game, I was close enough to say, "Arnold, it's like Babe Ruth. We would rather see Ruth strike out than watch an average Joe hit a homer." He acknowledged me but was not consoled.

In 2009 Arnie was still surrounded by fans. I could not get near him. I had been carrying around a book, *Grand Slam*, to various tournaments for years. I had obtained the signatures of over 90 major winners, but the name Arnold Palmer was a conspicuous absentee. At length, Arnie broke free from the crowd and into the Bermuda Dunes clubhouse. I had a pass to the clubhouse, but by the time I got there the Great Man had disappeared. A marshal told me that Palmer had gone downstairs to the locker room. I showed him my military ID and told him about the list of major winners and that I had been trying to get a Palmer autograph "for years." I asked if it would be all right if I waited till Arnie came upstairs again. I was pleasantly surprised by the marshal's reply. He must have been one of Arnie's thousands of friends.

Sure enough, Arnold Palmer came up from the men's locker room just to sign my book. He asked about my Navy service, and I asked the same about his in the Coast Guard. It must have been good duty for Arnie. I think he won the U.S. Amateur while he was in the service. He signed his picture with that beautiful eminently readable signature. He was, and is, The King.

Paul Azinger

— Paul Azinger, Golfer
Bermuda Dunes, California — 1980's

Again watching the Hope, Paul Azinger, a cancer survivor, was also a top pro golfer. While playing a par 5, trying to reach the green in two, he hit a horrendous hook that landed in another zip code. A lady spectator tried to console him, "Oh, too bad."

"No lady," Azinger answered, "just bad."

Pádraig Harrington

"It's not life or death."

— Pádraig Harrington, Golfer
Sherwood Country Club – Tiger Woods Challenge
Thousand Oaks, California – 2006

P ádraig Harrington, the ever-smiling Irish golf professional, was formerly an accountant. This came in handy in assessing his assets after three major tournament wins and a highly successful career on the European and U.S. golf tours. I had a friend, Ray Kennedy, an old rocker lead singer, who invited me to the Tiger Woods tourney at Sherwood. I lived there and we walked over to the course.

Ray had arranged through Pádraig's caddy, Ronan Floyd, both rock and roll music buffs, to meet with the golfer after the Sunday round. Pádraig was leading the tournament that Sunday and was ahead on the 18th, until he suffered a duffer-like double bogey and lost by a stroke. This cost him several hundred thousand dollars, and, worse, put our meeting with the Dubliner in peril.

After the round, Pádraig Harrington went straight to the practice putting area. Cautiously, Ray Kennedy approached Ronan Floyd to commiserate about the loss. To our surprise, Pádraig was more than willing to come over and talk and pose for pictures. Both the golfer and his main man Ronan appeared unaffected by the loss. I could hardly believe it.

"Aren't you... the slightest bit disappointed and angry?" I asked looking closely for Pádraig's reaction. He smiled that smile, and what he said was a lesson for me. I had been losing my temper on the golf course. It cured me. Who was I to get upset over a missed two-foot putt that cost me five bucks? My golf is getting worse, but it is more fun than ever. Will wonders ever cease? I have a signed picture of the event on my desk. We are all smiling.

Jim Furyk

"Sometimes we're afraid too."

— Jim Furyk, Golfer
Sherwood Country Club — Tiger Woods Challenge
Thousand Oaks, California — 2010

The 12th hole at Sherwood is a par three, with water all down the right side and sand traps on that side of the green which fall away sharply from the middle of the putting surface. I have played the hole many times, and never very well, even at a hundred-fifty yards. The pro's use the back tee, which is over two-hundred yards.

During a Pro Am, before the tournament I saw four amateurs in one foursome plunk four balls into a tiny creek no more than twenty yards from the tee. Presumably they paid 25 grand and up to make fools of themselves in front of a large gallery. It was lovely.

Jim Furyk played a shot to within fifteen feet of the hole. As he passed me, I mentioned that, when standing on the tee I was scared to death to bring the club back. He was good enough to say that professionals sometimes have thoughts of dread when facing such a challenge. Furyk is one of the more accessible of the PGA tour members. He has a loopy-doopy swing that flies in the face of golf instructors since time immemorial. It is very repeatable though, and whatever flaws the purists might find in it, it has kept the likeable Jim in the top ranks of pro golfers for more than two decades.

Ian Poulter

"I'm afraid I can't help you with that sir."

— Ian Poulter, Golfer
Sherwood Country Club — Tiger Woods Challenge
Thousand Oaks, California — 2010

Ian Poulter is a British golfer who has made a habit of spoiling the hopes of the United States Ryder Cup Team by sinking putt after putt from everywhere in sight during several of the bi-annual classics. Ian had fallen off a bit in the past few years and had not made a Ryder Cup appearance for a while. A colorful dresser, Poulter has his own line of golf apparel, and we who root for the American side were hoping that he would stick more to business than to golf.

That changed in the last months. Ian has won again on the U.S. PGA tour and has contended a few other times. He looks a sure bet to make the European team, bringing his accursed putter with him. We shall see, but it is not a comforting thought. In the midst of his assault on American golf supremacy in 2010, I approached Ian Poulter with a request that he take it easy on us the next time we met the Europeans. He answered with a sly bit of English humor. I hope it is not an augury of future Ryder Cup matches. This man is dangerous.

Tiger Woods

"I'll sign for you after the round."

— Tiger Woods, Golfer
Sherwood Country Club – Tiger Woods Challenge
Thousand Oaks, California – 2010

Tiger Woods is a great golfer. For the longest time, it appeared he would be the greatest ever. Only injuries stopped him. As a personality, Tiger reminds me of a Hall of Fame baseball pitcher named Steve Carlton. Carlton is also one of the all-time greats. He regarded America's pastime as an inner game, exclusively between him and the catcher. The opposing team, the press and, perhaps, even his teammates and the fans were an intrusion on his private game.

Carlton could be snappish and surly, especially to the press. Cue Tiger Woods.

The love affair between Tiger and his fans often was a one-way street. Since his back surgeries, he seems to have mellowed somewhat. At this annual event at Sherwood, I would approach him during the Pro Am before the tournament and ask for an autograph in my sacred book of major winners. Almost all the other pros would sign on Pro-Am day, as it was merely a practice round for them before the actual tournament. Tiger would not sign then, or, as it turned out, ever for me. I would slog up the hills of Sherwood to stand beside the scorers' tent in order to be first in the signing line. He never failed to zip by me, signing as few autographs as possible, speeding away from the rabble as quickly as he could.

I am not a fan.

Epilogue: I give up. Tiger just won the Masters. I said he would never win another major. This prediction joins three other gems of mine. I said the *Titanic* would be a flop because we all knew how it came out. *Godfather* would be a flop because since Little Caesar there had been so many shows about Italian gangsters. Oh, and Mel Gibson's movie about Christ would tank because everyone in it spoke Aramaic or Etruscan or whatever. Sign me up for the, sigh, Tiger Woods fan club.

Warren Spahn

"I tried to keep half the ball on the black."

— Warren Spahn, Pitcher
Biltmore Hotel, Los Angeles, California – 1990s

Warren Spahn was the most successful left-handed pitcher who ever lived. He won 363 games AFTER the age of 25, having taken time out to enlist in the Battles of the Bulge and the bridge at Remagen. He won a Purple Heart and a battlefield commission. To show how times have changed, the most money he ever made in a season was 60 grand. He made more later from autograph signings and other events, like the national convention of candy makers, which is where I met him. I also got to meet an old friend from my boyhood, the Sky Bar. Not only were they giving candy away, but I got to go to lunch with Warren Spahn.

With Baseball Hall of Famer Warren Spahn

For old times' sake, we went to the Biltmore Hotel, where the Milwaukee Braves, Spahn's old team, had stayed when they were in Los Angeles. The conversation was about old-time baseball.

In Spahn's early years, the teams traveled by train. There was card playing and occasional horseplay but also a lot of baseball talk. Hotel lobbies were also conversation pits with more talk about the Great American Game.

It was two to a room in those days. Spahn's roommate was fellow pitcher Lew Burdette, and that meant more baseball discussions.

As a modestly successful high school and college pitcher, I was most interested in Spahn's theories of pitching. He had a beautifully deceptive motion with a high leg kick, and when his fastball lost a few inches, he developed other pitches. He was a big winner in his forties, going 23–7 at age 42. His approach to hitters was to come at them in three or four pitch combi-

I was lucky enough to have met and talked baseball with two baseball Hall of Famers: Ernie Banks, Mister Cub (pictured here) and Warren Spahn, the winningest left-hand pitcher of all time.

nations, each with a certain purpose. Then he talked about putting half the ball on the black, the rubber border around the plate. It was too much. I felt like a third-grade math teacher listening to Einstein explain relativity.

Darrell Evans

"I have seldom seen such horseshit baseball."

— Darrell Evans, Baseball Player/Manager
Long Beach, California — 2003

Darrell Evans will never make the Baseball Hall of Fame. He did, however, play 21 years in the major leagues for the Giants, Braves, and Tigers. He did hit 414 home runs. He also was one of the few players to hit 40 home runs in a season — after the age of forty. The most amazing statistic about Evans is that, in 21 seasons, he never once went on the DL, the dreaded Disabled List. This is hard to believe, given the myriad injuries to major league players in this day and age. Darrell also coached in the majors and managed in the minors. One of the teams he managed was the Long Beach Armada.

A friend of mine, Bob Case, was a close childhood friend of Darrell Evans. As a young man, Bob had served as Casey Stengel's business manager, had played the game and been around baseball all his life. We took in a Sunday game in Long Beach, and before and after the game we were invited to spend time in the Armada locker room and the adjacent manager's office.

Sadly, on that day the Armada put on a woeful exhibition of fielding, running, and hitting in a losing cause. Not even the presence in the lineup of former major league slugger Jose Canseco could save the Armada from sinking. In an odd, rather sad happening during the game, the opposing pitcher managed to break his arm while throwing a pitch in the sixth inning, thus being the only pitcher in recorded history to win a game with a broken arm.

After the disaster, manager Darrell Evans was livid. With a friendly word or two to Bob and me, he stormed out and into the players' locker room, slamming the door shut as he did so. I could hear him yelling through the wall, but not clearly, so I walked over and put my ear to the door, the better to gain a writer's knowledge of what is said and done in such situations.

Through the door I could hear Evans as he hurled a variety of epithets and obscenities at his subdued charges. Some I had never heard before, and some may have never been used in connection with the game of baseball. It was an expletive explosion.

Suddenly, there was total silence.

I pressed my ear even closer to the door. This proved to be a mistake as Darrell had concluded his sermon and stomped my way, which was the way the door happened to open — on my ear. I was not badly hurt, just a scar or two, and a ringing in my head that lasted for the better part of a week.

I had breakfast with Bob Case today, some fifteen years later, and he kidded me about the incident. It was worth it. For my pains, Darrell Evans gave me two signed baseball cards.

Pee Wee Reese

"I just hope I ain't next."

**— Pee Wee Reese, Baseball Player
Los Angeles, California — 1993**

Who could not love a major league player whose name is Pee Wee? For those who wished to look a little closer, his first name was really Harold. Ever since his boyhood as a champion marble shooter in his home Louisville, Kentucky, the world knew him as Pee Wee Reese. Like many of his peers in their early twenties when World War II came along, Pee Wee's major league career was interrupted by military service. This did not stop the Brooklyn Dodger great from being elected to the Baseball Hall of Fame.

After his playing days, Reese became a radio and television broadcaster and was also a representative of the iconic Louisville firm of Hillerich & Bradsby, the world's foremost maker of baseball bats. Under normal circumstances, I never would have seen or met Pee Wee Reese, whose financial success precluded having to make appearances at autograph shows and the like, but circumstances were not normal.

I am fuzzy about the occasion, but I know the year was 1993, and Pee Wee Reese was in Los Angeles to honor the memory of two of his Dodger teammates. Both Roy Campanella and pitcher Don Drysdale had recently passed within a month or so of each other. Pee Wee and his former teammate, gritty right-handed reliever Clem Labine, were seated near enough to me so that between innings of a Dodger game, I was able to engage them in conversation. I said what an honor it was for me to meet them, but that I regretted that it had to be on an occasion such as this.

As things turned out, Pee Wee wasn't next but he did not survive the 20th Century. He will live on though, and not just for his prowess on the diamond.

In 1946, Reese as a Southerner had been greeted before the baseball season that year with the news that the Dodgers had signed Jackie Robinson, a black man, to a contract. This was breaking the color line, which had been in place for decades. Not only would Pee Wee be expected to play with a Negro, that Negro was an infielder, which threatened Reese's job directly. Many of Pee Wee's friends and later some of his teammates expected him to take a stand for "Southern values" and refuse to play beside Robinson. A petition was drawn up by some players who said they would not play on the same team with one of another race. Reese refused to sign the petition, and the disgruntled players were sent elsewhere.

In 1947, after a fine year in Montreal, Robinson went to spring training with the team. He endured insults, threats, and more from fans, and sullen silence from many of his teammates. To the contrary, from Pee Wee Reese, Robinson found acceptance and something more. In Cincinnati, it was either in '47 or early 1948, Robinson took the field to the usual hoots and catcalls. Reese went over to his teammate and, in a simple gesture of friendship, put his arm around this black pioneer.

It seems so little, but it meant so much.

Discrimination was not ended in baseball, but Pee Wee Reese gave it a pretty good whack. Pee Wee Reese was small in stature, but in human and racial terms, though he might disagree with any comparison to the Dodgers hated baseball rival, Pee Wee was really a Giant.

Joe Namath

"Happy to."

— Joe Namath, Quarterback
Bel-Air, California – 1977

It was late in 1977. I was playing golf in a threesome at Bel-Air Country Club. Our group was just getting ready to tee off on 10, the famous bridge hole at Bel-Air, a short iron shot over a very deep canyon. The starter approached us and asked if it would be possible for a fourth to join us on the back nine. The newcomer turned out to be Joe Namath, playing his last season in the NFL for the Los Angeles Rams.

The football season was still going, but Joe Willie would not start another game. He had been benched after a poor performance against the Chicago Bears. It had been eight years since Namath had made good on his boast, and the American League New York Jets had beaten the NFL champion Baltimore Colts in Super Bowl III. The Jets had gained respectability for their league, and Joe Namath became a sports hero.

And here we were, playing golf with a legend, a banged-up legend, but a legend nevertheless. Joe was wearing a knee brace and his swing was affected, but he was still a good player. Nothing special about the round. Our conversations were mostly about golf. We did not press Joe for stories of his heroics, and he did not offer any. It was just a pleasant morning on the golf course and our celebrity guest was a far cry from Broadway Joe. He was just a nice, warm guy to play golf with. On the 18th we shook hands after our game, and we all headed for the men's grill, a sanctuary for males only in those days. The room lit up when Namath entered — half the place wanted Joe to join them. Broadway Joe made his first appearance on the scene, and we soon lost him in a crowd.

The fawning over fame on that day, and many others, created a revulsion in me that I have never lost, though I too feel drawn and fascinated by their talent. Years later, at Lakeside Country Club, I was sitting in the bar with one of my business partners and a few strangers. Roman Gabriel was the Rams quarterback by then, and as he moved past us, the guy seated beside me, a sycophant first class, uttered something like "Hey Quarterback, how are things, Big Guy?" Gabriel eyed us briefly and strode by without a word. My unknown neighbor whispered in my ear, "He's a fag!"

Well, fuck you too, buddy. It was as if, disgusted by his own ass kissing and boot licking, the jerk decided to tarnish the object of his affection. Weird.

Anyway, I got up and left.

Back to Bel-Air and 1977. My two golf partners were actors who had just appeared in a film of ours. We sought out a quiet corner and had a drink or two. One of them, Joe, the Dodge Sheriff in a series of TV commercials, noted the fact that I did not drink alcohol and wanted to know about it. I gave a two-minute version of my drinking history. The other man, who played the sheriff's deputy in our movie and the medic on *Combat*, a long-running, successful show on ABC, had been nodding his head as I spoke. "That's me. I drink like that," he said.

Later, he would ask me how I did it. I told him, and he took my advice. Conlan Carter quit acting, became a commercial pilot, moved to Florida in his work, bought an orange grove, sold it, and became a millionaire. He lives quietly in Branson, Missouri, owns two beautiful houses there, one for his wife and one for his mother-in-law. Conlan spends some of his time on a motorcycle and at his condo in Florida. He has been sober for over 40 years.

Sorry, back to Namath again, still in the midst of a mob. While Joe, Conlan, and I were leaving, Namath spotted us and waved goodbye. I could not pass up this opportunity.

My son Richard, fourteen, was a huge Namath fan. I asked Namath if he would sign a photo to Rich Frederick. He did, and though the "green flies" were all over him, he took Rich's name and address down on a bar napkin and stuffed it in his back pocket, saying he would send a photo along. I thought this would be the end of it till two weeks later, when a protected brown envelope marked "Do Not Bend" arrived in the mail.

Joe Namath had kept his promise. Am I a Namath fan? Don't ask. Two weeks ago, forty years later, I asked Rich what happened to the signed photo. He looked at me blankly. "Have no idea," he said. Shakespeare was right, "How sharper than a serpent's tooth," a careless 55-year-old child. I decided to forgive him. He is quite a nice man, and Joe would understand. He is part of our sober circle now, making the best of today.

Broadway Joe is doing just fine.

Bob Welch

"Nothing happens out there until I throw the baseball."

**— Bob Welch, Pitcher
Los Angeles, California — 1980**

Bob Welch was a 21-year-old pitcher for the Los Angeles Dodgers when he struck out Reggie Jackson in a dramatic confrontation in the 1978 World Series. The next year's headlines for the young right-hander were more personal. Welch had entered a treatment program for alcoholism prior to the 1979 season, becoming one of the first athletes in sports to do so. Because of my own interest in this subject, in 1980 our company, FMS Productions, produced a film *Comebacker: The Bob Welch Story*. There was a double meaning to this title. In baseball terms, a comebacker is a ground ball hit directly back to the pitcher. The second *Comebacker* traced the beginning of Welch's journey from addiction to recovery.

The project was brought to my attention by Ed Schuman, an award-winning documentary film maker who, ironically, knew almost nothing about baseball. Ed and I attended a Dodger game in which Bob Welch pitched a 27-out one-hitter against the Atlanta Braves. The game would figure prominently in the upcoming film, but not by design. One of the inside stories in our movie was the friendship between Bob and his teammate and fellow pitcher, Rick Sutcliffe.

At Dodger Stadium with Cy Young winner Bob Welch

Rick Sutcliffe had observed Welch's drinking with mounting concern, when his friend showed up drunk at Candlestick Park before a game with the San Francisco Giants. Rick, Dusty Baker, and a few other players managed to hide the obviously intoxicated Welch in the faraway Dodger bullpen, out of sight of the manager, Tommy Lasorda. From this time on, Rick Sutcliffe encouraged his friend to seek treatment, and when Welch did so a few months later with the support of the Dodger front office, Rick was the first person to visit Welch and to assist in the recovery process.

We did some filming at The Meadows, the treatment facility where Bob Welch was a patient. Most of the other scenes were shot at Dodger Stadium, thus fulfilling a lifelong fantasy for me. Our cameras followed Welch as he drove to the stadium, parked in the players' lot, walked through the park to the clubhouse, donned his uniform, and walked down the tunnel to the bullpen. These shots were all done when the park was empty, and I walked together with Bobby, step by step. In civvies we walked to the mound and I was able to throw a few balls from the pitching rubber. "How good can it get?" I thought.

When it came time for Bob to take his regular turn on the mound that year, we contracted with Major League baseball to use their photographer to film batting practice, warmups, and interviews with Tommy Lasorda, Dusty Baker, Rick Sutcliffe, and other Dodger players, and then to film the game itself. The game went as if I had scripted it. Again it was another game with Atlanta. Bob had a three-run lead and held it until the 9th. Rick Sutcliffe came into the game in relief to save the day, just as he had helped save Bob's life. Unfortunately, Jeff Burroughs hit the only home run he had all year, a grand slammer, and the Dodgers lost — and I lost my closing scene. We were over budget in our little picture anyway and this one about killed us.

After moping about for two or three days, I developed a Plan B. Had the one-hit game been televised? We could transfer it from tape to film, more money, but that game held our happy ending. The answer was "yes, sort of." It had not been televised for the LA audience but was televised as a feed to Atlanta and baseball fans there. This meant Atlanta announcers had called the game, and this would not do for Los Angeles fans. On to Plan B-1. Was the Dodger radio call available? Yes. We had Vin Scully, but now we had to marry his words to the Atlanta TV coverage. More money. I had been enjoying my middle-aged fantasy, we had overcome many problems, and now fiscal reality entered the picture. We got the footage of Bob striking out Reggie Jackson, a great opening scene. Major league baseball was cooperative. They also wanted money. Finally, we had our game footage stitched together.

And how was Bob Welch doing in the midst of all this? For starters, he was sober. In spring training there had been a team meeting where Bob took responsibility for his problem and for the distraction that his treatment had created in the press. All he wanted to do now was to play baseball. The players, good teammates, rallied round and voiced their support. Sandy Koufax, a spring training pitching coach, was an understanding ally. Manager Lasorda and his coaching staff were more guarded. They disliked any element that took away from the game itself. They would wait to see what happened.

Tommy Lasorda, for one, did not like the word alcoholic connected with any of his players. Lasorda had a gay son. He did not want to hear about that either. Lasorda was adored by the great majority of fans — around Dodgertown itself, not so much. He arrived bearing a stack of 8x10s, prepared to sign autographs for all and sundry. He wanted to talk about "bleeding Dodger blue." The Meadows staff, a confrontational bunch by nature and training, wanted to probe a little deeper into the life of a person who would have a large say in the post-treatment life of their client/patient. The Hall of Fame manager's departure was abrupt, though he did leave a number of signed photos.

Our movie was now coming together, till we hit another bump in this long road. I had written the script for Bob to narrate his own story. This did not work. He could not clearly project words that were written for him. He could only speak his truth in his own voice.

On to Plan B-2. We had to find the right words in four hours of tape that Ed Schuman had recorded before we entered the project. There was no record of what was on the tapes, so it became a baseball audio game of seek and find. This took time and more money, but there was enough there to make it work. During this period, Bob Welch and I had a few meals and a few rounds of golf together, but he was a hard person to get to know. Basically, Bob was a very shy person, but as a star athlete in basketball and baseball, he had developed a certain sense of entitlement. This caused him to be late for production meetings. At least once, he did not show up at all. More money, which reminded me of an old moviemaker's saying, "In feature films, the director is God; in documentaries, God is the director." – Alfred Hitchcock. The writer and producer are just along for the ride.

One of the last scenes to be filmed was to recreate a confrontation between Bob and Dodger icon/exec Don Newcombe that resulted in Welch's accepting treatment. Amazingly, it was a one-take wonder.

Both Bob and Don turned out to be great role players. Professional actors could not have done better. It was smooth sailing the rest of the way.

The picture was a success. Bob Welch went on to win more than 200 games and become one of the top 100 pitchers of all time in major league baseball history. He won the Cy Young award in 1990, and, at this writing, his 27 wins in that year are the most for any major league hurler since. In an era of pitch counts and arm troubles from sliders, splitters, and cutters, this is a record that may stand the test of time.

I saw Bobby occasionally in his playing days, and when he was a pitching coach for the World Series champion Arizona Diamondbacks in 2001. He was doing quite well, had married his college sweetheart, Mary Ellen, had a couple of kids, and his recovery seemed secure.

In retirement, however, rumors about Bob began to surface about a cocaine problem. I hoped they were not true. Rumors can be such ugly things. His marriage ended, which was another bad sign. I was surprised — not shocked, just surprised — when news of his death in a fall at his home reached me from a mutual friend. It is one thing for a 100-year-old George Burns to slip and fall in a shower, but in the case of a healthy, athletic, youthful, middle-aged man, there will always be doubts. Alcoholism is cunning, baffling, powerful, and most of all patient.

Bob Welch was 57 years old.

Thomas Henderson

> ### *"Guilty? Of course he's guilty — guilty as hell!"*
>
> ### — Thomas Henderson, Football Player/
> ### Motivational Speaker
> ### Austin, Texas – 1994

Thomas "Hollywood" Henderson was the National Football League's first cocaine casualty. The fast and powerful special teams and strong side linebacker for the Dallas Cowboys and San Francisco 49ers was much

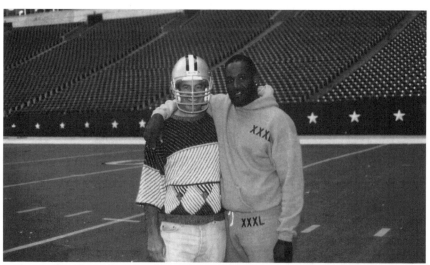

Texas Stadium for the film, *Second Half*. I could not get the helmet on without an assist from NFL great "Hollywood" Henderson.

more than that. For a few short years, he was one of the most exciting football players in the world, but he was more than that too. His wild and colorful ways, coupled with a motor mouth almost always in motion, made Hollywood a kind of P.T. Barnum and Dizzy Dean clone, with some self-destruction thrown in on top of his great talent. Though it was almost impossible not to like Thomas, his behavior drove his teammates and his Eagle Scout coach Tom Landry to the brink of anger and despair.

It all came to a head just prior to Super Bowl XIII, between the Cowboys and the Pittsburgh Steelers. Thomas had taunted Terry Bradshaw, "Bradshaw couldn't spell "cat" if you spotted him the 'C' and the 'A'." The Cowboys lost and Hollywood was snorting cocaine from an inhaler while on the field. It was downhill from there. The funny, good times with Hollywood tying some sheets together and sneaking out of the Cowboy training camp to party were over.

Thomas played for a few more years, but the magic was gone. It ended in a crack house with Hollywood being charged with sexual assault on two young girls. After one stint in rehab and an attempt at the marijuana maintenance approach to recovery, Thomas came under the care of Dr. Joe Pursch, who had headed up the intervention team that brought Betty Ford to recovery. Though Thomas had no medical insurance by then, Pursch, who was the medical director for the Care Unit system, moved his patient around until he had 120 days of sobriety under his belt.

Thomas had been convicted of the sex crimes and was on his way to prison in San Luis Obispo, California. Prison is normally not a place to get or stay clean and sober, but Thomas had embraced his new life and he made it through. The NEW Thomas was born in November 1983, and he has been clean and sober ever since.

Baseball had been my game, and we had made a film with Dodger pitcher Bob Welch that had turned out well. Football... that was something else again. Our high school football coach had seen me catching passes in an intramural game and asked me to come out for the team. "Football is a stupid game," I told him. This coach often took part in the gym class games, and he spent the next year trying to deck me. I was too cowardly and fast for him.

By 1990, our company, FMS Productions was facing a challenge. Our major market, addiction treatment programs in hospitals, was in trouble. Insurance companies, weary of the high rate of relapse and, as always, anxious to save money, had turned off the bucks. There was another market out there — the prison system. A large number of the incarcerated had gotten into trouble while under the influence of alcohol or drugs, or had committed robberies and thefts in order to get money for drugs.

My son Randall had been in touch with Hollywood Henderson with the idea of making a movie for that prison population, a large percentage of which were minorities, and Hollywood had been a very famous black athlete. I was doubtful. To make a film with a leading personality, and then see him or her relapse or possibly even die, would be counterproductive, not to mention bad for business. I would, I told my son, meet with this Hollywood Henderson, and so it was arranged. Thomas was living at the time in nearby Costa Mesa, and we met on his turf at his favorite restaurant, The Palms, fittingly enough in Hollywood. I learned in the first few minutes of our conversation that you did not meet with Hollywood; you were overwhelmed by him. His personality, if anything, was bigger than he was. I could see and feel the power in him.

Before he turned that power loose on me, I had two questions. I asked if he was guilty of the crimes that had put him behind bars. Like most inmates, he said he was innocent. A crimson flag popped up, but what he said next lowered the pennant as quickly, "Even though I didn't do it, I got away with so much I wasn't caught for that I figured it all evens out." Score one for Hollywood. I then asked about his nickname. "Man, there's lots of Thomas Hendersons, but only one HOLLYWOOD!" I was sold, but just to make sure, I called Dr. Pursch, a former Navy psychiatrist and friend with whom I had made several award-winning films, both before and after the Betty Ford intervention.

No doctor in the field would ever think of predicting the outcome for an alcoholic or addict after treatment, but it was apparent that Joe was sold on "Hollywood's" chances. So, we took a chance and made the movie. It was called *Second Half* and stressed the recovery part of Thomas' life. We used

NFL footage from his glory days, and the Cowboys were good enough to let us use old Texas Stadium for half a day. I got to run around on the field, age 52, catching passes and punting the football. The next day I could hardly walk. The artificial turf was less than a quarter-inch thick over concrete. Pro games there should have had broken bones on every play. Anyway, the film was a big success, which was a personal relief, since I had put my house in Lake Sherwood up to finance it.

Thomas, having learned a thing or two about making movies, decided to eliminate the middle man and make and sell his own films, which he did and has continued to do so with positive financial results that also helped heal countless members of his unseen audience. Thomas "Hollywood" Henderson is still out there. He has spoken to groups all around the country, many without charge. He has created a Youth Foundation and aided the inner city in his home Austin especially, by building playgrounds and recreational areas where none had been before. Thomas got 25% of the gross on our film, which put a nice amount of cash in his pocket. He was his own best negotiator.

Thomas had also authored a book about himself called *Out of Control*. It really should have been titled, as Bing Crosby's autobiography was, *Call Me Lucky*. With all his gifts, the fates were on his side as well. Thomas hit the Texas lottery for 26 million bucks. He actually scored twice, but the second was only 20 grand and can be dismissed.

Luck is often sought but seldom captured. Napoleon, on St. Helena, was asked what particular quality did he most prize in his marshals. Was it audacity, bravery, tenacity? His answer was to the point, "I wanted them to be lucky," he said.

Good and lucky, that's Thomas Hollywood Henderson.

Though bad and good are just general, qualitative terms that are often inaccurate, I have found in my life when a "bad" person turns "good," he or she can be a positive force in the ledger of life. Ledger of life sounds ostentatious, but high-flown clichés have helped me through life, and doubtlessly have aided Thomas too. Not that he needs much help these days. I stayed in touch with Thomas for a few years after our filming. He had meetings on addiction and the criminal justice systems with politicos like George W. Bush, then governor of Texas, and whom he found "pleasant but stubborn and unyielding."

I happened to glance at daytime television one day in June 1994 and watched with the rest of America as a white Bronco slowly toured the freeways of Southern California. I knew that the NFL had retained Hollywood to counsel players and former players who were having trouble with substance abuse. O.J. Simpson was one of them, but he wasn't buying what was being offered — sobriety and recovery. I called Hollywood and asked his opinion of Simpson and what had just transpired. His reply was graphic and brief. It did not surprise me.

Thomas is above race.

He meets every one of any color with a cool eye and completely open mind as to how he or she will fit into the Henderson game plan. I truly believe that Hollywood Henderson would be Governor of Texas if he did not have a felony conviction — at worst, mayor of Austin. He would be a good one too.

Mo Freedman

"You'll know when you know that you don't know."

— Mo Freedman, Football Player/Coach
Los Angeles, California — on numerous occasions

Mo Freedman was a center on the gritty little Bruins, a college foot-ball team that won the 1966 Rose Bowl game against the big, pow-erful, undefeated Michigan State Spartans. UCLA had no chance, everyone had said. They were out-weighted, out-manned, and probably out-coached. It turned out that they were none of those things, and their swarm-ing defense and inspired team play produced one of the biggest upsets in football history. Many of that group became football coaches themselves. Mo Freedman was one of them.

Crespi High is a small, Catholic preparatory school in Los Angeles, California. In the years 2015–2017, Crespi won a total of five football games. In the early 1980s, the Crespi Celts were not doing much better. When Mo Freedman became their coach in 1983, he had high hopes and little else. The small enrollment at the school and its reputation for scholastic excellence were regarded as positives, but not for the football program. Demographic changes and a greater emphasis on athletics by school administration were signs of progress, but there was a problem.

Crespi suddenly had a large number of black athletes. Their color was not the problem. It turned out that many of these players had an affiliation with two gangs, the Crips and the Bloods. Their bloody rivalry has been well documented. These young men loved the game of football, but not one another. A Bloods quarterback would rather assault his Crips wide end than throw him a pass. The Crips offensive guard saw no reason to open up a hole in the opposing line for a Bloods halfback. These were problems that seemed insoluble.

Mo and his staff worked tirelessly to promote a team concept. "We are a team. We work, we play as a team. We win as a team." It was not all Knute Rockne pep talks. Mo Freedman dealt in life lessons. Over days and weeks they took effect and the Crespi Celts bonded as a team. Mo took young men, "hip, slick, and cool," who thought they knew it all and taught them that football and life was a learning experience only enjoyed by individuals with an open mind, ready to learn and grow. They were undefeated in conference play that year and played the championship game at the Los Angeles Coliseum.

They lost, but Mo thought later that the realization that they were playing on a field where the USC Trojans and the Los Angeles Rams had performed was almost too much for the team, that they could not themselves believe their success and, consequently, did not play their best. Still, it was another life lesson, another learning experience. For Coach Mo, he knew for a fact that his words and his philosophy had hit home when he would run into his former players through the years and they would rush up to him saying, "Coach Mo, we know that we don't know, and we're learning to know."

Football can be more than a game.

Muhammad Ali and Miguel Cabrera
1980s/2011

My contact with these two sports heroes was about as incidental as it gets. Nice vignettes though.

In the late 1980s, I attended a California boxing awards luncheon in downtown Los Angeles with my old friend Bob Case. Bob was a vice president in the International Boxing Association, headed up by his old baseball buddy Dean Chance. It was the usual rubber chicken and long speeches kind of thing with not a lot of excitement going on until there began to be a buzz around the large dining room. There were several hundred attendees, former and current champions, but this was something special. Muhammad Ali had entered the building and was greeted with a long ovation. I didn't get to see him — he was surrounded by fans and well-wishers — until the affair ended.

Outside on the street, Muhammad was still in the midst of an adoring crowd, but I walked through them, right up to the Great Man, and offered him a handshake. Playfully, he went into a boxing stance and pretended to do battle. I raised my hand in the air in surrender. He smiled, clapped me on the shoulder, and finally shook my hand. Ali had Parkinson's, that was obvious, but it did not own him. The old, life-loving Muhammad shone through, and I felt privileged to see it.

In 2011, Miguel Cabrera of the Detroit Tigers was fast becoming the most feared slugger in baseball. His DUI run-in with the Florida Highway Patrol in spring training that year had put a temporary damper on things, but he had gone through a rehab program and all signs were positive. The Tigers visited

Dodger Stadium early that year, and thanks to my old standby Bob Case, who had many friends in the Dodger front office and broadcasting booth, I found myself with him on the field before the game as the Tigers took batting practice.

Miggy was looking idly into the stands when a three- year-old in a front-row box seat got his attention. The little boy made faces at the player wearing number 27 in a Detroit uniform. Miguel looked rather like a very large child himself. As quickly as that, Miggy started making faces back. For over a minute, these two partners in childhood exchanged grimaces and smiles, giggles and waves. It was as fun to watch as it sounds.

Roy Campanella had it right when he said that "it takes a man to play baseball for a living, but you got to have a lot of little boy in you too." Amen.

Dean Chance and Bo Belinsky

"Bob, we're too old to make new friends."

**— Dean Chance, Baseball Player, Boxing Executive
Wooster, Ohio – 2006**

"I read the Bible every day."

**— Bo Belinsky, Baseball Player
Los Angeles, California – 2004**

The ubiquitous Bob Case is the hero of this story. Bob was a batboy for the Los Angeles Angels baseball team in the early 1960s. He began what would become lifelong friendships with the disparate partnership of Dean Chance and Bo Belinsky, pitchers and playboys united.

Chance was a milkshake-drinking, married farm boy; Belinsky a hard-living pool hustler and lady killer from New Jersey. They both loved nightlife, fun and games and, while they were at it, made headlines and won quite a few ballgames for the Angels.

Belinsky, for a year or two, got more ink than Hall of Famer and Dodger legend Sandy Koufax. Two more opposite personalities than Sandy and Bo do not exist on this planet. Both Dean and Bo are gone now, though through Bob Case I was able to meet them both. Dean Chance won a Cy Young Award and was a 20-game winner twice. Personally, he was warm and folksy — the kind that left city slickers shaking their heads and counting their money after being outsmarted in a business arrangement. Staying close to his 400-acre Ohio ranch, Dean found time to be a carnival barker and run a large number of midway games, always coming out ahead, until he tired of the traveling life. He founded the International Boxing Association, promoted fights, and managed some fighters, always on the plus side of the ledger.

In talking with Dean about baseball, if you had played the game as I had, he made you feel like an equal, as if you could have made the big leagues if you had his luck — or a micro-version of his great curveball that drove Mickey Mantle and many others to the nearest bar.

The above Dean Chance quote came from a weekly phone call between Case and Dean after the former complained about being screwed in a deal with a person he had known and trusted. Dean was really a corn-fed philosopher who had many such wise and pithy sayings for all occasions such as, "The guy found himself on third base and thought he hit a triple." He was the Will Rogers of baseball.

If everything Dean Chance touched seemed to come out on the plus side. Bo Belinsky's life was headed in another direction. Bo still had a way with women. He married a Playboy Playmate, Jo Collins. They had a daughter, but the marriage did not last. Next, he married an heiress to the Weyerhaeuser lumber fortune. Bo's drinking and drugging when the party was over drove wedges between his wives, children, and many of his friends. He ended up living under a bridge.

When things looked their darkest, with encouragement from Bob, Dean, and many others, Bo found recovery and religion, two separate entities, not always united. He became a born-again Christian and entered a 12-step program. He had found his spiritual side and a new life. The new Bo was quiet and reserved — a sharp contrast to the brash and cocky ballplayer. He found employment in, of all places, Las Vegas and worked tirelessly to help others to recover from their addictions and pain. He carved out a whole new reputation for himself, that of a responsible and giving human being.

Bo passed away having a host of friends, both old and new. Bob and Dean, who had been there through it all, were there for Bo at the end, taking charge of the funeral arrangements. Bo Belinsky was 64 years old. A Greek philosopher once said that the most important victory in life is the one over oneself.

That was Bo's story.

Five Good Ones to Quit On And More

Five Good Ones to Quit On and More

How did anyone in prehistoric times, before computers, cell phones, and social media learn to get along and make one's way in the world? If you were lucky, as I was, your learning tree came from many sources — parents, peers, teachers, and other authority figures. Then, there were the movies and baseball. The movies taught me about history, heroes, and heroines, not always accurately, but far more interesting than a classroom. The violent, sociopathic antihero would have to wait his or her turn.

We played sports, which were games and not life or death. My sport was baseball. Uniforms were Levi's and a tee shirt with the name of a laundry or an auto dealership. I didn't get to wear a uniform till American Legion ball, when I was fifteen or so. There was one coach with perhaps a parent assistant. Advice from other parents was neither sought nor accepted. Parents and players both behaved themselves — no temper tantrums. It is odd but I remember baseball games fifty-five or more years ago but cannot recall local, state, or national events of the day with any real clarity. To some extent, we were shielded from them. Even when television arrived, national and world network news were given only fifteen minutes, which was probably enough to touch on the real news of the day. Now we get news 24/7. Are we really more informed or better off?

Back to baseball. Even in college there was only one coach, John Lewis, and an occasional part-timer who had played some pro-ball. I was expected to know how to pitch when I made the team as a freshman. There were no base

273

coaches, bullpen coaches, bench coaches, ad infinitum. The training room had no whirlpool spa or ice-down treatments available. All we had was a giant tub of Atomic Balm, a cure-all for sore arms or muscle aches or pains. I don't remember anyone missing a game or a serious injury of any kind, though if you got Atomic Balm on your genital area as a result of carelessness or a prank, you became an instant screamer. I never had a sore arm in all the years I pitched. Today, you have kids getting Tommy John surgery in high school. There were too many sliders, cutters, and splitters for the arm to handle.

I do wax nostalgic about baseball, which is why my two cousins and I head for spring training in Arizona, as we have for decades. I still can hear the calls of the game, most of them sent to the verbal showers, and the lessons they taught. "Just meet it." "Don't over swing or try to do too much." "Eye on the ball." "Focus, get in the game." "Don't let your mind wander." "Take five and lay one down."

You got five swings and bunted. If your fifth swing was a miss, a pop up, or a dinky grounder, I can still hear coach say, "Quit on a good one," by which he meant a well-hit ball, preferably a line drive. If I hit a liner and coach wasn't looking, I would ask the batting practice pitcher for another pitch or two.

One day, I remember hitting four line drives in a row before he caught me at it. I am going to do one better than that now.

The last five stories involve individuals who have performed in or directed some of the greatest films or most popular television programs in history. They are still with us, they have not gone away; their work still being watched and enjoyed by millions: Charlton Heston, George Burns, Francis Ford Coppola, John Frankenheimer, and Barbara Eden.

And after all this, a special sneak preview.

Charlton Heston

"I think Tom has to step up."

— Charlton Heston, Actor/Author/Activist
Beverly Hills, California – 1991

I f you meet or happen to bump into a movie star, the experience may be disappointing, not at all what you expected. In the flesh is not like looking at them on a sixty-foot-high silver screen. This in-person view is true in other fields as well. Politics, sports, and dating websites come to mind.

Back to the movies. These illustrious idols are not always larger than life and not just physically. George Burns was larger than life, and he could not have been taller than five feet five. A very few will surpass your expectations. My two were John Wayne and Charlton Heston. I have written of Wayne elsewhere in this book, so I will merely mention that his handshake could crack walnuts, and the liver spots on the back of his hands were as large as quarters.

The Naval Reserve Recruiting Command had prepared a script that highlighted the contributions of Naval Reservists in both their civilian and military careers. I had a hand in the preparation of that script, was about to retire from the Reserves as a captain, and this would be a nice capstone to my career. The name of the film was *Twice a Citizen*, words said to be uttered by Winston Churchill in tribute to the Reserves in the Royal Navy and other services. Charlton Heston had agreed to do the project, gratis, but there were months of delays until a hole could be found in his still busy schedule.

Many stars do not live up to their images.
Charlton Heston did, and he was larger than life.

The hole was found in late spring of 1991. As these things often go, we were given one day's notice: the narration to take place at Heston's home tomorrow morning. Fine for me, but our sound recordist, Commander Stephen Fisch, had to drive the night before to San Diego to pick up the equipment from Combat Camera Group at NAS Coronado. Plus, after the recording the next day, he had to return the damn thing to CCG that evening. All I had to do was show up tomorrow in mid-morning, which I did, with the sleepless yet alert Steve Fisch in tow.

We got passed through the gate and Mr. Heston met us just in front of the house. The home, a wonderful example of fifties modern, was set on three acres just under Mulholland and Coldwater at the very tip-top of Beverly Hills. The famous movie community lay unseen below, and there were Santa Monica Mountains across the canyon in every direction. A cantilevered

276

portion of the house hung over the canyon, suspended in space, impressive, as was the homeowner.

Charlton Heston was in his late sixties, bronzed, nearly as tall as John Wayne, and looked ready for three fast sets of tennis, the court being right there. We had arrived for work, however. Heston had his copy of the script, I had mine, and, as we ambled down to an out building behind the tennis court pavilion, he favored us with small talk and some thoughts on the script.

Small talk?

Charlton Heston was incapable of small talk. It was his voice, that, VOICE, that "Old Man River," "Rolling Thunder" voice. Every word was a pronounce-ment and every sentence a proclamation.

My God, I thought, he IS Moses! How could we miss with that voice? Getting that voice on tape proved a bit of a problem. A large room, a party or reception room, in that building seemed promising. It was empty for one thing, because too much clutter plays hell with the sound. Sound checks in the big room were less than satisfactory — too much reverberation.

The necessity of completion led us to a solution, thanks to Steve Fisch. There were a number of pillows scattered about, dozens, as a matter of fact. I have no idea what they were used for, but we appropriated them to build half a pillow igloo along the wall.

Mr. Heston, I could not stop calling him that, sat in our makeshift sound booth and read from the script. It tested perfectly. The narration reading went better, and the playback was gold.

With the pressure off, we all had some drinks, tea and lemonade, as I recall. Chuck (I could call him that now, but I didn't) held forth on his military service in the Army Air Corps in World War II. I nudged him into talking politics by pointing out that being an active, vocal Republican in Hollywood must be a very lonely business. His politics by then had moved from being a Democrat, who marched for civil rights with Martin Luther King, to being a supporter of Ronald Reagan and a conservative Republican. This is a mostly normal pattern as one ages, though I could not help thinking of my father, Paul Frederick, who grew more liberal with each passing year.

Dad and Mom's house in the Arizona desert, just south of Phoenix, was a socialist enclave, surrounded by rednecks who would have been Trump voters, had my parents lived that long, which they didn't. Heston swore he would march with King again, but there were many things about "that other party" that bothered him — like guns.

As a boy, mostly by himself, he had hunted and fished in the Michigan woods. As a man, he had amassed a magnificent gun collection. He believed fervently in the Second Amendment, which is why he accepted the largely conventional position of president of the National Rifle Association. He was not a quiet figurehead. I steered us back to his role as a lonely voice. There are plenty of Republicans in Hollywood, Heston claimed; they just won't admit it. I mentioned Tom Selleck, who had admitted his party preference very softly. Charlton Heston's comment on Selleck is the lead on this story.

Steven and I took our leave eventually. I was so happy with the day. If Heston had been Pope, I would have kissed his ring. I settled, we both did, for a hearty handclasp. Both Steve and I tried to outdo each other in thanking Heston for doing the narration. We could not have been more earnest. Stephen told me that six years later he attended a Navy event at the Beverly Hills Hilton. Heston and his wife were there, and he introduced himself to the actor and his wife, thanking him again and saying that all these years later, *Twice a Citizen* was still being shown throughout the country. Heston's eyes misted. Later that evening, finding Lydia Heston alone, Steve asked about that reaction. She replied, "He has done so many things for others, for other organizations, and he is so seldom thanked for those efforts. It touched him."

I saw Charlton Heston once more after this. It was at the *Los Angeles Times* Festival of Books on the UCLA campus. Heston was there to talk about his meeting the legendary author Ernest Hemingway. He mentioned going to Hemingway's home in Key West. Heston was just beginning to talk of his collection of signed Hemingway first editions when his talk was interrupted by a supercilious, sanctimonious, Beverly Hills liberal gas bag.

I believe in free speech, but this was too much freedom. "Throw the bum out," I found myself yelling. Heston never lost his cool, heard the man out beyond my limits, and told him that he had a right to his views, but he was here to talk about Hemingway. The yammering, sermonizing, asshole finally shut up. When he finished his talk, Charlton Heston got a nice standing O.

I think about Charlton Heston sometimes, and I will never forget the sound of that voice — that voice. They don't make voices like that anymore. And he is still Moses.

P.S., I told the following story to Charlton Heston during the taping of the narration for *Twice a Citizen*. He said he had never heard it before. My mind has an endless collection of odds and ends of little use until a proper situation presents itself.

In 1880, the book *Ben-Hur: A Story of the Christ*, written by Civil War General Lew Wallace, had become an enormous best seller, the biggest in American history. In fact, after the fifties movie version, its sales finally surpassed *Gone with the Wind*. The theatrical firm of Klaw and Erlanger was extremely eager to put it on the stage. Letters were sent to Lew Wallace outlining the benefits of a play, but he expressed little interest.

Abe Erlanger, who was Jewish, hurried to Indiana to meet Wallace in person. Erlanger described the power of a play, indicating that no expense would be spared, including putting the famed chariot race on stage, also giving the General a healthy advance plus a large chunk of the royalties. Wallace was not satisfied. His reply was roughly as follows: "I am aware of the potential financial rewards that may come from my book. I am more interested in seeing the great message of Jesus Christ be proclaimed. Tell me, Mr. Erlanger, do you believe in our Lord and Savior, Jesus Christ?" Abe Erlanger hesitated only briefly, "General Wallace, frankly I don't. My partner Klaw does, but he's up in Boston."

Klaw and Erlanger got to stage the play anyway.

Johnny Grant and George Burns

"George, it is my good fortune to announce the dedication of the George Burns and Gracie Allen stage here at Hollywood General Studios."

— Johnny Grant, Mayor of Hollywood
Hollywood, California — 1979

Hollywood General was the new name for General Service, which had been owned by the Nasser Brothers since 1950 or so. New name, same old studio, renting their stages and providing offices for small-time Hollywood concerns, plus George Burns.

In order to take advantage of the change, my old Navy pal, publicist Harry Flynn, came up with the idea of dedicating one of the old stages to George Burns, its longest living resident.

George had been around the place since World War II or so. His and Gracie's production company, McCadden Productions, was named for a street behind the old lot. George was more than willing to play along; and a handful of press, studio execs, and two major stars, George included, and many minor celebrities turned out for the proceedings.

Hollywood Columnist Marilyn Beck and George Burns hosted our Hollywood Outtakes show on NBC.

The Burns and Allen show actually had been shot on that stage, as had movies by Abbott and Costello, the Marx Brothers, and the many films of Hopalong Cassidy/William Boyd. It is still in use today.

In 1979, our company hired George for the second of two *Hollywood Outtakes* shows we did for NBC. Though by then George had reemerged as a movie star, he accepted 25 grand to co-host the program with columnist Marilyn Beck, who was there because the show was her idea. This was a great opportunity to get a good look at George Burns up close.

McCadden's offices were just around the corner from mine, and I would drop in occasionally, sometimes for business, often just for pleasure. These spaces reeked pleasantly of cheap cigars and Hollywood history, unlike Ernie Kovacs whose expensive tastes and allegedly twenty-five-dollar cigars, put his poor widow Edie Adams in such debt that it took her years to get out from under. Spurning celebrity charity, Edie worked her butt off and paid off Ernie's debts in full.

Blessed lady. I used to see her having lunch at a café around the corner, looking a tad more matronly than when I saw her on Broadway as Daisy Mae in *Li'l Abner* in 1957. Tina Louise and Julie Newmar were also in that show, which I watched from the balcony of the St. James Theater. Having spent the entire summer away from women while I was at Officer Candidate School in Newport, Rhode Island, I had to be restrained by my friends from leaping from the balcony, à la John Wilkes Booth, though with nothing dire, only sex in mind. It has been a long life, and I do tend to ramble.

Anyway, George Burns preferred El Producto cigars, and there were cases of them lying around. Jack, his invaluable assistant who had been with George almost as long as Gracie, once gave me a box.

To make George comfortable on the show, we hired two writers, Sy Jacobs and Fred Fox, who had been around since Ed Wynn and Joe Penner. The youth craze had taken over Hollywood. Having a track record and experience meant nothing anymore. Except in comedy. Humor remained a mystery to most of the newcomers, raised on shows that relied heavily on laugh tracks. Venerable comedy writers, who knew the "secrets," found a home in sitcom TV. On being a small part of this revelation, I walked around, with a T-shirt that read, "I smoke cigars and I know things."

On shooting day, I watched George work his magic. If he had been more relaxed he'd have been dead. Of course, those two martinis and half a dozen cigars may have helped. *Outtakes* was not bad as those things go, though it did spawn an endless series of pallid and often disgusting imitators. I must plead guilty to starting it all.

New to this biz and unfamiliar with its politics, we lost control of the show to the ever-popular Dick Clark. He knew how the game was played. Although I could have used the money, I did not weep. Confecting a chocolate-covered turd out of a turd is no fun, I can tell you that.

My lasting memory of George Burns was watching him drive on the lot in his new beige Cadillac with a green top. Observing this ritual one morning, I almost lost my life. He drove right at me as if I were invisible, or anyway not visible, and pinned me against a sound stage wall. I was within one or two inches of an unplanned emergency vasectomy. If he had not braked, you would probably not be reading this. I can still see those enormous, magnified eyes behind horn-rimmed glasses, peering at me from just above the steering wheel.

Say goodnight George and goodnight Gracie — together again.

Francis Ford Coppola

"Where is Jimmy Nasser?"

— Francis Ford Coppola, Director/Writer
Hollywood, California — 1980

Today, Francis Coppola is the highly regarded owner of a winery/resort in Napa, California. He is also considered a Hollywood genius, in the manner of Orson Welles. When not being a genius, Welles had problems completing his films. There were eight that had been started but never completed at the time of his death. Francis had his difficulties also. Though little remembered today, his mega hit *Apocalypse Now* had so many problems in shooting and post-production that it had been tagged by the nickname "Apocalypse Maybe" and "the kiss of death, Apocalypse Never." Check with Martin Sheen on the production problems therein. Its editorial delays came from Francis' endless search for the perfect final cut. As great as *The Godfather's* first two films were, it was widely rumored that editorial control of *The Godfather III,* in particular, had passed from Francis.

When I knew him, at any rate, Francis was a failure and a flop. Well, okay, I didn't really know him, and I actually only met him once. But, as usual, I'm getting ahead of myself. My attitude toward the Great Man and his work has more than envy and sour grapes. I had predicted failure for both *Apocalypse* and *Godfathers*. I must have been influenced by the producer who, in the late 60s, had observed that, in case of nuclear attack, one should seek shelter under Francis because, "He hasn't had a hit in years."

My disregard may well have come from that first meeting I alluded to. I was sitting peacefully and dreamily at my typewriter in our historic but humble offices at General Service Studios, a venerable but active relic that had been around since the silents. Francis announced his arrival by kicking in the door to my office, disturbing my creative reverie, and knocking the ash off my cigar. Obviously pissed, he uttered the line at the top of this story. Since I was alone in my room and Jimmy Nasser, the president of General Service, was at least ninety years old, I was momentarily answerless. Belaboring the obvious, I finally managed a reply, "He isn't here."

At the time Coppola was in negotiations with Nasser to acquire the studio. There seemed to be a problem with how things were going. In the end, Francis bought the place and immediately changed its name to American Zoetrope.

The first hint of the new regime's direction was the announcement that all of the old tenants would be relocated. Moving. That meant that I would no longer be able to walk to lunch past the *Ozzie and Harriet* bungalow or to see the *Incredible Hulk* greening in the sun or the *Beverly Hillbillies* and the residents of *Gilligan's Island* hanging out between takes.

The one exception to the departures was George Burns, who had offices there since God had so ordained.

I don't suppose George ever noticed any changes. We were given several months of grace, during which time I was able to observe how the new broom was faring. The new regime's first effort was a mystical romance set in Las Vegas. A neon-lit miniature Vegas backdrop was created on one of the stages. I watched one of the old hands look on in wonder as two feet of new concrete was poured on top of old concrete.

One from the Heart was a small film with a big budget, 20 million dollars — a lot of money at the time. It grossed a cool million, more or less. This was not an auspicious beginning. Another of Francis' ideas was to make the place into a film school to introduce youth to the joys and wonders of filmmaking. Suffer the little children to come unto him, so to speak. They weren't really children, just middle school students from a neighborhood school. It was not a great neighborhood. A grip or gaffer watching the proceedings said, "They came, they saw, and they stole everything in sight." More inauspicion, which ought to be a word even though it isn't.

By now, my business partner Herm and I were snugly in our new digs on Vine Street, across the street from Capitol records. We could still get on the lot, though, and get all the gossip. The stage that hosted *One from the Heart* now had a tail section of a 30s airliner sticking out of the front side of it. Presumably, part of the cabin was somewhere on the inside. This was for their new picture, *Hammett*, the life story of the famous writer of detective fiction and the creator of *Sam Spade*, Dashiell Hammett. Hammett, besides being a noted author was also a communist, an alcoholic, and in love with a playwright, Lillian Hellman. That mix sounds interesting, but the picture died a horrible death. This all meant financial disaster, and Francis Coppola and Zoetrope were facing bankruptcy.

To save himself and his company, Francis sold the studio back to Jimmy Nasser. Coppola's regime had been brief but colorful. However, Coppola's romance with Hammett had not ended. I noted that he had trouble letting go. Francis so believed in the film that he felt a few years later that if the picture could be re-edited and new scenes added, *Hammett* could be a hit at the box office. The principal players in the film had aged, thoughtlessly, their images did not match up, and the plan was abandoned.

With all the snitty things I mentioned in view, Francis Coppola deserves all of the Oscars, Golden Globes, and honors he has won. He earned them by a never say die, don't give up, and get-off-the-canvas-one-more-time attitude. He continued to reinvent himself and triumphed over all. I have seen his winery resort and eaten at his fine restaurant. He is to the Manor House reborn.

One of the things he should get more credit for is for shaming Universal Studios into releasing *American Graffiti* as a feature film. The Universal motion picture brass thought so little of the film that they were going to release it as a TV movie. Francis offered to buy the picture, probably with money he did not have, which made the executives take a second look. Francis boosted the movie careers of such actors as Harrison Ford and Richard Dreyfus, among others, made George Lucas a billionaire, and gave us *Star Wars* forever and ever. Oh, *Happy Days* too, which success led Ron Howard into directing films, which he wanted to do all along. Pretty big returns on a million-dollar bluff.

John Frankenheimer

"If I had my way, I'd have made them all that way."

— **John Frankenheimer, Director**
Brentwood, California – 1998

This will be as brief, as befits my association with the famed director, which lasted all of 95 minutes.

We met in a house of worship in Brentwood where people of like mind and former poor life choices attend a meeting to keep their heads on straight and their lives from spinning out of control. It should not be a surprise that many members of this community can be found among the performing arts. A friend and I were looking for seats when he spotted someone he knew. The man waved us toward the two vacant seats beside him. My friend whispered to me as we were moving along the pew, "John Frankenheimer." John Frankenheimer! Jesus!

It is an unwritten rule in our community not to be impressed by fame or notoriety. We are all equals, there for the same purpose. I knew this, but to borrow from *Animal Farm*, "Some people are more equal than others."

The name and the man might not mean much to many, but in the movie business, John Frankenheimer *was* a force. My buddy had followed protocol and spoke the name as if he were talking about Joe Doakes, but I could not help myself. I was impressed. The average person might not even recognize the name. This was Hollywood, though, and John Frankenheimer was Hollywood royalty. He had come from television in the late 1950s, the Golden Boy from the Golden Age of TV. His departure was the end of that Golden time.

I won't go into the Golden Age because it would take too long and consist of many other names you never heard of, except perhaps Rod Serling. Anyway John Frankenheimer was about the last from television to defect and head to Hollywood to make movies, most of them not as good as what we had been seeing on television. Still this was John Frankenheimer and he made great movies. We are speaking here of *Birdman of Alcatraz*, *Seven Days In May*, *The Manchurian Candidate*, *The Train* and *Seconds*, all of them filmed in glorious black and white.

Before the speaker showed up, I said to my new acquaintance, "I like them all — but I love the black and whites." That set John off. It turned out he felt the same way. He did most of the talking after that, which was the way I wanted. He explained that his first big movie in color, *Grand Prix*, was impossible to make in black and white, as it was a sprawling epic of European road racing, and the lack of color would make it look like an old documentary. After that he could not go back. He also tried to explain *Seconds* to me.

Seconds was a mystical sci-fi story of an old man taking a young man's body. I didn't understand his explanation any more than I did the movie. While he was talking, I was recalling Frankenheimer had a reputation for eating actors for breakfast, lunch, and dinner. He also insisted on total control of his films. This was fine, as long as he made pictures like *Birdman*, but by the 70s his star began to dim. The 80s were even worse, his output mostly uneven. It was said that his alcoholic womanizing was hurting his work. I would hope so. It devastated mine, albeit of a much more subterranean level. He certainly didn't look like a cannibal or a control freak. Although he could still take an actor to task, he had mellowed.

After a rocky patch in various rehabs, Frankenheimer had embraced the sober life, and that turned his life toward the top again. His comeback began with a return to his old home, television. There were two award-winning movies for HBO and more honors for two films for TCM, *Andersonville* and an

Emmy-winning series on George Wallace. A hit movie, *Ronin*, which starred Robert De Niro, reestablished John's reputation at the head of the class.

As part of his new life, he worked with others with the same problem. Ask Gary Sinise, Lieutenant Dan, who got aid and support from Frankenheimer when the actor was having an alcohol problem in his family. There was a happy ending for the Sinise family and for John Frankenheimer too.

Frankenheimer's final film, HBO's *Path to War*, was one of his best, and he went out a winner. He had been that for a long time. His comeback in mid-career, when many had counted him out, should be an inspiration to many.

It sure as hell was and is to me.

Barbara Eden

"It's him. It's HIM!"

— Barbara Eden, Actress/Singer/Author
Rancho Mirage, California – 1982

Barbara Eden is 89. Jeannie? Impossible! Where does that leave me? From Merriam-Webster, fossil is a person whose views have become outmoded. FOGY. I have no idea what Barbara Eden is up to these days, but I am certain of two things: she is not outmoded and definitely not a fogy. My association with Ms. Eden, as with many of these character sketches, was brief, but not without interest.

My wife Gayle and I met Barbara Eden at the 1982 Dedication for the Betty Ford Center. Many celebrities attended the event, including Bob and Dolores Hope and famed producer Hal Wallis and his wife, actress Martha Hyer. George H. W. Bush was the featured speaker.

Barbara's interest in the event was more personal. Her son, Matthew, an only child, was already wrestling with the heroin demon that would ultimately claim his life. She was also happy to get away from the divorce proceedings with husband number 2.

Things were not perfect in Jeannie's world. Her career path, on the other hand, had seemed trouble-free. She began, after an uncredited bit or two, as a movie star, albeit in films that could have best been described as light and frothy — *Ten Weeks in a Balloon* and *Harper Valley PTA* for example. Then

Roses in the Desert
Gayle Frederick and Barbara Eden
at the dedication of the
Betty Ford Center
October 1982, Rancho Mirage, CA

Barbara became Jeannie, which made her iconic.

There are performers who feel that roles where they are typed or are offered parts of less weight than that of Joan of Arc or Moses, say, are beneath them. These individuals are often very vocal in their displeasure, whining their way to fame and fortune. This has not been Barbara Eden's way. She took every role she played seriously, including Jeannie, and always gave whatever or whoever it was her best. Eventually she would be rewarded with a variety of roles in television movies and touring theatrical plays. She also had a night-club act and could sing. There was very little that our Barbara couldn't do. Well, there was one thing. She could not sit out in the sun. Her complexion was so fair that shade, even an umbrella, needed to be close at hand.

Gayle and I and Barbara and her girlfriend, Nancy Conway, were staying in the same Marriott, and we had some good times together. The local press buzzed around, which was annoying for me, but not for Barbara, who took it with grace and in stride. She has always been a Golden Apple type. But there was one reporter who was more than annoying. He was troublesome. Also he was more than a reporter. He was

292

the publisher of a magazine that concerned itself with addiction, drug and alcohol abuse. It was very popular in the field. Ignoring the fact that it would do little or nothing for her career, Barbara graciously granted him an interview. It had gone well till it became obvious that the gentleman was interested in more than words in a magazine. Not the slightest hint of scandal, sexual or otherwise, had ever touched Barbara Eden, and she was going to keep it that way, even when he exposed his clam-white body to the four of us as we sat around poolside. He was strutting about in our area wearing a Speedo. Now, if someone wants to go around showing off his genital goodies, that is his perfect right. It is also my right to think of how the statue of David or a medium-large farm animal would look in such attire. We hurriedly made for the nearest safe harbor. In this case it was my room where we could laugh off the situation without making fools of ourselves. The merriment ended with a loud knock on the door. Reacting like the heroine she was, Barbara leaped from her chair, turned and launched herself across the bed, sliding out of sight between bed and baseboard.

I answered the door.

It was *him*, but he had at least put on a white, terrycloth robe. My explanation for her absence was along the line of her having to rush to a movie location in Tasmania. Whatever I said he did not believe, and I did not care.

Barbara and company left town soon thereafter.

I will always have my memories of a beautiful blonde, arms outstretched, and flying across my bedroom like a base runner stealing second. I have not seen her since, but I am certain that she is as nice, sweet, and kind as ever. She said once that she was just a "square."

Let's hear it for squares; we could use more of them.

Sneak
Preview

Sneak Preview

In writing this book, while touching on the values, virtues, verities, and occasional vices of the stars of my era, the last half of the 20th century, it occurred to me that I had a lot more to say about those years — specifically, why everything has turned to shit. This puts me with geezers going back to Roman times, lamenting about kids of that day, and longing for the good old days. Well, what if the good old days were the good old days and today is a sorry mess? I put the decline in the early sixties, but I will not argue the point. Since then we have had Vietnam, Nixon and Watergate, drugs, local wars, ethnic cleansing, acid rock, more drugs — many prescribed — nuclear disasters, mass shootings, climate change, grunge, a king-sized worldwide depression, homelessness, poverty, flood and famines, partisan politics, sky-rocketing prices for basic needs like housing, pain pills, the Kardashian family, 24-hour news, Styrofoam, Alec Baldwin, 100-million-dollar movie budgets, global warming, the Kim Dynasty, unromantic airline travel with seats the size of upright baby coffins, gang violence, police shootings, police being shot, the loss of civil discourse, the Yugo, the destructive side of "progress" (cell phones, social Media — Twitter, texting), Facebook, five bucks for Coke in a theater, white supremacy, anti-Semitism, CEO salaries, Harvey Weinstein, gutless politicians, television and radio evangelists, the Alabama legislature with an IQ average 20 points lower than the Bama football team, Sarah Palin, Tom Steyer. Elizabeth Warren, Socialism, people who think Socialism and Communism are the same thing, corporate greed, too much union influence in elections, the lack of a sensible 3rd political party, AOC, Ted Cruz, Bernie Sanders, tofu, king-sized candy bars, fracking, ethanol, overregulation, under regulation, the Duggars, reality TV, The Great Pacific Garbage Patch, wars with no end game, and to top it all, Donald J. Trump as President of the United States. I rest my case. Enough is enough.

But this leads me to recall another highlight of fifties movie life, the sneak preview. If you go to a movie today and it is supposed to begin at a certain time, you can depend that it will start ten or fifteen minutes late, delayed by a blitz of ads, countless previews of the best scenes in the coming attractions, making it unnecessary to see the film since you have already seen it, as well as countless exhortations to shut up and watch the film. In the fifties, previews had titles that promised the moon without telling you anything. The scenes from the film seemed to be chosen at random, and we used to only show you who was in the picture. Plus, on special occasion, a Major Studio Sneak Preview would be announced. It could have been a turkey, or it could have been *Shane*, but it was always a surprise. Cliffhanger serials touted next week's episode by showing the impossibility of escape for our hero or heroine.

On radio or early TV you would always be told who the famous guests would be next week — Bogart, Crawford, Rin Tin Tin. Even books gave clues as to what the author would do next. Take a look at a writer like Franklin W. Dixon, who authored over countless decades the *Hardy Boys* series. FWD did not actually exist, although the books kept coming. At the end of each adventure there would be a description of the thrills to come. "In their next exciting adventure, the Hardy boys will encounter action and adventure aplenty as they try to solve the Mystery of the Dyslexic Ghost."

So I am giving you a view of tomorrow by looking at yesterday. These essays and observations would not fit in this book, no matter how I tried to shoehorn them in there.

The Sneak Preview begins on the next page.

The American Society for the Prevention of Progress
Santa Rosa, California – 1950s

Families are proud of their family members. The Fredericks are no exception, even though "famous" could be stretching it.

Way back, there was a John Frederick, the Elector of Saxony who hid Martin Luther in his castle when Luther was summoned to Rome. It probably would have been a one-way trip. My family's links to that John Frederick are tenuous, but who knows?

Another John Frederick fought in the Revolutionary War, and another namesake, still a boy, marched with Meade's army.

We Fredericks were from Pennsylvania. On the other side of our family, the Hedgpeths of Missouri were with the first wagon train on Beale Road, which led to California. Some in the party were looking to duck the Civil War, which was only a year away. They could not avoid combat, however, and were attacked while crossing the Colorado River by Mojave Indians, who had been stirred up by Mormon settlers, who predicted a white flood coming to settle, when my relatives were merely trying to get to the Golden State. There is a 20-page journal of crossing the Plains still in our family. The Mojaves, future casino owners, do not come off well in this tale of the early West. When you are ducking Indian arrows, it is difficult to be objective.

A Hedgpeth descendent (my grandmother's family) is the subject of this story. Dr. Joel Hedgpeth could speak and sing in three different languages — English, Welsh, and Latin. His wife, a Stanford graduate, could do so as well, although Doctor H. could play the lute and lyre also.

I was visiting Dr. Joel and his lovely wife in the mid-90s. As we were going out to lunch, on the doorstep, Mrs. H. whispered softly to him in Latin, something that made him swear in Latin and return to the back of the house.

"What did you say to him?" I asked.

"I told him to go back and comb his hair," she answered.

Unruly hair aside, Joel Hedgpeth was a famed marine biologist who authored two-inch tomes on Pacific tidal pools. He successfully protested the intrusion of nuclear power into several environmentally sensitive areas of the West, palled around with John Steinbeck and Ed Ricketts on the Sea of Cortez, and still found time to head three large oceanographic laboratories and institutions.

In my view, Dr. Hedgpeth's greatest accomplishment was the founding of The American Society for the Prevention of Progress (ASPOP). Dr. Hedgpeth was the only member of this fine organization since, as is obvious, an additional member could have only meant — progress.

Oddly, this legendary achievement was not mentioned in the fulsome obituaries Dr. Hedgpeth received on his death at age 95 in 2011. How the London, New York, and Los Angeles Times could have missed this event is beyond me.

As far as ASPOP goes, more than ever noble negativity is needed today. I know I am behind on this, but take Myspace for a good example. Personally, I have all the space I require and have no need to view, poach, or acquire anyone else's. This kind of thing leads to invasions, wars, nationalism run amok, and the like. I understand Myspace is no longer popular, but "no" on Myspace anyway. Take Facebook, please! It has not only killed the handwritten letter, which for the most part is a symbol of love and intimacy among friends and family members, Facebook has proved, without contradiction, that the lives of its members are meaningless, dull and boring, besides being a new and novel way to waste time. It also puts to rest the idea that ten million monkeys sitting at keyboards will come up with prose that will rival Shakespeare. Even Sidney Sheldon and Jacqueline Susann, though dead, are safe.

My computer and cell phone are (and I am far from being alone) possessed by dark and sinister forces that are ruining my life, which is in its final quarter. I must amend that last statement. I am in overtime — well into overtime, and what is left of my life is too precious to leave to devices that type words with which I am not familiar, turn my texts into any one of two dozen foreign languages, randomly dial up people with whom I do not wish to speak, and because I do not know how to delete from my contact list, are constantly trying to hook me up to the departed.

I am considering restarting ASPOP and changing the bylaws. If I can somehow avoid the onus of progress, maybe honorary memberships, there may be hope for the country yet.

About the Author

J ohn Charles Frederick was born August 20, 1938, in Salem, Oregon, to parents Paul and Dorothy Frederick. He attended schools in Salem and graduated in 1961 from Willamette University, majoring in history and baseball. He was commissioned an Ensign in the United States Naval Reserve, beginning a 36-year career that included ten years of active duty. While on active service, he served as Executive Officer for the Office of Information for the Armed Services in the Pentagon, as Public Affairs Officer for the United

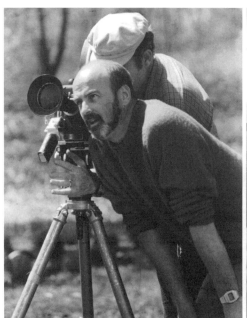

Directing a film in the 80s.
I preferred writing and producing.

Traveling and enjoying life now!

States 2nd Fleet and the NATO Striking Fleet Atlantic, and finally, as a Motion Picture and Television Officer in Hollywood, where the movie bug got him. On leaving active duty, John remained in the active Reserve where he served as Executive Officer and, for three years, as Commanding Officer of the Pacific Fleet Naval Reserve Combat Camera Group. He retired from the Navy in 1991 as a Captain, USNR.

He embarked on a new career of writing and producing educational and documentary films. In 1975, he co-founded, with Hollywood producer Herm Saunders (*F Troop* and *Adam-12*), FMS Productions — a company that is still going 45 years later. FMS produced and distributed a number of award-winning films that dealt with social issues and problems, proving "solutions to negative situations."

His marriage to the former Sharlene Bailey, a fellow student at Willamette, produced three children, Randall, Richard, and Elisabeth. In 1986, he married his former high school sweetheart, Gayle LaBranche, who passed away in 2014.

Frederick is a life member of the Writers Guild of America, West. He has produced nearly 50 informational and documentary films. *StarCatcher* is his first solo literary effort. He was hugely supported in the writing by Irene Robertson, Gayle's best friend and a former neighbor, who has become something more. They have traveled widely and continue to delight in each other's company. John would like to have it known that a) it is never too late to fall in love, and b) it is never too late to write a book or to complete a major project that one has always planned to finish, but never got around to it.